Lear[illegible]ove Knitting and Crochet

Introduction

All you ever wanted to know — and more — about knitting and crochet. From basic beginnings to more advanced techniques. A treasury of information written in a clear and precise way.

Included in this book are instructions for learning how to knit and crochet, advice on what to choose for your first project, how to decide what yarn to buy, what size to make, how to look after your finished article when washing or pressing, and so much more.

We hope this book will encourage you to pursue a hobby which has delighted and fascinated many, many people for many, many years.

Index

How to Knit . . . . . page 2
The Basic Stitches . . . . . page 4
Knitting Accessories . . . . . page 7
Reading Your Knitting Pattern . . . . . page 7
Lace and Eyelet Patterns . . . . . page 10
Cable Patterns . . . . . page 11
Fairisle Patterns . . . . . page 12
Fishermans Rib . . . . . page 13
Working Notes . . . . . page 14
Finishing and Making Up . . . . . page 14
Extra Hints . . . . . page 17
Sample Knitting Stitches . . . . . page 20
How to Crochet . . . . . page 24
The Basic Stitches . . . . . page 25
Crochet Accessories . . . . . page 28
Reading Your Crochet Pattern . . . . . page 28
Fancy Stitch Techniques . . . . . page 30
Working Notes . . . . . page 36
Finishing and Making Up . . . . . page 39
Sample Crochet Stitches . . . . . page 41
Choosing Your First Knitting or Crochet Project . . . . . page 46
Washing and Caring for Your Handmade Garment . . . . . page 47
International Knitting and Crochet Terms . . . . . page 47

How To Knit

First of all you need to beg, borrow or steal a ball of any double knitting or 8 ply and a pair of 4mm (UK 8) needles.

We will explain in more detail about yarn and needles in a later section (see pages 7 and 46) — for now we just want to get you actually knitting.

Hints and Tips
Left-handed people may find it easier to prop the book up against a mirror to see the illustrations in mirror image, while still being able to read the text from the original page.

Holding the needles

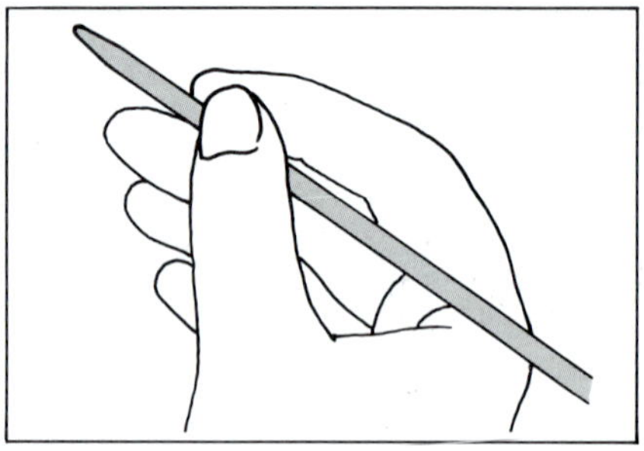

The right needle is usually held from underneath in the same position as holding a pencil. When working the first few rows the knitted piece will pass over the hand, between the thumb and the index finger. As work progresses let the thumb slide under the knitted piece, grasping the needle from below.

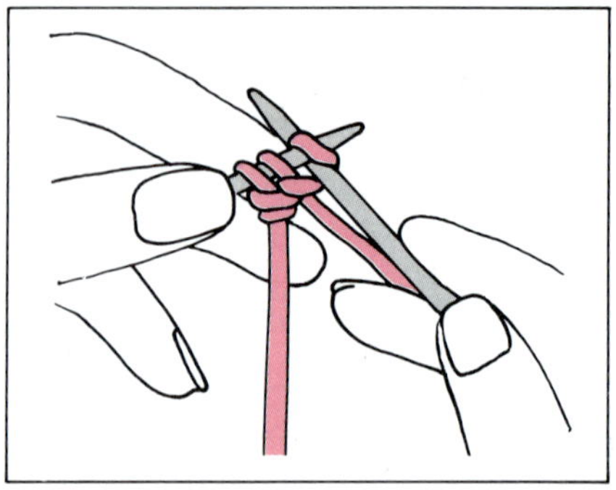

The left needle is held lightly over the top, using the thumb and index finger to control the tip of the needle.

Holding the yarn

Method 1

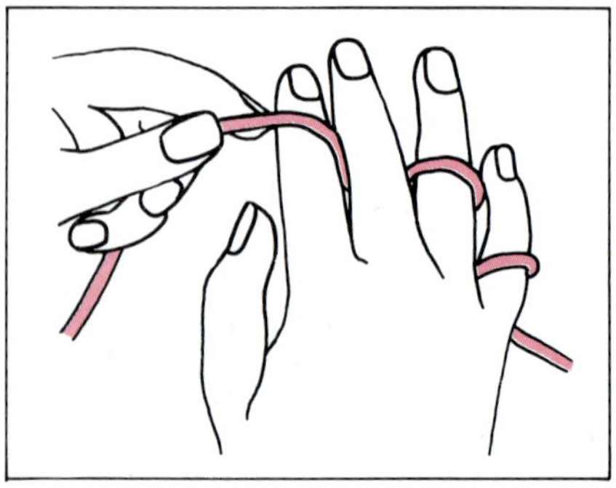

Holding end of yarn in left hand, pass yarn under the little finger of right hand, then around same finger, over third finger, under centre finger and over index finger. The index finger is used to pass the yarn around needle tip. The yarn circled around the little finger creates the necessary tension for knitting evenly.

Method 2

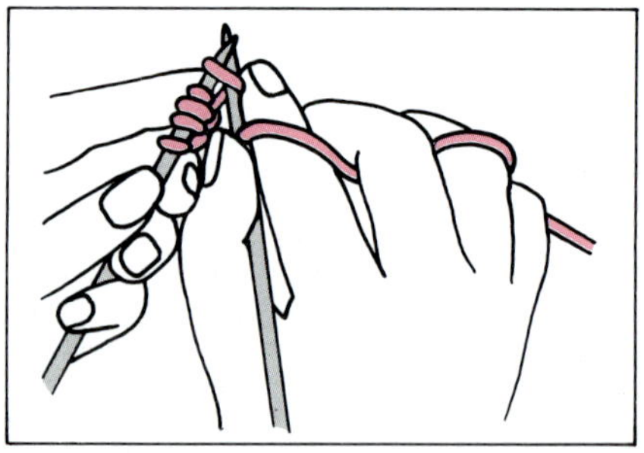

Holding end of yarn in left hand, pass under the little finger of right hand, over third finger, under centre finger and over index finger. The index finger is used to pass the yarn around the needle tip. The tension on the yarn is controlled by gripping the yarn in the crook of the little finger.

Casting On

There are several ways of casting on, all serving different purposes. Thumb Method and Cable or 'Between Needles' Method are the most widely used, and are explained in detail here. **Thumb Method** is used whenever a very elastic edge is required or when the rows immediately after the cast-on edge are to be worked in garter stitch. **Cable Method** (or 'between needles' method) gives a very firm neat finish and is best for use before ribbing or any other firm type of stitch.

Both these methods commence with a slip knot and this is the starting-off point for almost everything you do in knitting.

Slip knot

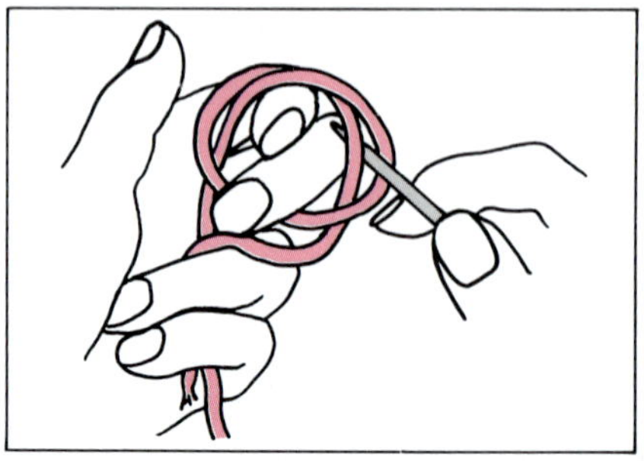

(a) Wind the yarn around two fingers of left hand from front to back and over the two fingers again to the left of the first thread. Using a knitting needle pick up second thread through first loop.

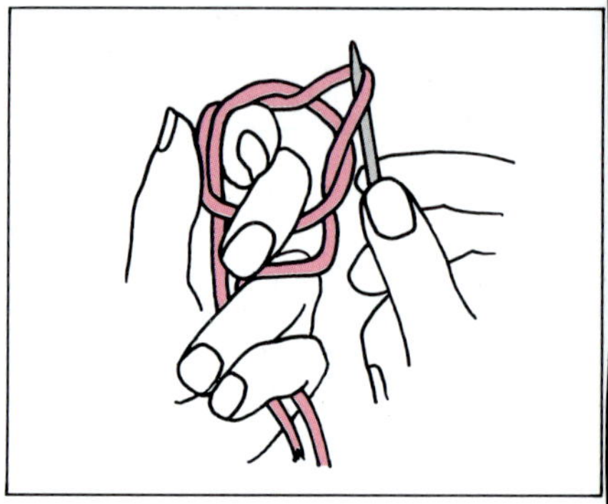

(b) Pull the second thread through the first one to form a loop.

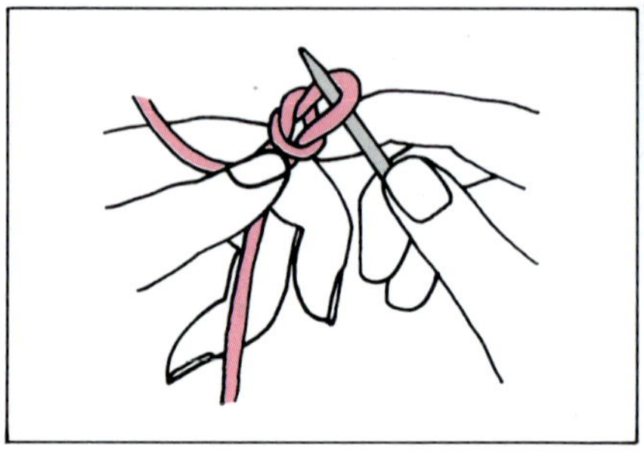

(c) Pull end to tighten the loop.

Thumb method

This is the best method to use if you are going to be working in garter st, or need an elastic edge. You will need one needle.

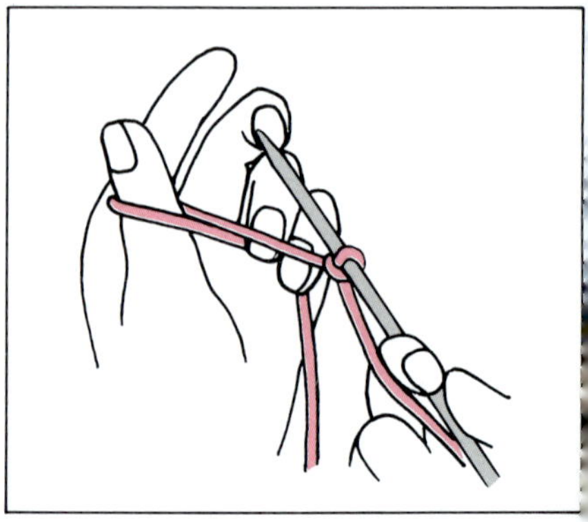

(a) Make a slip knot about 30 cm [12 ins] from the end of the yarn. (NB — This is sufficient to cast on approximately 20 sts in double knitting or 8 ply yarn). Place the slip knot on a needle and hold the needle in the right hand with the ball end of the yarn over your first finger. *Wind the loose end of the yarn around the left thumb from front to back.

K1, P1 rib

Cast on an odd number of stitches Cable Method — for example 19 stitches.

1st row:

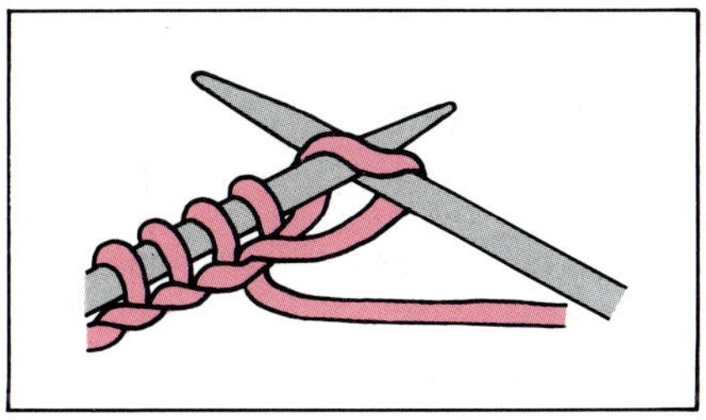

(a) Knit first stitch on left needle.

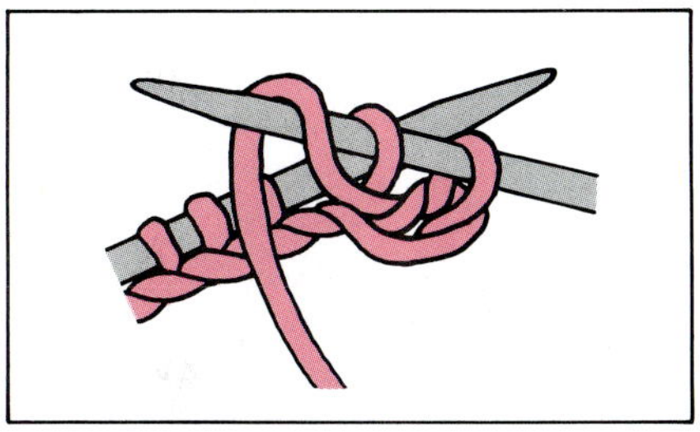

(b) Purl next stitch on left needle.

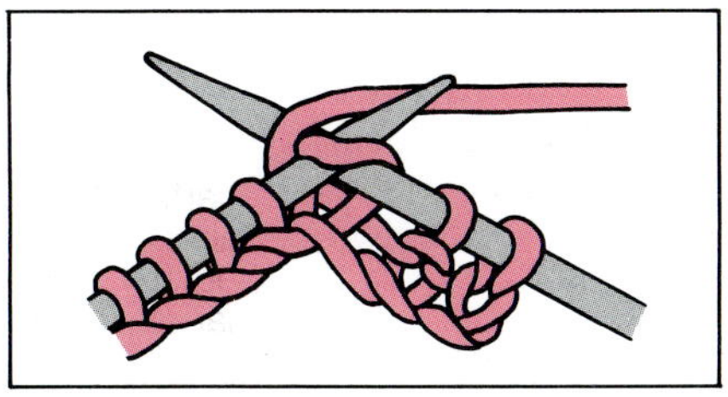

(c) Knit next stitch on left needle.
Repeat steps (b) and (c) until all stitches have been transferred to right needle.

2nd row:

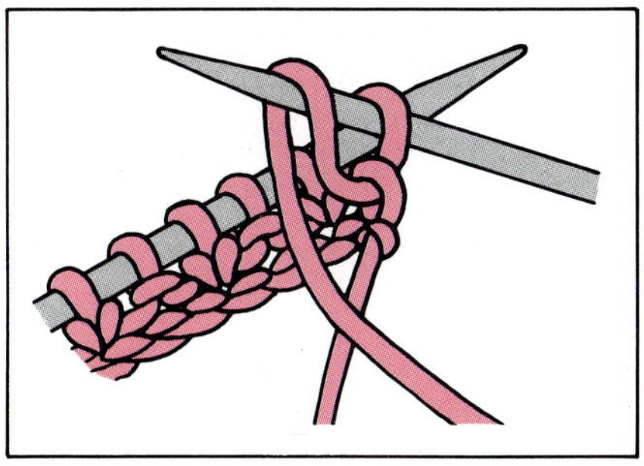

(a) Purl first stitch on left needle.

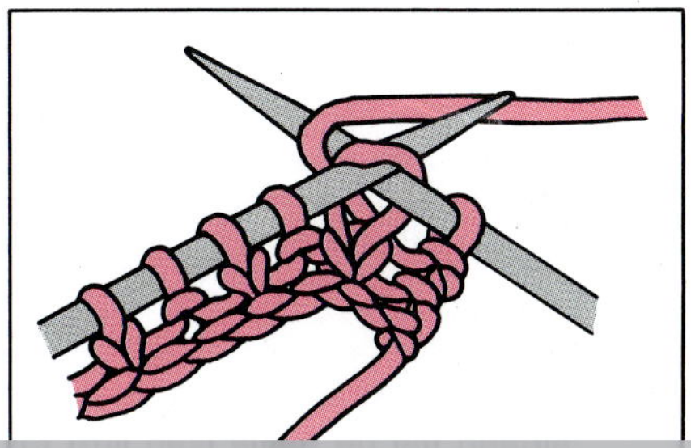

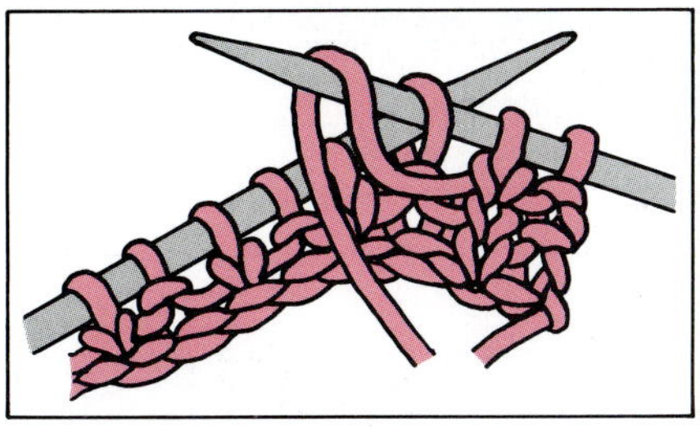

(c) Purl next stitch on left needle.
Repeat steps (b) and (c) until all stitches have been transferred to right needle.

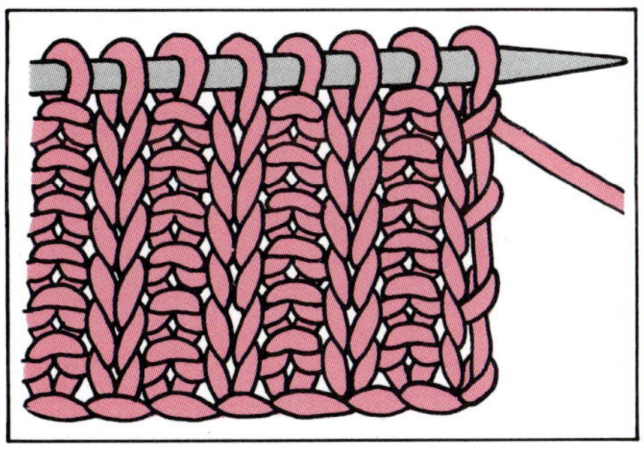

These 2 rows form K1, P1 rib and can usually be found written in a pattern as follows:

1st row (right side): K1, *P1, K1; rep from * to end.

2nd row: P1, *K1, P1; rep from * to end.

K1, P1 rib may also be written as follows with a garter st edge st for sewing up:

1st row: K2, *P1, K1; rep from * to last st, K1.

2nd row: K1, *P1, K1; rep from * to end.

K2, P2 rib

Cast on a multiple of 4 stitches plus 2 Cable Method — for example 18 stitches.

1st row:

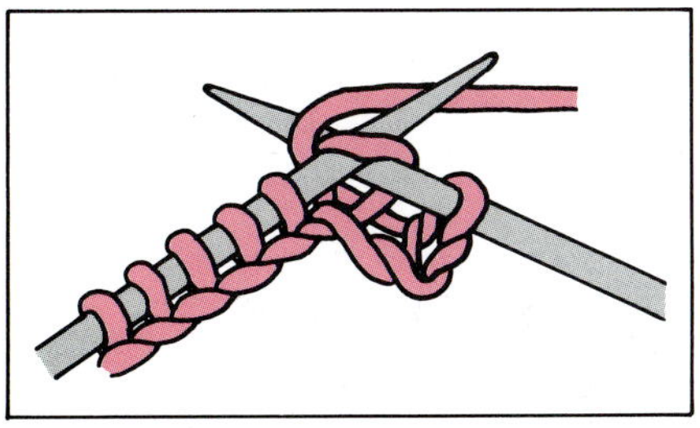

(a) Knit first 2 stitches on left needle.

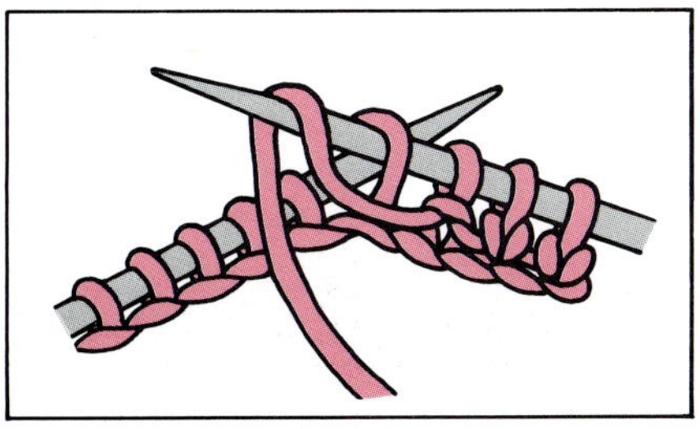

(b) Purl next 2 stitches on left needle.

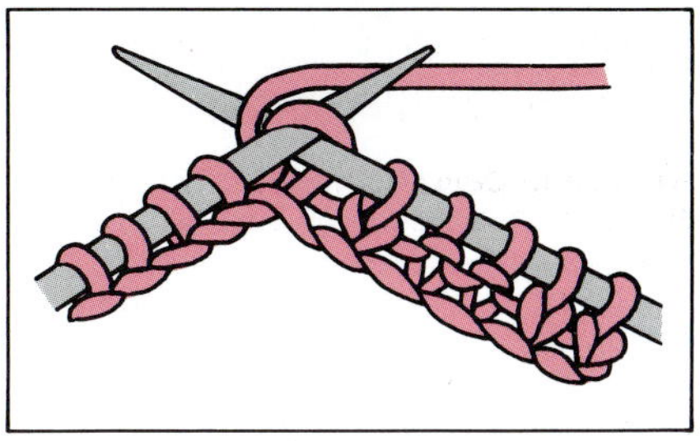

2nd row:

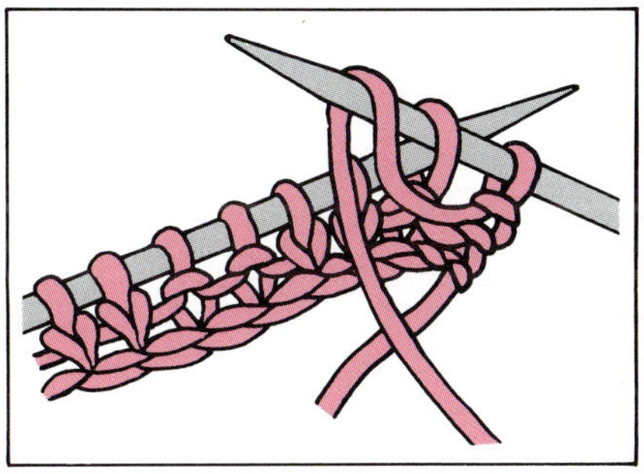

(a) Purl first 2 stitches on left needle.

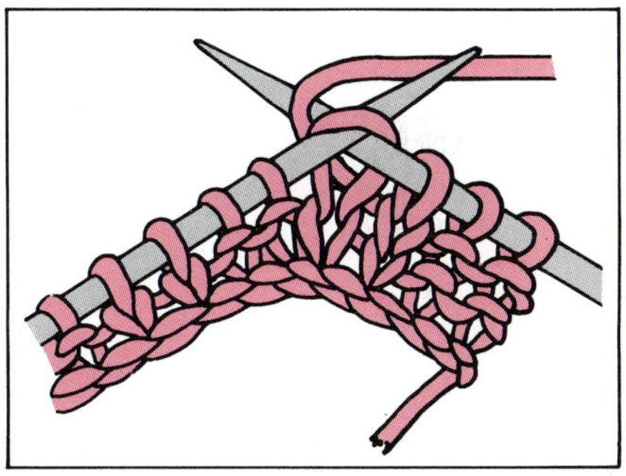

(b) Knit next 2 stitches on left needle.

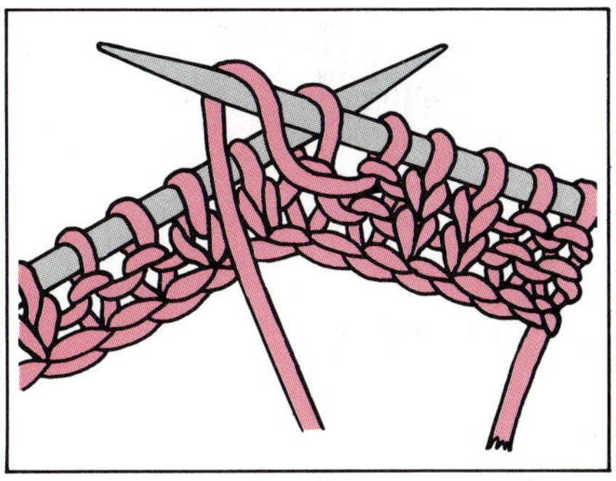

(c) Purl next 2 stitches on left needle.
Repeat steps (b) and (c) until all stitches have been transferred to right needle.

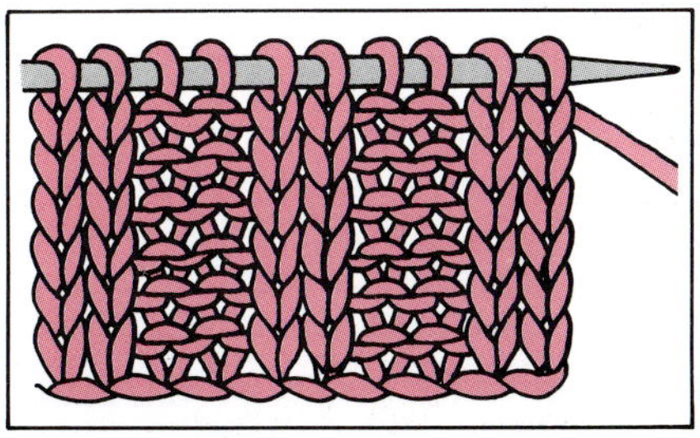

These 2 rows form K2, P2 rib and can usually be found written in a pattern as follows:

Casting off

Always cast off in pattern. This means that in stocking stitch you cast off knitways on a knit row and purlways on a purl row. Casting off ribbing should always be done as if you were continuing to rib and most pattern stitches can also be followed during the course of the casting off.

Knitways

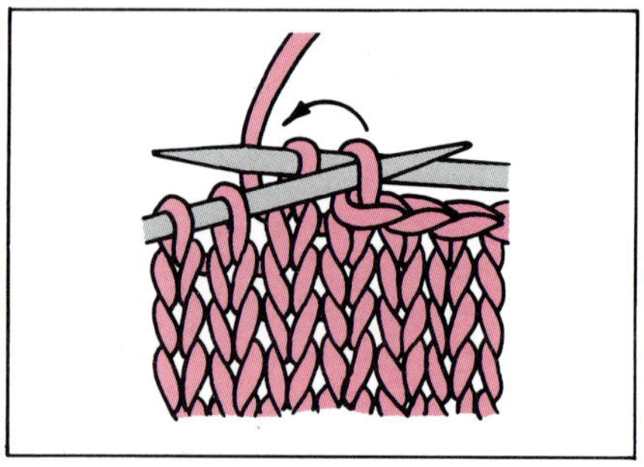

Knit the first two stitches. *Using the left needle lift the first stitch over the second and drop it off the needle. Knit the next stitch and repeat from * until all the stitches have been cast off and one stitch remains on right needle.

Cut the yarn leaving an end of about 8 cm [3 ins], and draw the end through the last stitch on needle.

Purlways

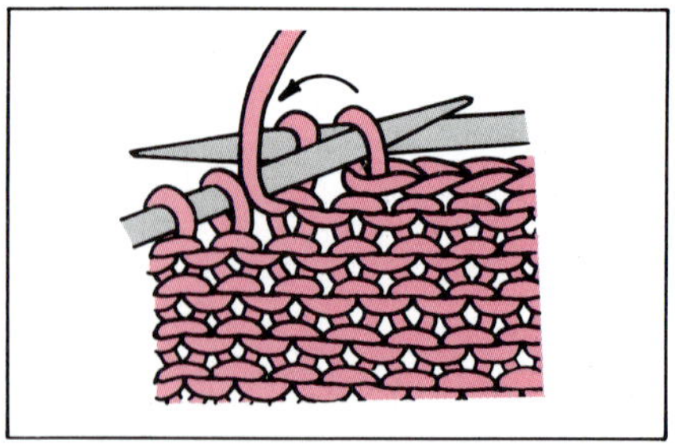

Purl the first two stitches, then *using the left hand needle lift the first stitch over the second and drop if off the needle. Purl the next stitch and repeat from *. Complete as for Knitways.

In K1, P1 rib

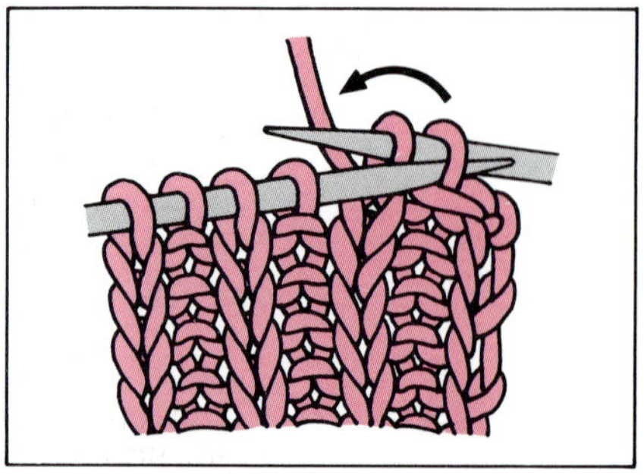

Knit the first stitch, purl the second stitch, then *using the left hand needle lift the first stitch over the second and drop it off the needle*. Knit the next stitch and repeat from * to *. Purl the next stitch and repeat from * to *, and so on until all the stitches have been cast off and one stitch remains on right needle. Complete as for Knitways

In K2, P2 rib

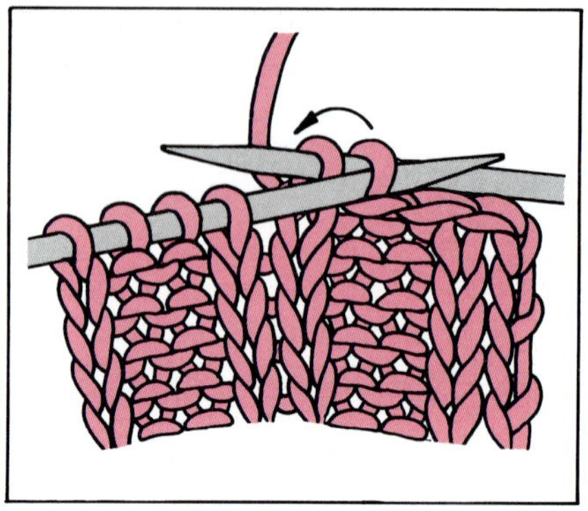

Work in a similar way to casting off K1, P1 rib but knit the first two stitches, then purl the next 2 stitches and so on to keep the rib correct. Complete as for Knitways.

Hints and Tips

Using a crochet hook to cast off can be extremely time saving. Treat the crochet hook as if it were the right hand needle and knit or purl the first two stitches in the usual way. *Pull the second stitch through the first, knit or purl the next stitch and repeat from *. This method is extremely useful when a loose elastic cast off edge is required as you can gently loosen the stitch still on the crochet hook to ensure that the elasticity is retained.

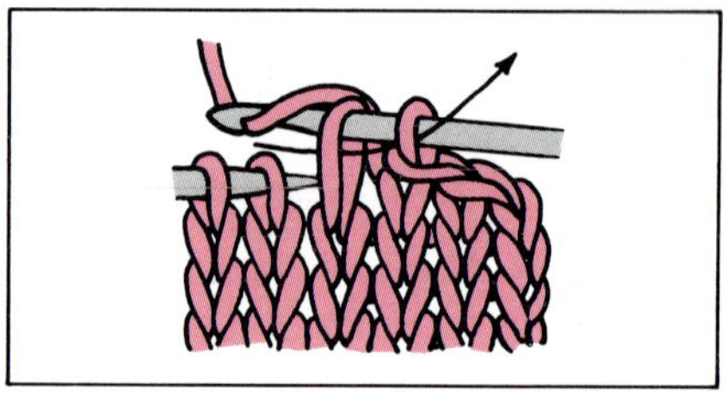

Continental Knitting

With practice this method can be quicker than the English method but care must be taken to achieve an even and regular tension. Both hands play an active part, so it is suitable for right-handed and left-handed knitters.

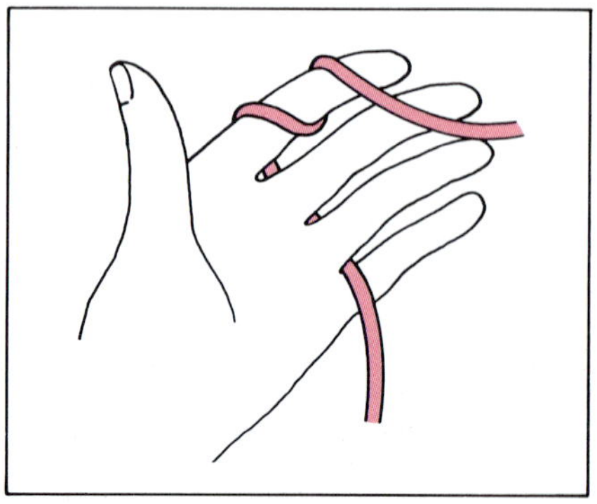

(a) The left hand controls the yarn and is looped round fingers as shown. The right hand controls transfer of stitch to right needle.

Knit

The needles are held with hands placed over the top of work. The left needle is held between thumb and second finger so that first finger is free.

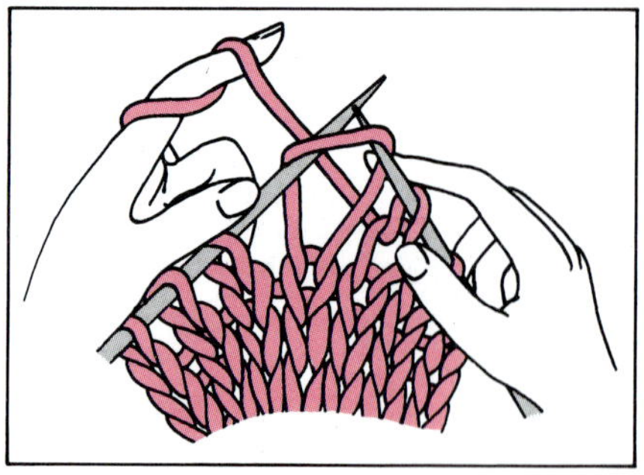

(a) Insert point of right needle into front of first stitch on left needle.

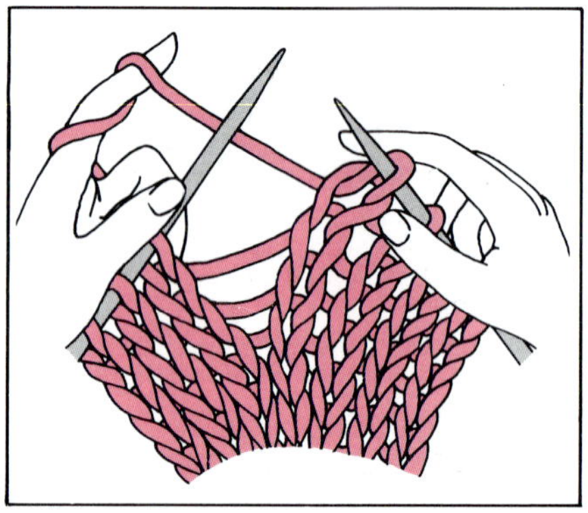

(b) Pick up yarn lying at back of stitch and with a slight twist bring this loop through to front of work, letting stitch slip off left needle and leaving a stitch on right needle.

Purl

The needles are held in the same way as for knit but the yarn is kept at front of work.

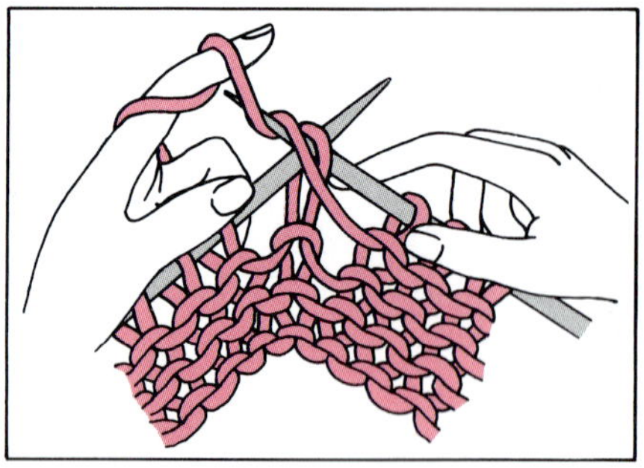

(a) Insert right needle purlwise into first stitch on left needle. Take yarn over and round needle.

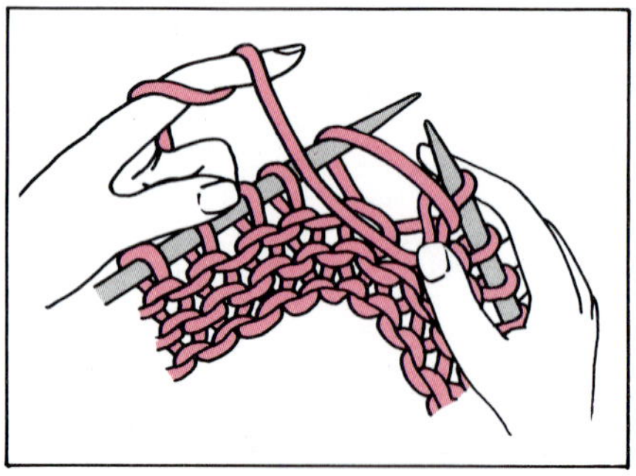

(b) Take a loop through to back of work controlling with right hand as shown, then slip stitch off left needle.

Congratulations!! You have now discovered **how to knit.** Next we will explain how to make sure that the garment or item that you decide to knit as your first project ends up as the size and shape it was meant to be!

Knitting Accessories

The pattern will tell you what you need to be able to complete the garment or item, but as well as the needles and yarn you will also need to have a basic kit of accessories.

Knitting needles are used in pairs to produce a flat knitted fabric. They are pointed at one end to form the stitches and have a knob at the other end to retain the stitches. They may be made in plastic, wood, steel or alloy and range in size from 2mm to 10mm in diameter (UK 14 to 000). There are also even larger needles available for 'odd pins' knitting (using one standard size needle and one giant needle to produce a loosely knitted fabric that keeps its shape). See page 48 for a complete needle conversion table. Needles are also made in different lengths. Choose a length that will comfortably hold the stitches required for each project.

It is useful to have a range of sizes so that tension swatches can be knitted up and compared. If possible buy a complete set of needles with a case to keep them in, so that one needle doesn't go missing and you always have the size that you need. There's nothing more infuriating than settling down to knit, and then finding that you haven't got the right size needles! Discard any needles that become bent. Points should be fairly sharp — blunt needles reduce the speed and ease of working.

Circular and double-pointed needles are used to produce a tubular fabric or a flat circle (see page 19). Many traditional fisherman's sweaters are knitted in the round. Double-pointed needles are sold in sets of four. Circular needles consist of two needles joined by a flexible length of plastic. The plastic varies in length. Use the shorter lengths for knitting the sleeves or neckband, and the longer lengths for larger pieces such as sweaters and skirts.

Cable needles are short needles used to hold the stitches of a cable to the back or front of the main body of the knitting. They generally come in two thicknesses and can be either straight or with a U-bend to stop the stitches slipping off. Try to use the cable needle which is smaller than the needles you are using, to prevent stretching the stitches.

A ruler and tape measure are essential for checking tension swatches and for measuring the length and width of completed knitting. For an accurate result, always smooth knitting out (without stretching) on a firm flat surface before measuring it.

Pins (with coloured glass heads if possible to avoid losing them in the knitting!), are used to measure the tension swatch (see page 8) and also when picking up sts evenly along an edge — for example on a front band (see page 15).

Stitch holders resemble large safety pins and are used to hold stitches while they are not being worked, for example, around a neckline when the neckband stitches will be picked up and worked after back and front have been joined. As an alternative, thread a blunt-pointed sewing needle with a generous length of contrast-coloured yarn, thread it through the stitches to be held while they are still on the needle, then slip the stitches off the needle and knot both ends of the contrast yarn together.

A row counter is used to count the number of rows that have been knitted. It is a cylinder with a numbered dial that is pushed onto the needle and the dial is turned at the completion of each row.

Wool sewing needles or knitters needles are used to sew completed pieces of knitting together. They are large with a broad eye for easy threading and a blunt point that will slip between the knitted stitches without splitting and fraying the yarn. Do not use sharp pointed sewing needles to sew up knitting. A tapestry needle is also suitable.

A crochet hook is useful for picking up dropped stitches and can be used for casting off (see page 6).

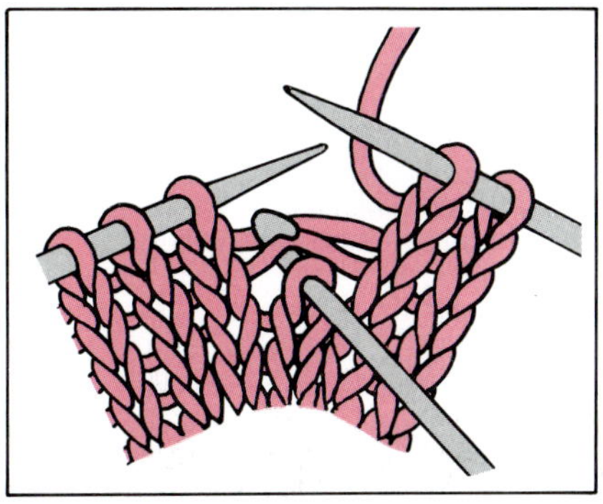

Reading Your Knitting Pattern (and understanding it!)

Now that you know how to knit and purl, the next stage is to learn how to read your pattern, and how to interpret the information given. At first glance it can all look like a foreign language, but don't despair .... read on!

Measurements

Most knitting patterns have an allowance for movement or ease over and above the actual bust or chest size. The amount of ease varies with the style of garment and fashions of the time. In other words a pattern may be 'To Fit' bust 85 cm [34 ins], with a 'finished measurement' of 95 cm [38 ins]. This garment has a 10 cm [4 inch] 'allowance' or ease. Generally jackets or cardigans have more allowance so that they can be worn over other bulky garments. The photograph or make, you may find the following tip helpful. Choose one of your own sweaters that is a size you feel comfortable in, or is suitable for the style of garment that you are going to make.

Lay the garment out flat on a table and measure the width across the body. Double this measurement to find the finished size all round. Compare this with the actual size or finished measurement printed on your pattern. Knit the size that has the nearest finished measurement to the one you want. Don't worry if the 'To Fit' size doesn't correspond with your actual size. These are only given as a guide.

There are of course exceptions to this general guide, for example when a garment is influenced by thirties or forties styling, and is intended to have little or no allowance in order to fit closely to the figure. In this case it would be best to fol-

Tension

The correct tension is the most important contribution to the successful knitting of a garment. The information under this heading given at the beginning of all patterns refers to the number of stitches required to fill a particular area; for example a tension indication may be '22 sts and 30 rows = 10 cm [4 ins] square measured over stocking st on 4mm (UK 8) needles'. This means that it is necessary to produce fabric made up of the proportion of stitches and rows as given in the tension paragraph in order to obtain the correct measurements for the garment you intend to knit, regardless of the needles **you** use. The needle size indicated in the pattern is the one which **most** knitters will use to achieve this tension but it is the tension that is important, not needle size.

knitting. Although this may seem to be time wasting and a nuisance it can save the enormous amount of time and aggravation that would result from having knitted a garment to the wrong size!

The finished size is based on getting the correct tension. If your knitting is too loose the garment will be too big. If your knitting is too tight the garment will be too small.

Tension Piece

The instructions given in the tension paragraph of a knitting pattern will be either for working in stocking st or in pattern stitch. If they are given in pattern stitch it is necessary to work a multiple of stitches the same as the multiple required in the pattern. If in stocking st any number can be cast on but whichever method is used this should always be enough to give at least 15 cm [6 ins] in width. Work in pattern or stocking st according to the wording of the tension paragraph until the piece measures at least 15 cm [6 ins] in depth. Break the yarn about 20cm [8 ins] from the work and thread this end through the stitches, then remove the knitting needle. To check the stitch tension place a pin vertically into the fabric a few stitches from the side edge. Measure 10 cm [4 ins] carefully and insert a second pin. (NB: diagram shows 5cm [2 ins]). Count the stitches. If the number of stitches between the pins is less than that specified in the pattern (even by half a stitch) your garment will be too wide. Use one size smaller needles to knit another swatch and measure the stitches again. If there are more stitches than specified the garment will be too small. Change to one size larger needles, knit another swatch and measure the stitches again.

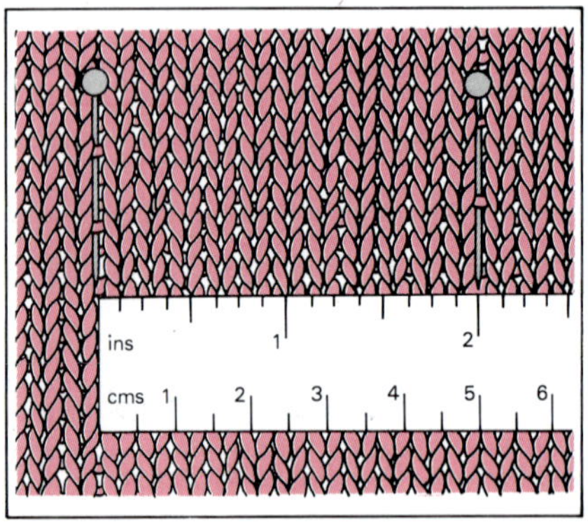

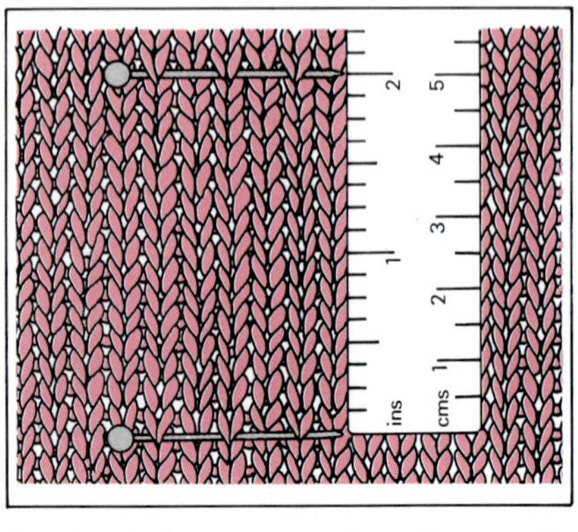

To check the row tension place a pin horizontally in the fabric a few rows from the cast on edge. Measure 10 cm [4 ins] carefully and insert a second pin. (NB: diagram shows 5cm [2 ins]). Count the rows. If the number of rows between the pins is less than specified in the pattern your garment will be too long. If the number of rows between the pins is more than specified your garment will be too short.

Hints and Tips

If you can't get tension exactly right on sts **and** rows, decide which is more important. Generally it is better to get the width measurement correct as lengths can usually be adjusted during the course of knitting by adjusting the length to underarm or sleeve length, which are frequently given as a measurement and not in rows. An exception to this would be when the garment is worked sideways from wrist to wrist, in which case the rows would be more important, in order to get the correct width of garment.

Your tension will become more even the more you practise knitting. Experiment with different methods of holding yarn in right hand in order to gain best even tension. Once you have found the most comfortable method for **you** — stick to it. Everybody holds the yarn and needles in different ways, so don't worry if you feel that you look awkward. It's the tension that counts!

Standard Knitting Terms

To keep instructions brief, most patterns use abbreviations for standard knitting terms. To help you make sense of the jargon, here are a few of the more common ones. Eventually knitting pattern abbreviations will become familiar as a second language.

Increasing and Decreasing

There are various methods of increasing and decreasing and they serve two purposes. The first is to make the knitting wider or narrower, to shape it. The second is to create decorative effects in lacy or textured patterns, and is explained in detail on page 11.

Using increasing and decreasing to shape

When shaping the various parts of a garment, increases or decreases are worked in pairs at each end of the row on the symmetrical pieces — (back, sleeves etc) to given a balanced shape. The fronts of a cardigan however are shaped differently on each side to give the correct shape for the armhole on one side and the neck shaping at the other.

It is very important to follow the instructions given in the knitting pattern carefully. The designer will have worked out the various shapings to give the best possible results for each piece of material, and to ensure that the pieces fit together correctly when made up.

Increasing

Used when making fabric wider, or when adjusting for different stitch tensions.

Inc in next st (working into front and back of a stitch)

knit row

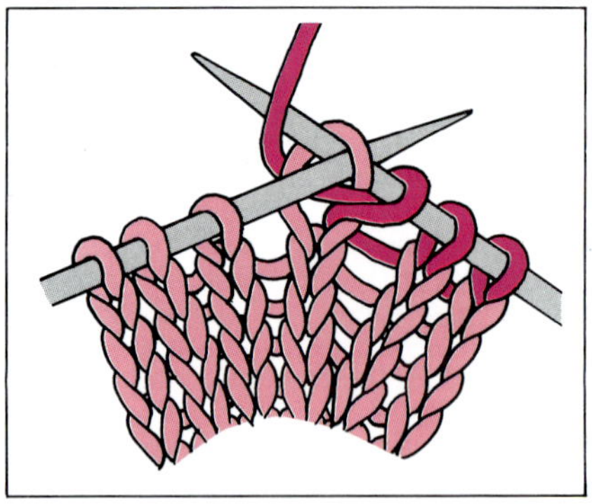

Knit into the stitch and before slipping it off the needle, knit again into the back of the loop. This is abbreviated in patterns as **Inc 1,** or **inc in next st.**

purl row

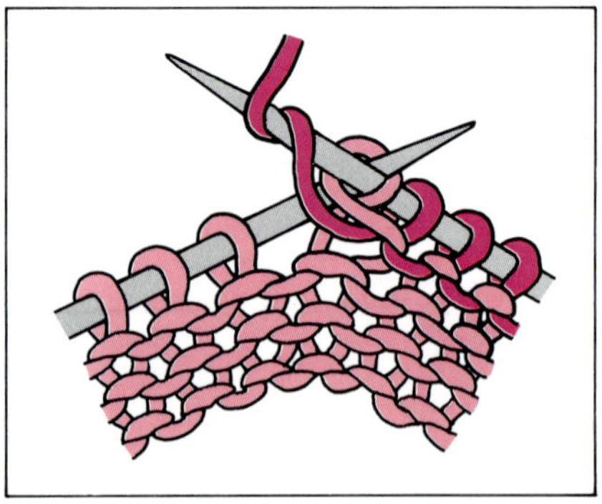

The method on a purl row is similar. Purl into the front of the stitch then purl into the back of it before slipping it off the needle.

To keep side edge of work neat and easy to sew, increase as follows at each end of row; 'Inc in first st, work to last 2 sts, inc in next st, work last st'. Work the increase as knit on right side rows, and purl on wrong side rows.

Make 1 (st made between 2 sts)

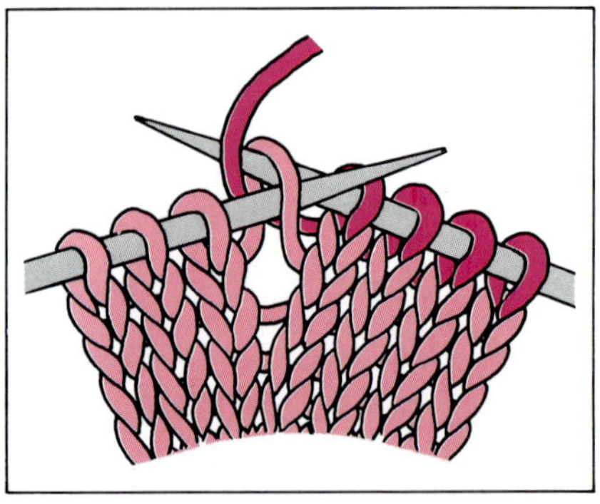

Lift the yarn lying between the stitch just worked and the next stitch and place it on left hand needle, then knit (or purl) into back of this loop. This increase is abbreviated as **M1** (make 1).

Yfwd or yf (yarn forward — makes a hole)

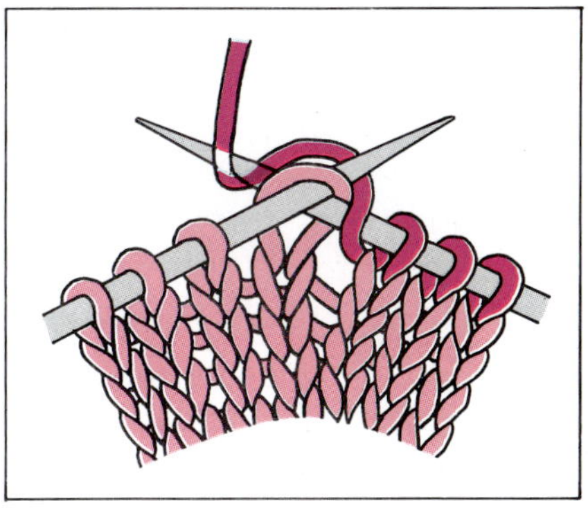

To make the yarn forward increase between 2 knit stitches, bring the yarn to the front as if to purl, take it over the top of right hand needle and knit the next stitch. The completed increase creates a visible hole and is often used in lace patterns.

Yrn (yarn round needle — makes a hole)

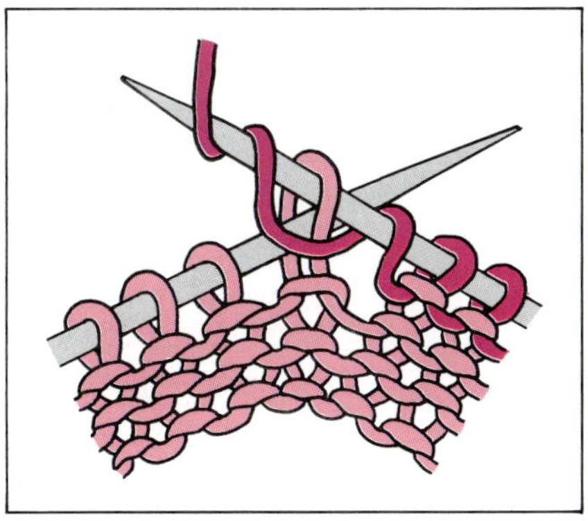

To make a stitch between 2 purl stitches take the yarn over the top of right hand needle to the back of the work, then under the needle to the front.

Note: The term **yo** (yarn over) for North American readers covers yfwd (yarn forward) and yrn (yarn round needle), and is a general abbreviation meaning to increase a stitch by winding the yarn round needle as opposed to the front and back method described above. It is necessary to ensure that you wind the yarn correctly. After working next stitch, ensure that an extra stitch has been made, and that you havn't just carried the yarn from front to back, or vice versa.

Decreasing

Used when making fabric narrower, or when adjusting for different stitch tensions. Different methods of decreasing give different effects. For example decreasing 1 or more stitches in from the edge on a raglan armhole gives a 'fully fashioned' decorative appearance, and a much neater edge for sewing up and for picking up stitches.

right needle without knitting it then knit the next stitch.

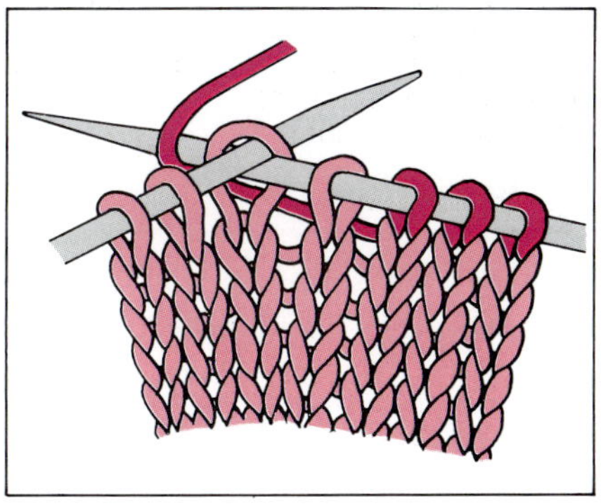

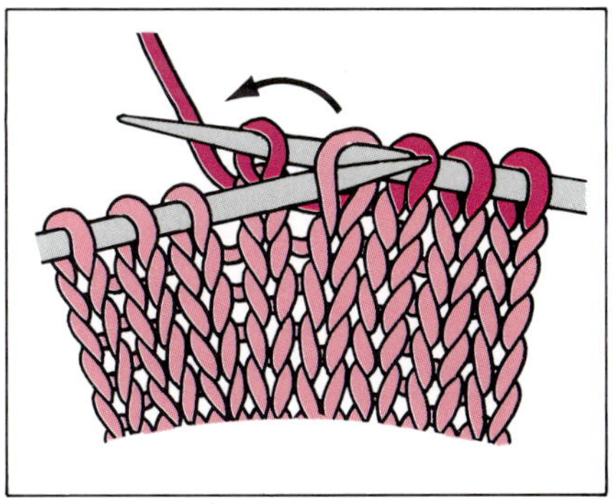

(b) Lift the slipped stitch over the knitted stitch and drop it off the needle.

The effect of this decrease worked on a right side row is to make the stitch slant to the left.

K2tog (knit 2 together)

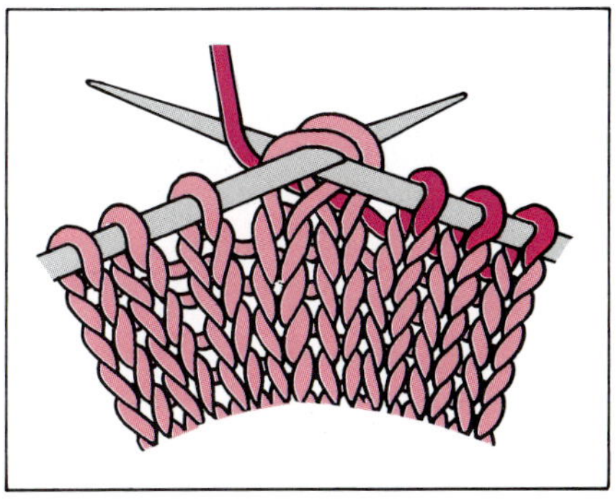

This decrease is worked simply by inserting the right needle through two stitches instead of one and then knitting them together as one stitch.

The effect of this decrease worked on a right side row is to make the stitch slant to the right.

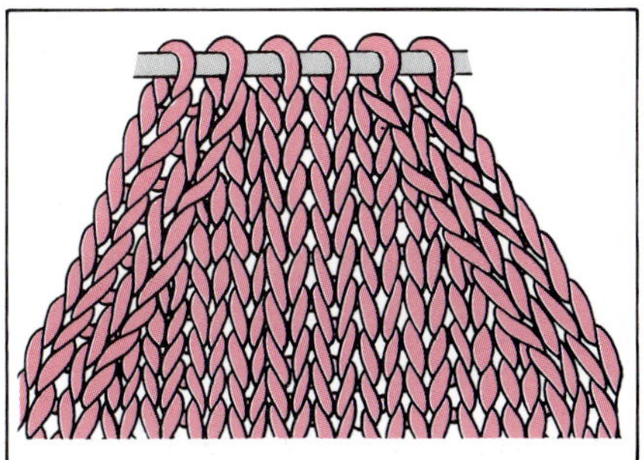

fashioning', on a raglan armhole for example. This will most commonly appear on a pattern as follows:

Next row: K1, sL 1K, K1, psso, work to last 3 sts, K2tog, K1.

K2tog tbl (knit 2 together though back loops)

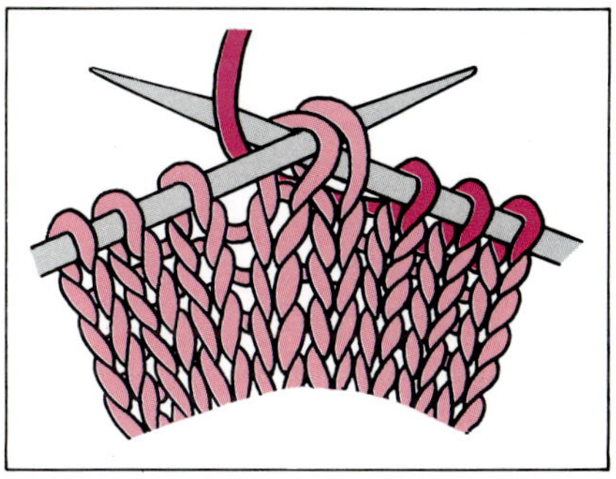

This decrease is similar in method to K2tog but is worked by inserting the right needle through the **back** loops of two stitches and then knitting them together as one stitch.

The effect of this decrease worked on a right side row is to make the stitch slant to the **left** and also twists the stitch.

P2tog (purl 2 together)

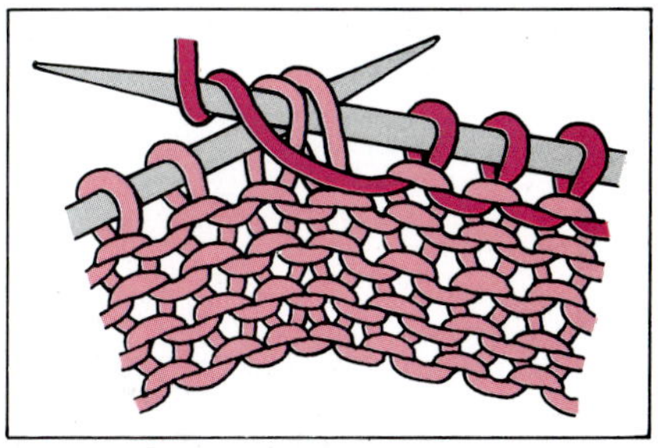

This decrease is worked simply by inserting the right needle purlwise through two stitches instead of one and then purling them together as one stitch.

The effect of this decrease worked on a wrong side row is to make the stitch slant to the right on the right side.

P2tog tbl (purl 2 together through back loops — see Hints and Tips on page 10)

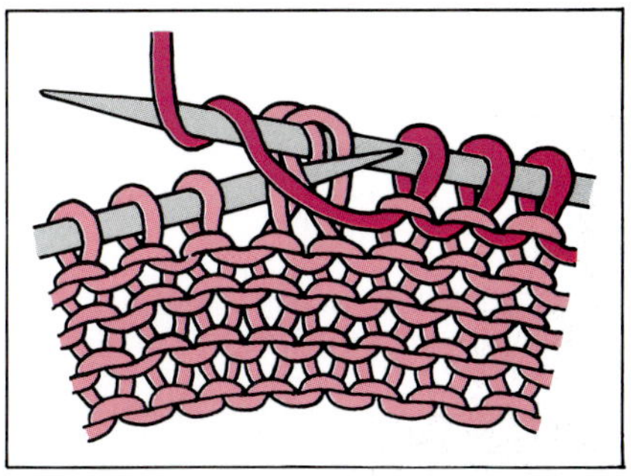

This decrease is similar to P2tog, but is worked by inserting the right needle through the **back** loops of two stitches from left to right and then purling them together as one stitch.

Hints and Tips

Be warned! P2tog tbl is a bit awkward to do, but important to get right so that the stitches slant the correct way, particularly when used in lace patterns.

SL 1K, K2tog, psso (slip 1 knitways, knit 2 together, pass slipped stitch over)

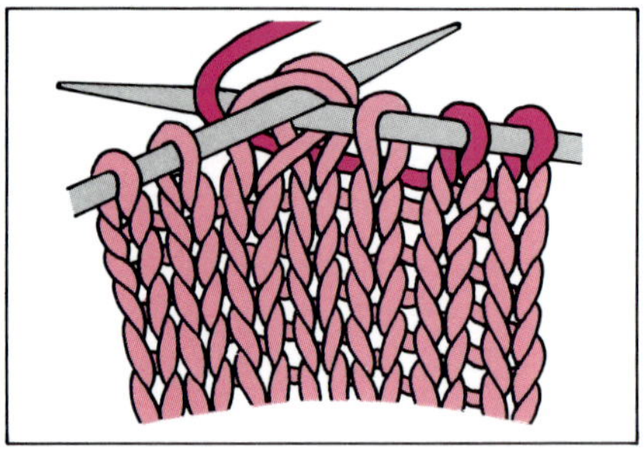

(a) slip next stitch onto right needle without knitting it, then knit together the next 2 stitches.

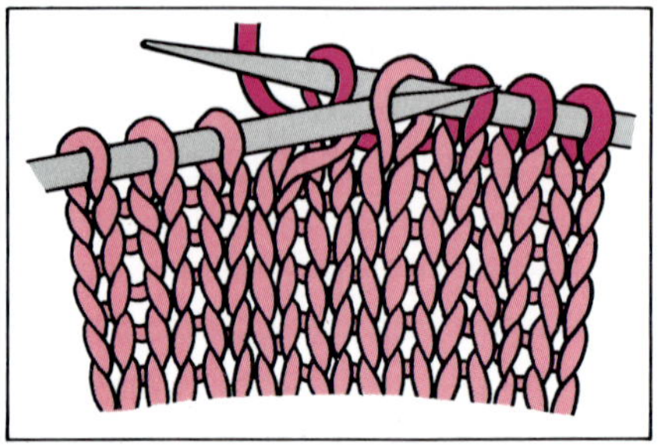

(b) lift the slipped stitch over the knitted stitch and drop it off the needle.

This decreases 2 stitches keeping the stitch slanting to the left.

K3tog (knit 3 together)

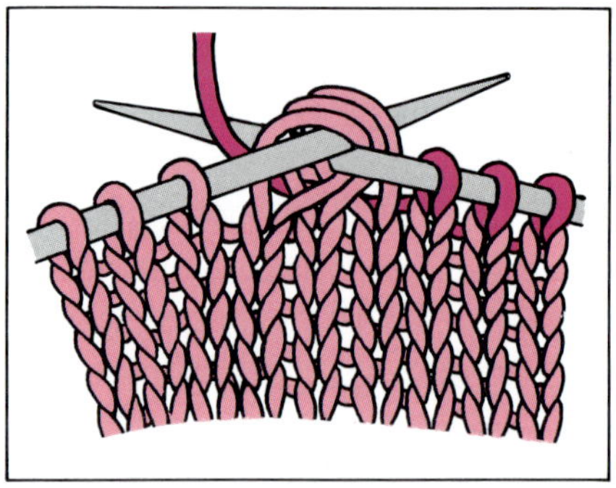

This decrease is worked by inserting the right needle through three stitches instead of one and then knitting them together as one stitch.

This decreases 2 stitches, keeping the stitch slanting to the right.

These two decreases can also be used at each end of a row, and worked 1 or more sts in from the edge, to form a 'fully fashioned edge'. This will most commonly appear on a pattern as follows:

Next row: K1, sL 1K, K2tog, psso, work to last 4 sts, K3tog, K1.

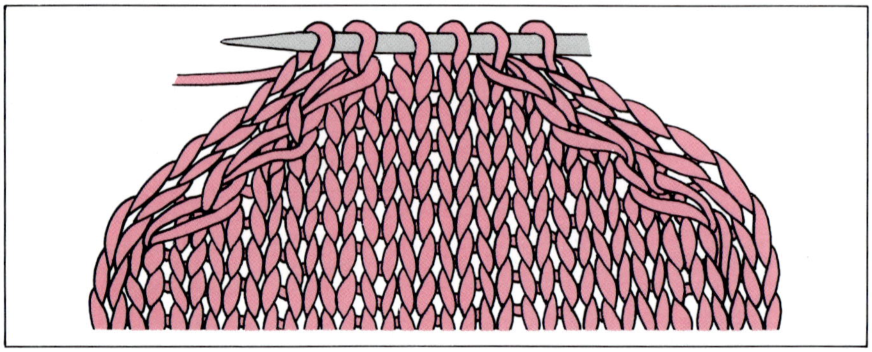

Sl 2tog, K1, p2sso (slip 2 together, knit one, pass 2 slipped stitches over)

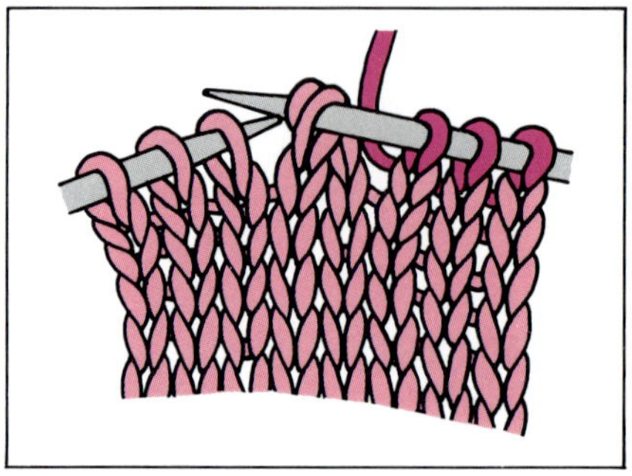

(a) insert right needle into next 2 stitches as if to knit 2 together but then slip these stitches onto right needle without knitting them.

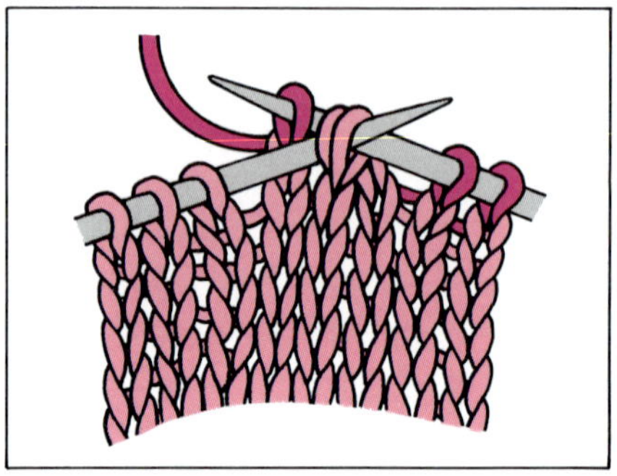

(b) knit next st, then lift the slipped stitches over the knitted st and drop them off the needle.

This decreases 1 stitch either side of a centre stitch, and keeps the centre stitch on top (sometimes used on V-neckbands).

Having discovered that you **can** knit without making a complete mess of things you may wish to do more than a plain stocking st or garter st garment! Do not be put off by lace patterns or cables as every design, however complicated, is really only a variation of knit and purl stitches and you have already taught yourself how to knit and purl..... and much more. So onwards to the next stage.

Lace and Eyelet Patterns

Lace patterns are all based on the same principle — a decrease worked in conjunction with an increase. The increase is made by winding the yarn round the needle, to make a hole or eyelet. The decrease is worked in order to keep the same number of stitches.

The decrease is either worked directly next to the eyelet, or a few stitches away, and can be either visible to form part of the design, or invisible.

Eyelets (on their own!)

Note: For North American readers the term **yo** (yarn over) covers all of the following abbreviations, and means that you should wind the yarn round the needle to make a stitch.

yfwd and yrn — you have already seen how to work yfwd (between 2 knit stitches) and yrn (between 2 purl sts) on page 9.

yrn (yarn round needle)

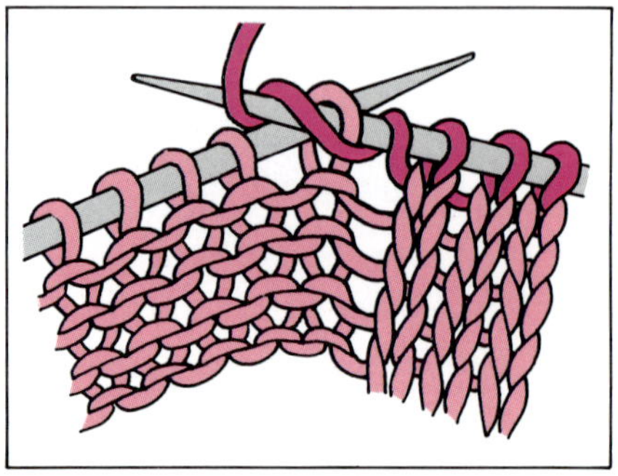

Yrn is also used to make a stitch after a knit stitch and before a purl stitch. Bring the yarn under the right needle to front of work, then over the top and back round under the needle to the front. Some patterns may use yfrn (yarn forward and round needle) as separate from yrn in this case.

yon (yarn over needle)

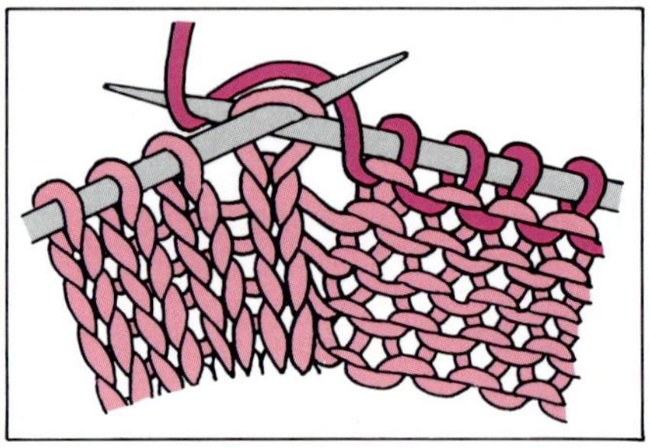

To make a stitch after a purl stitch and before a knit stitch, take the yarn over the top of the right needle and knit the next stitch.

Eyelets with decreases

Note: For North American readers the term **yo** (yarn over) covers yfwd (yarn forward) and yrn (yarn round needle).

K2tog, yfwd (knit 2 together, yarn forward)

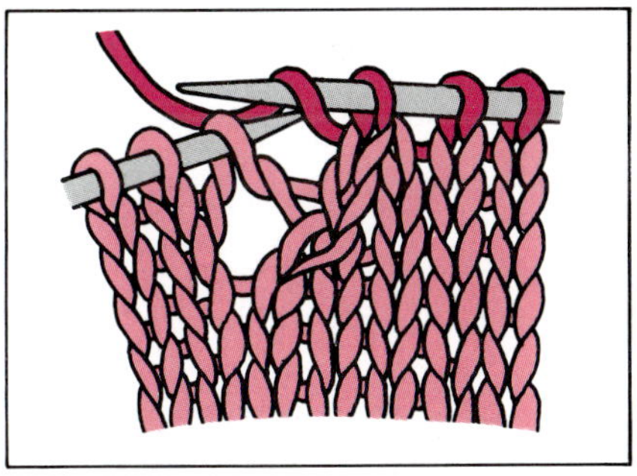

The decrease slants to the right with the eyelet on the left.

yfwd, sL 1K, K1, psso (yarn foward, slip 1 knitways, knit 1, pass slipped stitch over)

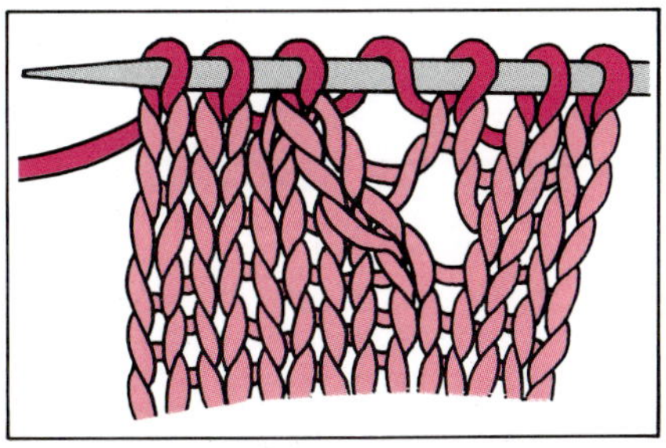

The decrease slants to the left with the eyelet on the right (i.e. the exact opposite of K2tog, yfwd).

yrn, P2tog (yarn round needle, purl 2 together)

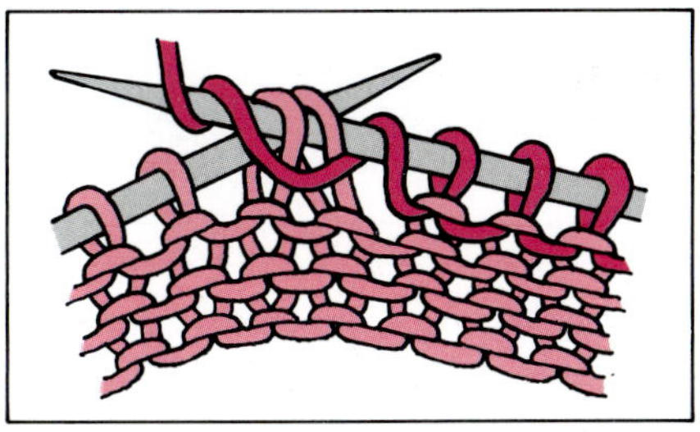

When worked on a wrong side row, this produces the same effect as K2tog, yfwd on a right side row.

P2tog tbl, yrn (purl 2 together through back loops, yarn round needle)

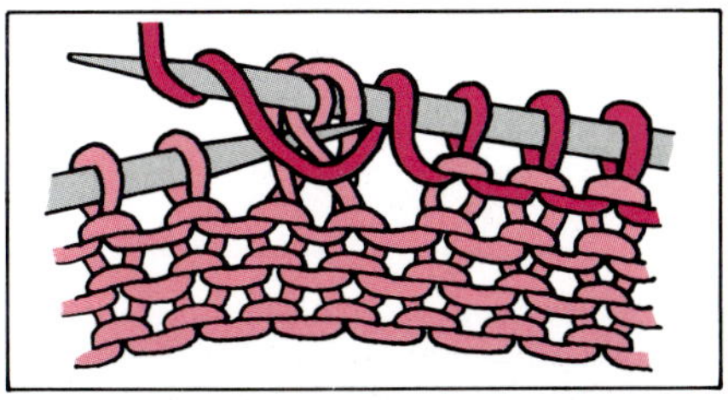

Again, when worked on the wrong side row, this produces the same effect as yfwd, sl 1, K1, psso on a right side row.

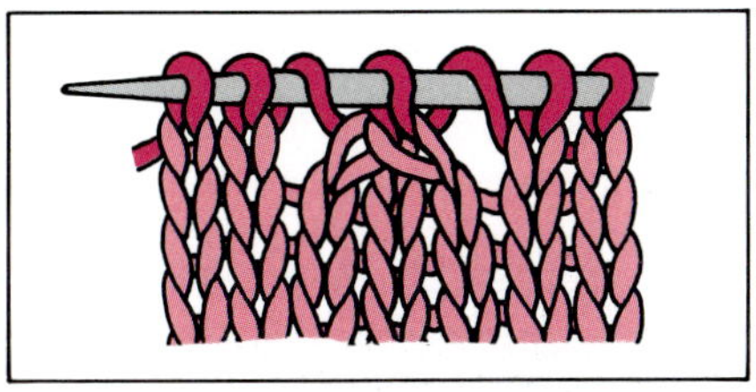

yfwd, sL 1K, K2tog, psso, yfwd (yarn forward, slip 1 knitways, knit 2 together, pass slipped stitch over, yarn forward)

This makes an eyelet either side of a 'double' decrease at centre.

Keeping pattern correct or shaping over lace patterns

Make sure both the eyelet **and** decrease can be worked in order to keep correct number of stitches. If this is not possible work the odd stitches in the main background to the pattern — for example, stocking st (knit on right side rows, purl on wrong side rows).

Before you start shaping, first mark the centre stitch with a coloured thread. As the shaping progresses check that the same number of stitches have been decreased on each side of the work by counting the stitches either side of the marked stitch. The thread marking the centre stitch is moved up as each row is worked. If only a few stitches are to be decreased, e.g. for a set-in sleeve armhole, before starting, count in from each edge the number of stitches to be decreased, place a marker and work as before. Most successful lace patterns rely on the fact that for every 'yfwd', which makes an extra stitch, there is always a 'K2tog' or 'sL 1K, K1, psso' to keep the number of stitches constant. When shaping, you should regard these as pairs of stitches and not work a 'yfwd' unless you have enough stitches to work two together.

Where the eyelet is not always next to the accompanying decrease this is not so easy, in which case it is better to work the remainder of the **complete** pattern repeat in the background stitch.

Cable Patterns

Cabling is simply a method of working the stitches in a different order so that the stitches cross over and give a rope or twisted effect. Once you have overcome the basic methods of cabling, the sky is the limit as all cables are based on the same principle.

Basic Cables

Basic cables are usually worked in stocking stitch on a reversed stocking stitch background in order to stand out. The same stitches are crossed all the time.

You will need a cable needle, or double pointed needle approximately the same thickness as the needles that you are

C4B (Cable 4 Back)

Worked over 4 sts in stocking st, on a reversed stocking st background.

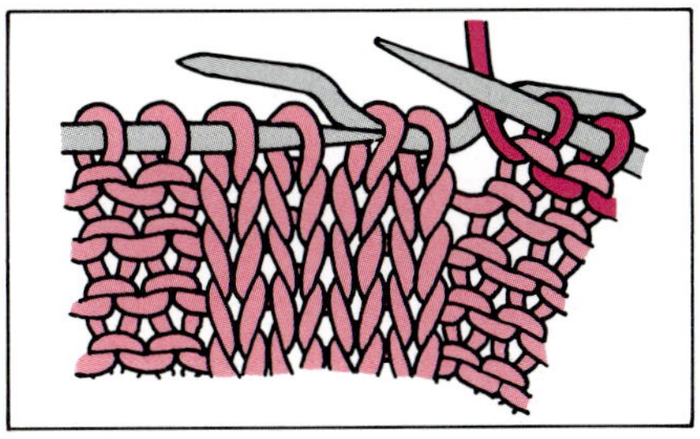

(a) slip next 2 sts onto cable needle and leave at back of work.

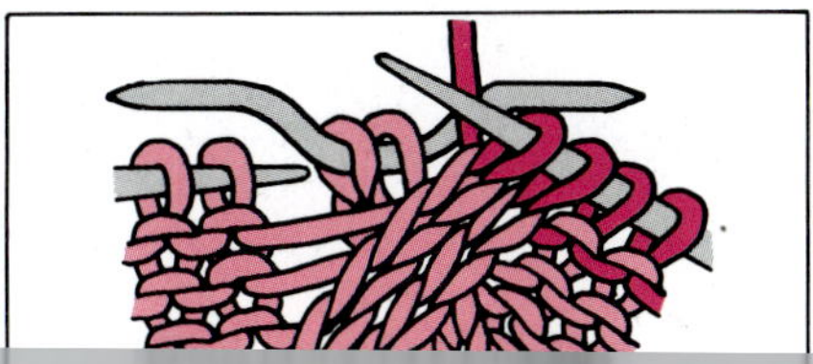

(b) knit next 2 sts from left-hand needle.

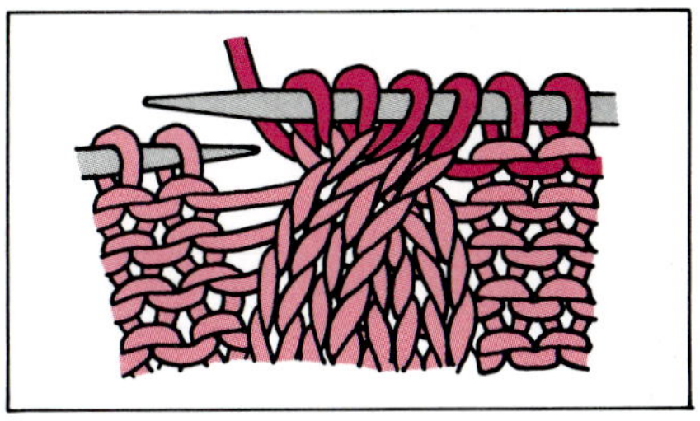

(c) knit sts from cable needle.

This crosses the cable to the right.

C4F (Cable 4 Front)

Worked over 4 sts in stocking st, on a

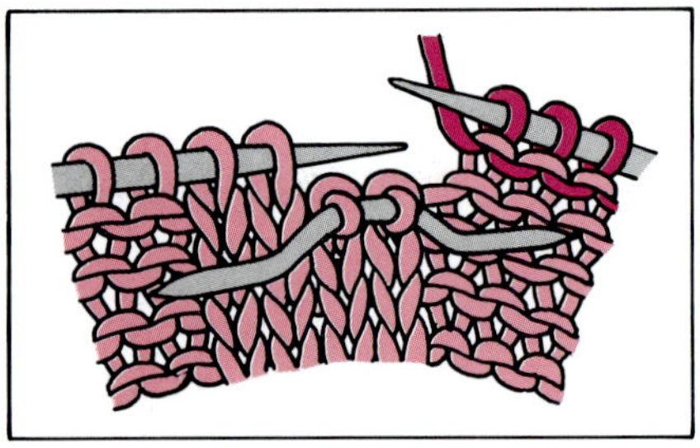

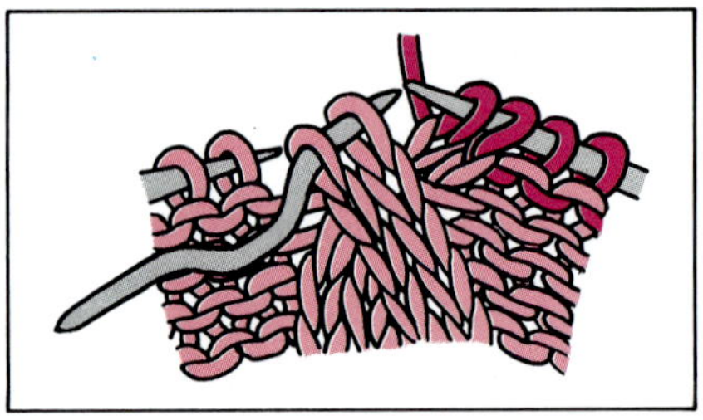

(b) knit next 2 sts from left-hand needle.

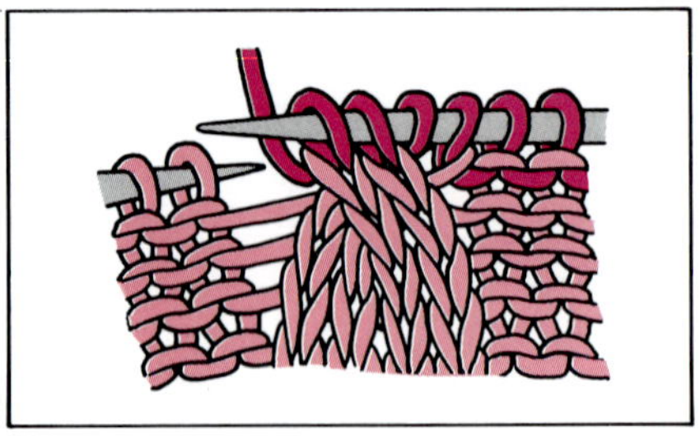

(c) knit sts from cable needle.
This crosses the cable to the left.

Having mastered the technique, any cable or twist is worked in the same way, sometimes crossing different numbers of stitches and working in knit and purl. As you can see depending on whether the stitches on cable needle are held at front or back of work, so the stitches can cross to left or right.

Many cable patterns also involve stitches travelling across a background pattern. On these patterns the stitches cabled are not the same every time. For example:

T3B (Twist 3 Back)

2 sts in stocking st on a reversed stocking st background. Work to 1 st before the 2 knit sts.

(a) slip next st onto cable needle and leave at back of work.

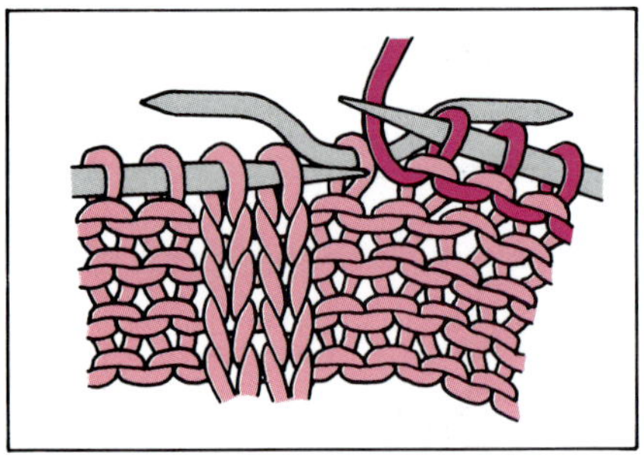

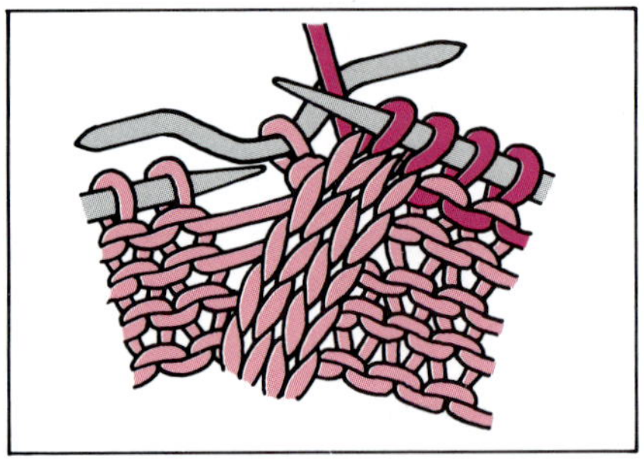

(b) knit next 2 sts from left-hand needle.

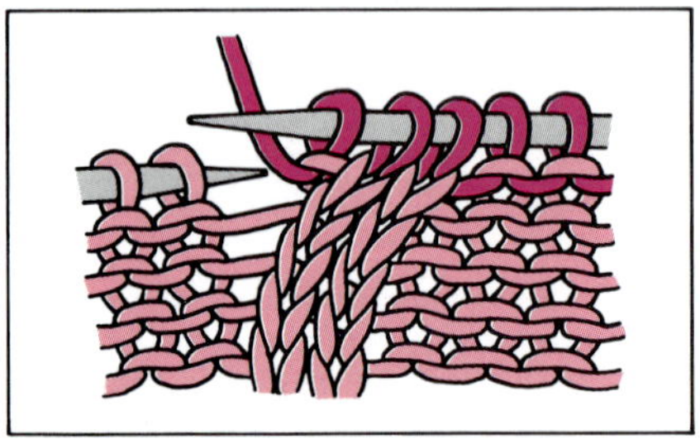

(c) purl st from cable needle.
This twists the 2 sts to the right.

T3F (Twist 3 Front)

2 sts in stocking st on a reversed stocking st background. Work to the 2 knit sts.

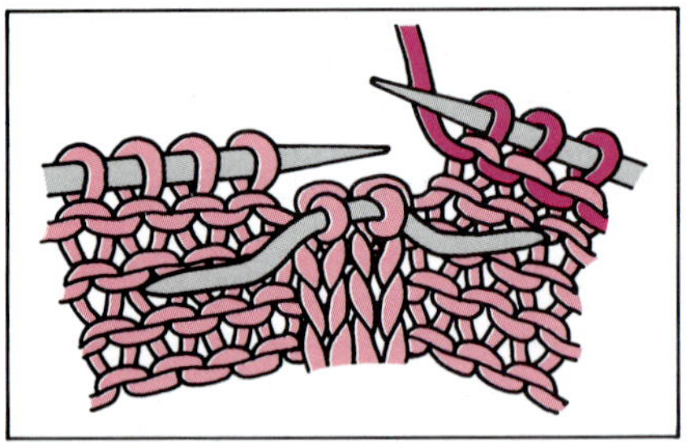

(a) slip next 2 sts onto cable needle and leave at front of work.

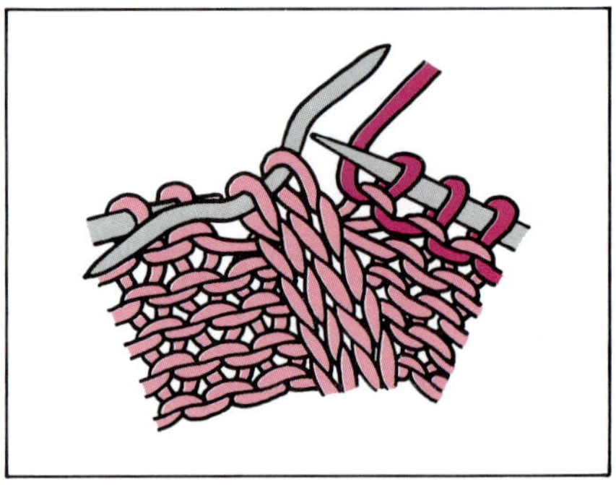

(b) purl next stitch from left-hand needle.

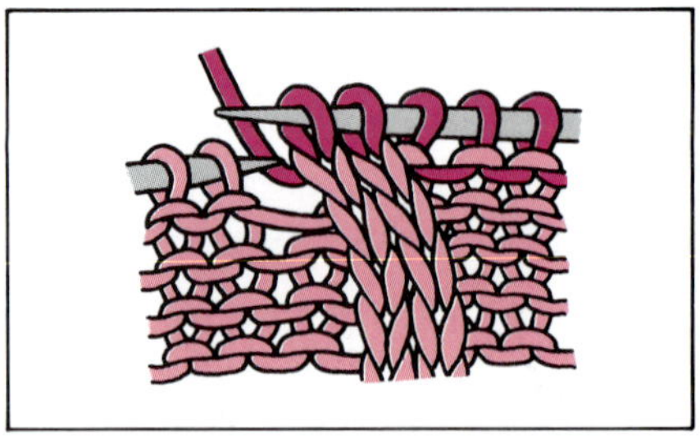

(c) knit sts from cable needle.
This twists the 2 sts to the left.

Keeping pattern correct or shaping over cables

When there are not enough sts to work the complete cable, work the odd stitches in stocking st, or whatever pattern they have been worked in until now.

Hints and Tips

When shaping over cables (either side of a V neck for example), try to keep the pattern symmetrical by ceasing to work the cables in the same place on both sides of the neck.

Fair Isle Patterns

Fair Isle is a general term for patterns where 2 or more colours are used on one row. This can either be as small repeats, or as large blocks of colour. Each of these require slightly different methods of working.

Stranding colours

Use this method for colour patterns with small repeats.

(a) Knit row — hold the second colour in the left hand and carry it loosely across

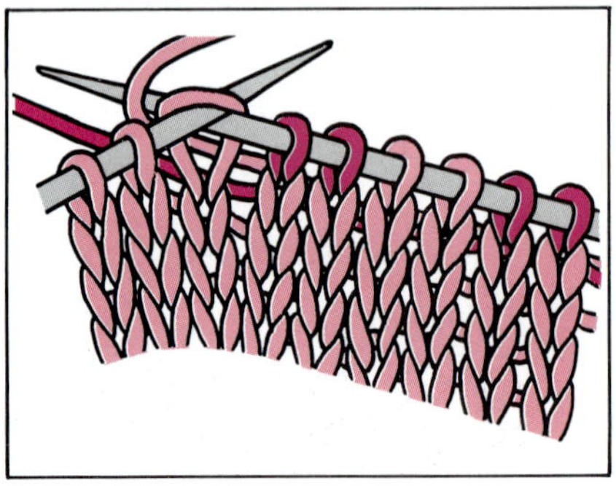

the wrong side of the work.

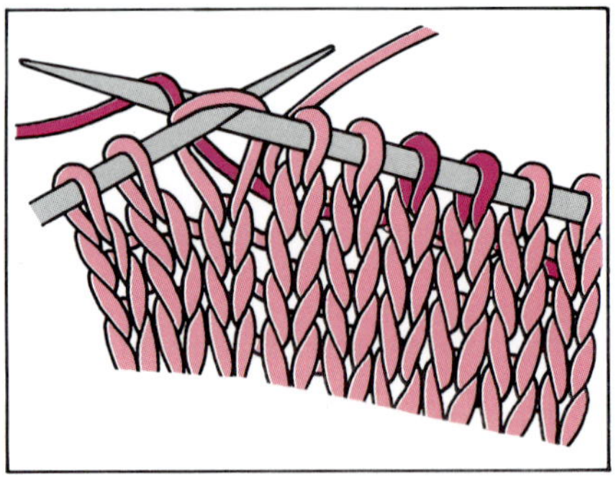

(b) To knit second colour lay yarn over

needle as shown and draw through a loop.

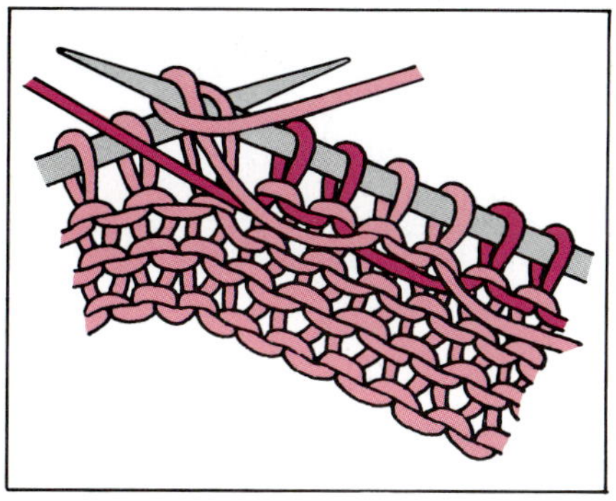

(c) Purl row — hold second colour in left hand.

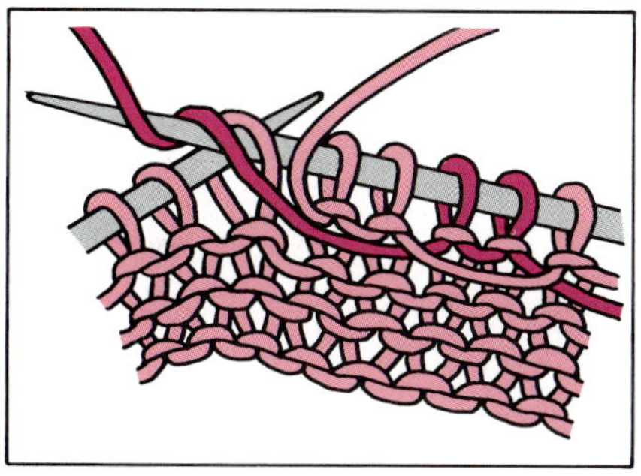

(d) To purl second colour wind yarn round needle as shown and draw through a loop.

Twist yarns together every 3rd or 4th stitch where more than 6 sts are worked in one colour by laying colour not in use across colour in use before working the next stitch. This avoids long floats at the back of work which can easily get caught when putting the garment on.

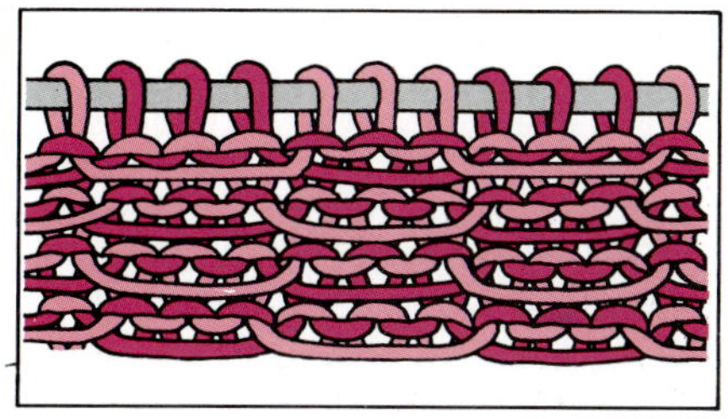

(e) A more professional appearance can be gained by keeping the same colour at the top on the wrong side and carrying colours to ends of rows.

Carry the colours not in use loosely up side edge of work.

Hints and Tips

The secret of working good 2-colour knitting is to carry the colour not in use **loosely** across the wrong side of the work and take care not to pull it tight when changing the colours over.

Weaving

It is possible to twist yarns together on every alternate stitch of a fair isle pattern as given above for Stranding. This gives a neat appearance at the back of the work but distorts the shape of the stitches and alters the tension. Unless the pattern specifically calls for this method it is not recommended.

Blocks of Colour

Where colours are used in large blocks or over large areas at a time, it is best to use a separate ball of yarn for each section.

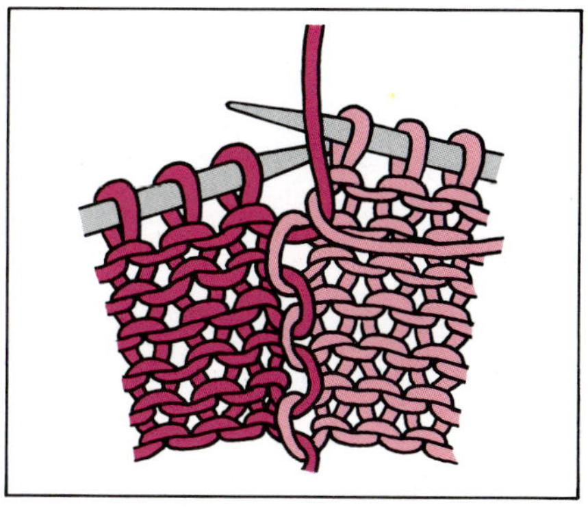

When using separate balls of yarn, the yarns must be twisted over each other when changing colour, otherwise a hole will be formed between the colours. When the colour change is in a vertical line, cross the yarns on both knit and purl rows.

When the colour change is on a slanting line, the yarns need be crossed only on alternate rows.

(a) When the colour change slants to the right, cross the yarns on the knit row. Take the first colour in front of the second colour, drop it, then pick up and knit with the second colour. On the purl row the diagonal slants in such a way that the yarns automatically cross.

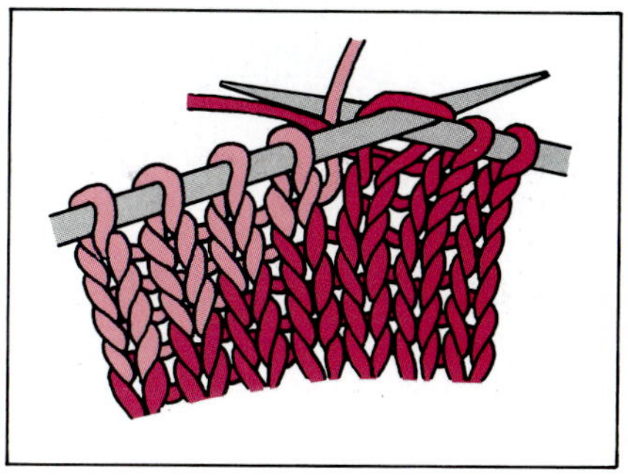

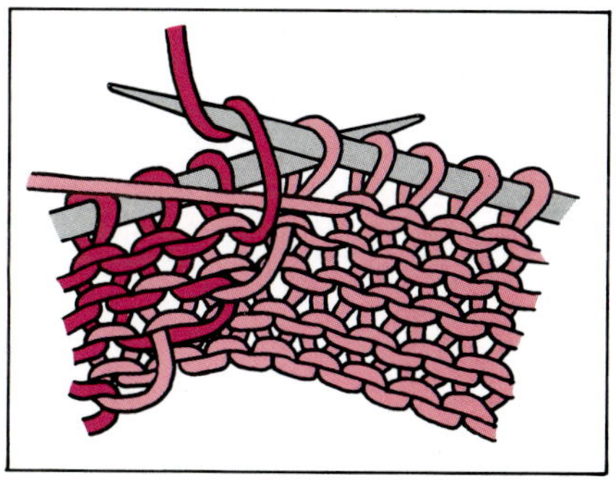

(b) When the colour change slants to the left, the yarns must be crossed on the purl row. On the knit row the diagonal slant causes the yarns to cross automatically.

Working from Charts

Fair Isle or colour patterns will either be given as rows written out, or in the form of a squared chart. One square usually represents one stitch and one row. When working from a chart, always read the notes concerning the method of working very carefully. You should find clear instructions for direction of reading the chart, when to twist yarns together and so on.

Hints and Tips

Where areas of colour are small and many, it is easier to use Aero, Milward or Susan Bates 'Yarn Bobbins'. These are shaped pieces of plastic with a slit at one end. Wind a length of yarn onto bobbin and pass end through slit to stop it unravelling. Unwind short lengths at a time, allowing bobbin to hang on wrong side of work when not in use.

Fisherman's Rib

This is a very popular stitch, and easy to do once you get the knack!

Here, we show you how to work 'knit 1 below', a common stumbling block with fisherman's rib.

Insert right needle through centre (to back of work) of stitch **below** next stitch on left needle. Wind yarn round needle and draw through a loop, dropping **both** stitches off left needle. This is sometimes abbreviated as K1B (Knit 1 Below).

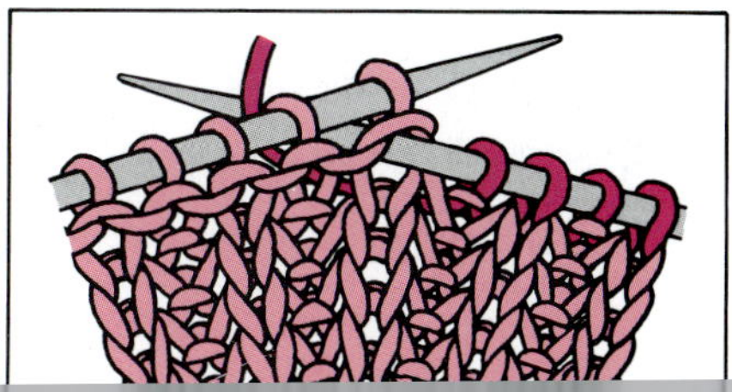

See page 22 for a full explanation of one version of fisherman's rib.

Working Notes

This section contains general information to help you while you are knitting.

Following a Pattern

Knitting patterns are written in a language all of their own. Abbreviations are used for many of the repetitive words which occur in the instructions and although all manufacturers do not use exactly the same abbreviations, an experienced knitter can follow the jargon.

Before starting to knit any pattern, always read it right through. Even if you are not experienced, this will give you an idea of how the pattern is structured and you will know what to expect. After knitting one or two patterns you will understand how the pattern works.

Where imperial and metric measurements are given always work **either** in inches throughout **or** centimetres throughout, (for example when checking tension or measuring lengths).

Asterisks, *, and Brackets, ( ) [ ]

These are used to indicate repetition of a sequence of stitches. For example: *k3, p1; rep from * to end. This means you repeat 'knit 3 stitches and purl 1 stitch' over and over to the end of the row. When instructions appear within brackets, they are worked for the number of times required as stated afterwards. For example: [k3, p1] 4 times. This means that the stitches within the brackets are worked 4 times in all.

Work Straight

This instruction means that you continue with the number of stitches on the needle for the required length or number of rows without increasing or decreasing.

0 = no stitch, row or time

Some patterns may include the figure '0'. The abbreviation section will tell you whether this refers to stitches, rows or times. For example, if you are following the 2nd size and the instruction for your size reads 'K2, (yfwd, sL 1K, K1, psso) 1[0-1-1] time, K1', you should knit 2 stitches, (K2), then skip the instruction in round brackets and go straight on to the next part of the instruction. If the instruction reads e.g. K2[0-2-2], it means that you should not knit any stitches for the 2nd size, but those knitters following the other sizes should all knit 2 stitches. By using this method, our designers ensure that texture or lace patterns go right to the side edges of the work on **every** size and that the sizes all have similar ease.

General Abbreviations

Below are the most common pattern abbreviations. Most of them have been explained in detail in earlier sections.

Alt = alternate

For example: increase 1 stitch at end of next and every **alt** row until there are X sts. This means that, counting the next row as row 1, the increase is worked on rows 1, 3, 5, 7 etc., until the required number of stitches is reached.

Beg = beginning
Cm = centimetres
Dec = decrease (see page 9)
Inc = increase (see page 8)
Ins = inches
K = knit
P = purl
Psso = pass slipped stitch over
Rep = repeat
SL 1K = slip 1 knitways
SL 1P = slip 1 purlways
St(s) = stitch(es)
Stocking st = 1 row K, 1 row P (see page 4)
Tbl = through back of loop (see page 9)
Tog = together
Ybk = yarn back — take yarn under needle from front to back
Yft = yarn front — take yarn under needle from back to front
Yfwd = yarn forward (see page 9)
Yon = yarn over needle (see page 10)
Yrn = yarn round needle (see pages 9 and 10)

Joining in a new ball

Always finish at the end of a row. Avoid joining in a new ball halfway through a row, as the sewing in of ends can spoil the appearance on the right side, and can lead to holes appearing if not done properly.

Measuring lengths

The most accurate method of measuring wide pieces (for example when the width of your knitting is more than the length of one needle), is to work halfway across a row, lay the work flat on a table and spread the sts evenly across the 2 needles.

Always measure at centre of work, never at side edge which is usually looser than the main work. Place a marker (a safety pin or piece of yarn) at centre of last row before start of armhole shaping. This makes it easier to measure the armhole length when you come to it.

Counting rows

You will achieve a much more professional finish if you work the same number of rows on similar pieces, particularly when they are to be joined together at the side edges — for example the back and front. It is helpful either to make a note of rows in the margin of your pattern for each section, or the number of times a pattern is repeated.

It can also be easier to place the start of neck shaping in the correct position (if it is given in rows below shoulder) if you know how many rows you have in the body length or armhole length.

Hints and Tips

Underline your size throughout before you start — this makes life much easier and avoids the possibility of following the wrong instructions and having to undo all your hard work!

Finishing and Making up

Once all the separate pieces for a garment have been knitted, and before they are joined together or edgings are worked, the pieces need to be pressed or blocked to the correct size and shape. For general instructions see page 46. Once pressed the pieces are much easier to sew together.

Joining seams

Running stitch seam (or invisible stitch)

You will see in the diagram to the right a visual description of the running stitch that we use for almost every seam in the garments we make as this gives the neatest, most professional finish.

Running stitch is worked one stitch in from the edge.

Thread a wool or tapestry needle with the knitting yarn. Work under two rows at a time.

The secret of good running stitching is to keep the seam elastic without allowing it to stretch too much. The best way to do this is to work the running stitch loosely for a few stitches and then pull the thread very firmly so that the stitches are held together quite tightly. Now stretch this seam slightly to give the required amount of elasticity, then continue with the next

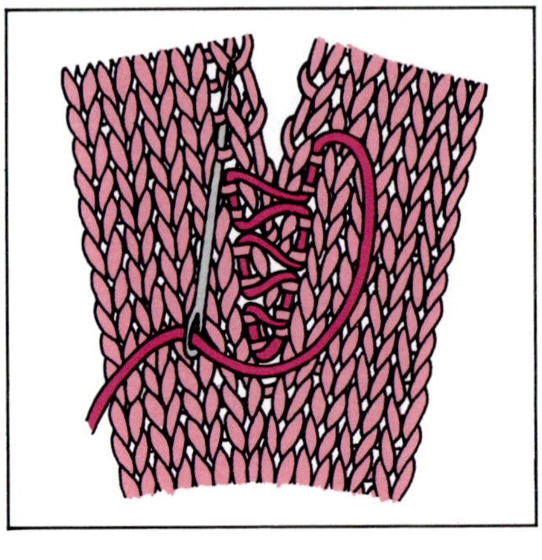

section of the seam.

If you are used to sewing your knitting together by other means it may take a little while to get used to using running stitch. However — practise makes perfect and the professional finish you will achieve will make it worth while. As you can see, it is important to have the same number of rows in pieces to be joined, as mentioned on page 14 and to carefully match pieces together row for row.

Another advantage of running stitch is that it can be used to sew shaped edges together quite easily; because you are working on the right side of the work all the time it is much easier to see where you are and to keep the seam neat.

Backstitch seam

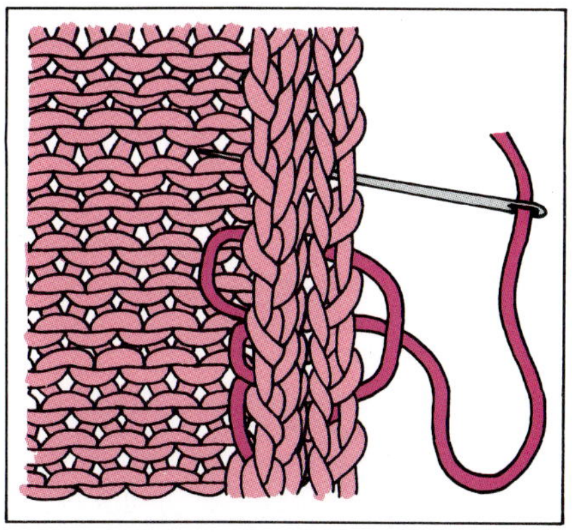

Place the pieces to be joined right sides together. Ensure that they match pattern for pattern and row for row. Thread a wool or tapestry needle with the knitting yarn and work backstitch along the seam close to the edge.

Slip Stitch

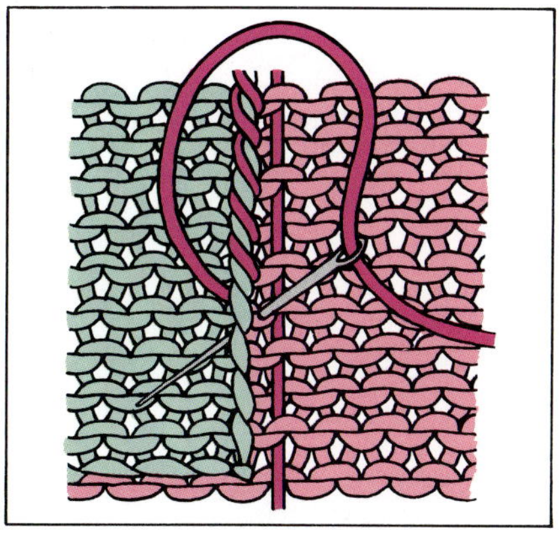

This method is neatest for sewing pocket linings and edgings in place. To make sure that linings are sewn onto the wrong side in a straight line it is helpful to run a line of stitches in a contrast colour down the centre of the edge stitch of pocket on main piece of garment. This line of stitching can then be used as a guide. To avoid stitches showing on right side insert needle through centre of the thread on main part of garment, rather than under whole thread.

Flat seam

with loose stitches matching ridge for ridge.

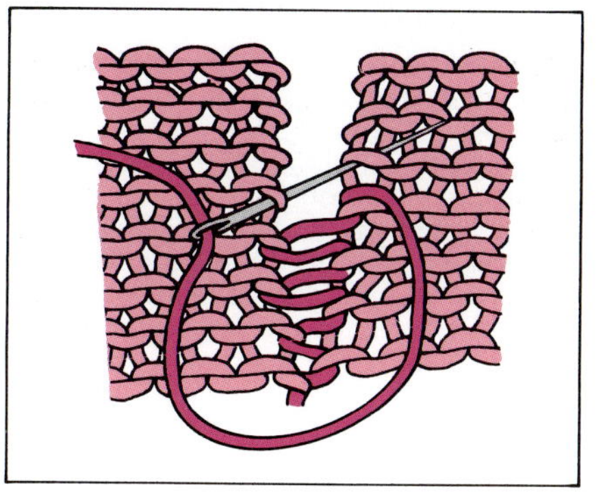

Oversewing

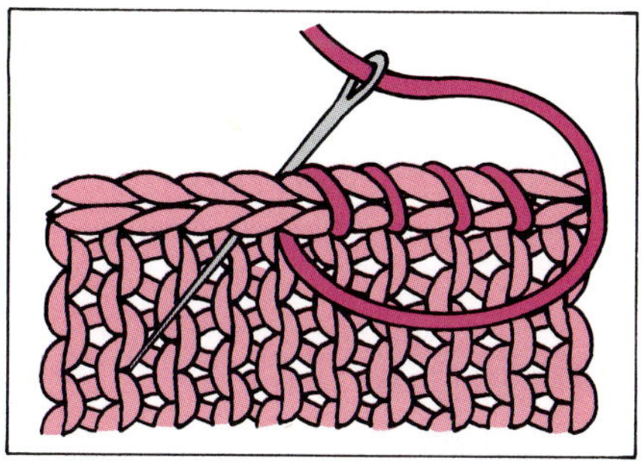

Place pieces to be joined right sides together making sure rows and patterns match. Work an oversewing stitch close to the edge, using a wool or tapestry needle threaded with the knitting yarn.

Hems

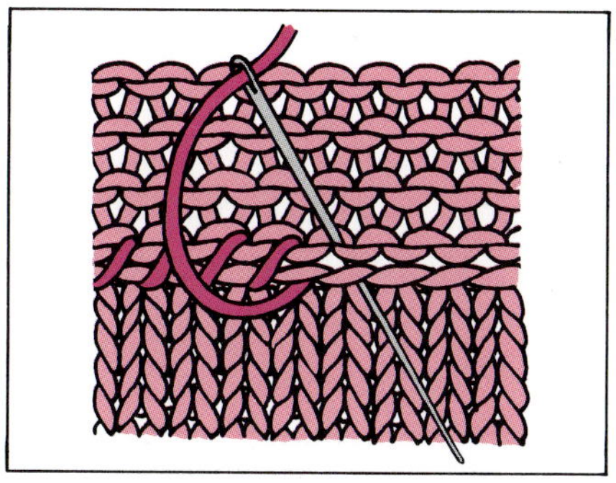

Fold work in half to inside along fold-line. Using either a wool or tapestry needle threaded with the knitting yarn, or a sewing needle and thread, slip stitch carefully in place taking care to match stitch for stitch, so that the edge lays flat and is not twisted.

Knitting up stitches along an edge

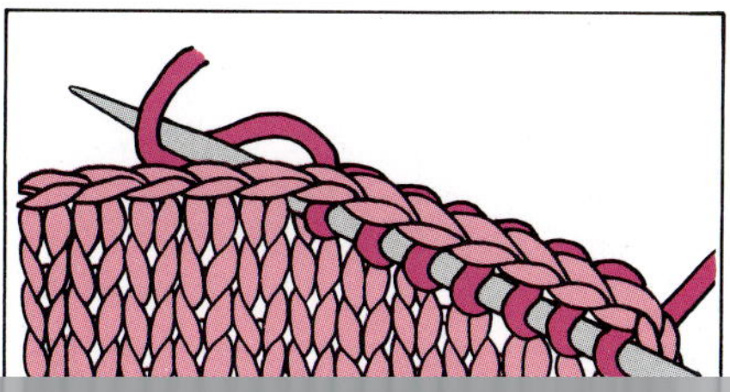

To knit up stitches along a cast on or cast off edge — for example to add a border or to work a collar — insert the point of the knitting needle under both loops of the first stitch, pass the yarn around the needle and draw a loop through to form a stitch. Continue for as many stitches as are required.

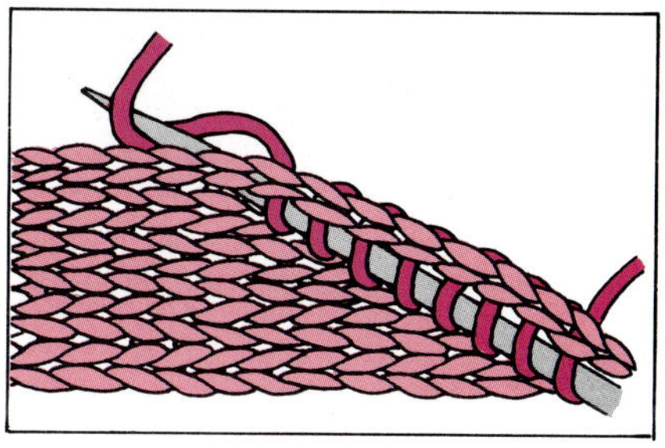

To knit up stitches along side edges — for example the button band on a cardigan — insert the point of the needle between the first and second rows 1 stitch or half a stitch in from the edge, pass the yarn over the needle and draw a loop through.

Often, the number of stitches that must be picked up is not the same as the number of stitches or rows along the edge.

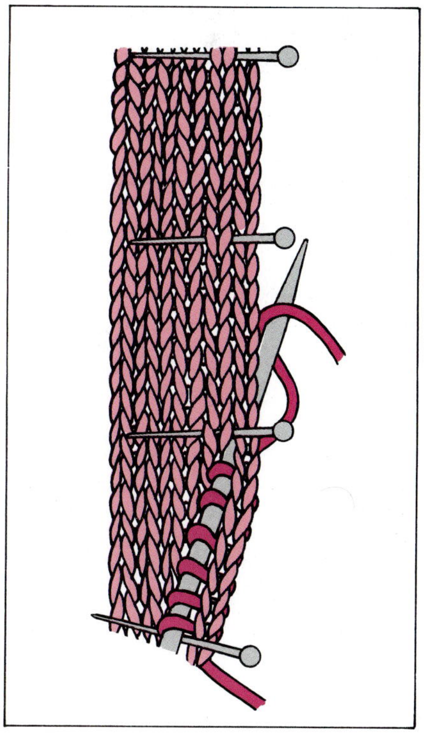

It is easier to pick up the stitches evenly if you divide the length of the edge in half, then in half again and again, so the edge is divided into eighths. Mark each division with a pin. Divide the number of stitches to be picked up by eight and pick up approximately that number of stitches in each section to total the number required.

Buttonholes

A simple way of making a small buttonhole suitable for baby garments is by making an eyelet by the 'K2tog, yfwd'

Horizontal Buttonhole

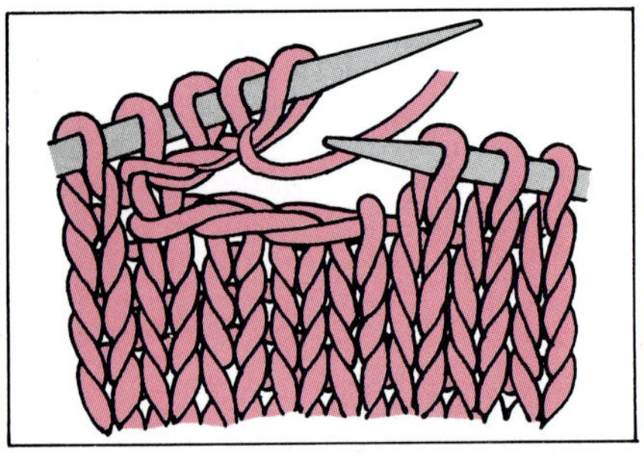

Work to position of buttonhole, cast off given number of stitches (depending on size of button and thickness of yarn), work to end of row. On next row work to cast off stitches, turn and cast on same number of stitches cable method, but before placing last stitch on left needle, take yarn from back to front between points of needles, then turn and work to end of row. The opening can be neatened by working buttonhole stitch round the edge.

Vertical Buttonhole

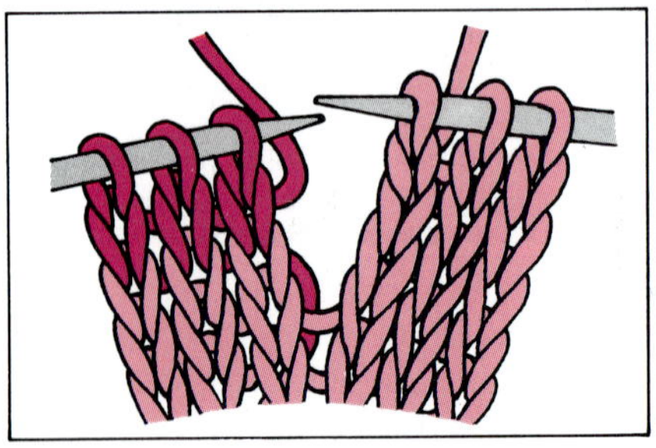

Divide stitches at position of buttonhole and work an equal number of rows on each set of stitches then join up with a row worked right across.

Sewing in Zips

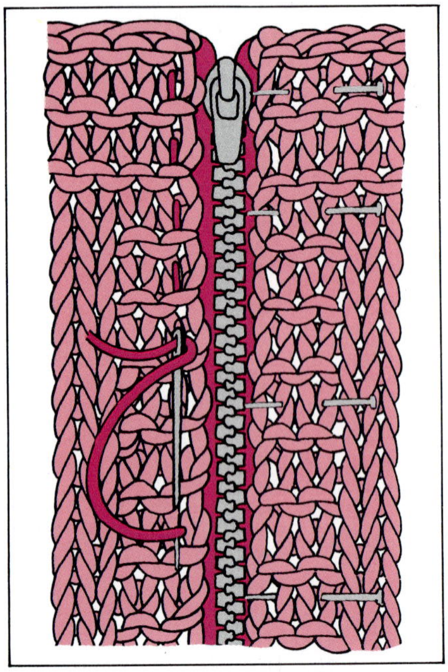

When putting a zip in a cardigan or jacket it is best to have a firm edge to sew the zip to (for example 2 sts worked in garter st), but on a skirt the zip can be sewn to the edge of main fabric in order to keep it unobstrusive. Match depth of zip carefully with depth of opening. Pin zip in position on wrong side of fabric taking care that top ends are folded neatly inside, and tack.

Using a sewing needle and thread backstitch in position on right side with small stitches close to teeth of zip, then oversew tape on wrong side all round the edge. If required, a row of double crochet can be worked all round the edge of opening on the right side to cover teeth of zip when closed.

Hints and Tips

It may not be possible to get an open-ended zip of exactly the length you require. In this case either get a shorter one and end slightly lower down at neck edge than originally intended, or a longer one and take the end slightly higher up. Do not stretch or gather the edge to fit zip length as this will spoil the appearance of the finished garment.

Sewing in set-in Sleeves

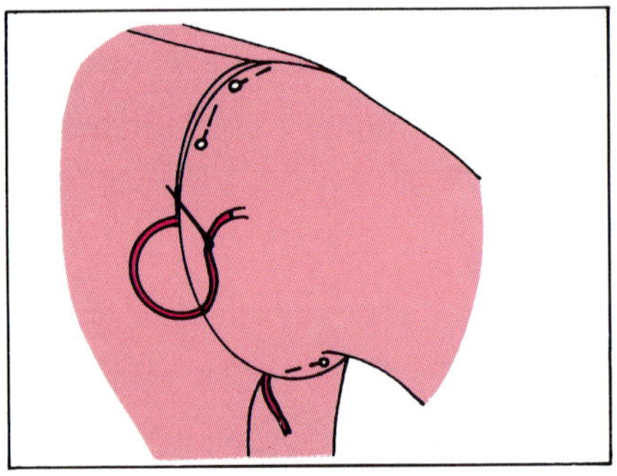

Pin sleeve into position in armhole, matching underarm seams, and centre of top edge with shoulder seam. Either sew from right side using running stitch (see page 14), or from wrong side by backstitching (see page 11).

Elastic Waistbands

Cut elastic to required waist size and join into a circle. Elastic should fit comfortably allowing a slight stretch. Lay elastic in position on inside of waistband. Elastic is held in position with a Herringbone or Crochet Casing.

Herringbone Casing

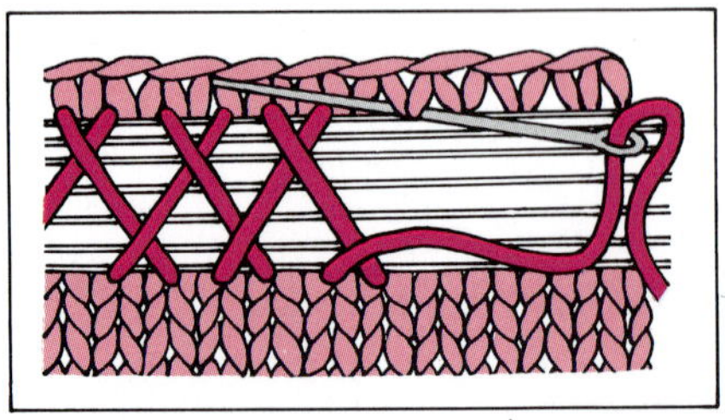

Use a tapestry needle and matching yarn (1 or more thicknesses as required) and work Herringbone stitch over the elastic, working into every alternate stitch of knitting. Stitch just inside top edge and just below elastic as in diagram. Take care not to catch the elastic as this must be left free to move within the casing.

Crochet Casing

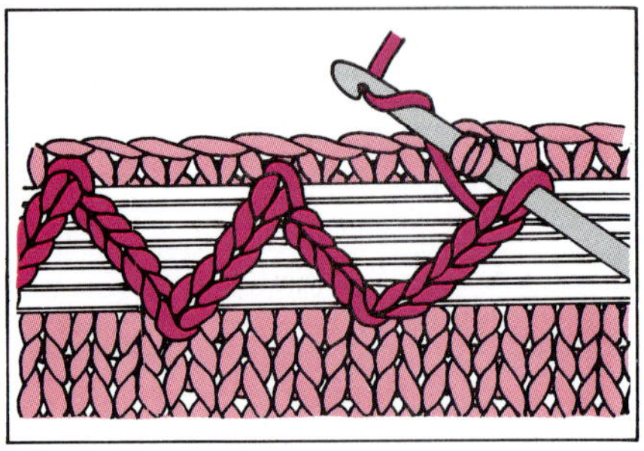

Using a medium crochet hook and correct yarn work a zig-zag chain as follows: Start at side seam and work a slip stitch into top edge, make 6 chain (or number of chain required to take width of elastic), work slip stitch below lower edge 2 sts along; continue thus as in diagram until casing is complete. Fasten off neatly.

Sewing in Front Bands

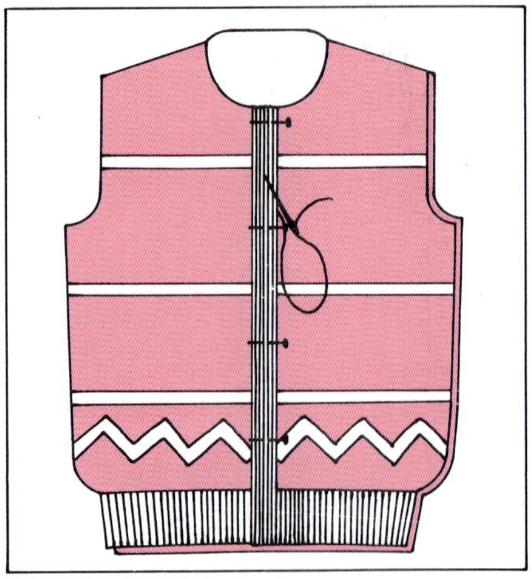

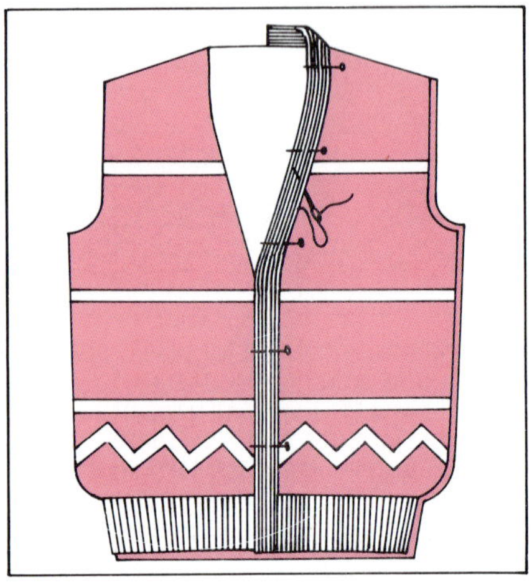

Knit the band as instructions. Lay fronts on top of back flat on a table, making sure cast on edges are level and that shoulders match. Any horizontal patterning should be level across garment. Pin band in place stretching evenly. On most stocking stitch garments the band can be sewn to the main garment row for row. The neatest method is by running stitch.

Where the band cannot be sewn row for row, miss a row every so often on the side which has more rows (how often depends on how much tighter the rows are).

Grafting

Grafting invisibly joins two pieces of knitting. The edges are not cast off, and the knitting can be joined either while it is still on the needles or after it has been taken off.

Knitting on the needles

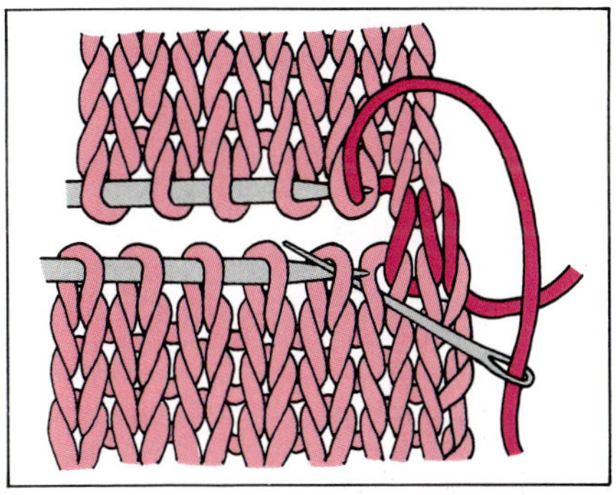

Thread a wool or tapestry needle with a length of the knitting yarn. Place the two pieces to be joined with wrong sides together and hold the knitting needles in the left hand. *Pass the wool needle knitwise through the first stitch on the front needle and slip the stitch off the knitting needle. Pass the wool needle purlwise through the second stitch on the same needle, leaving the stitch on the needle. Pass purlwise through the first stitch on the back knitting needle and slip the stitch off, then pass knitwise through the second stitch on the same needle, leaving the stitch on the needle. Repeat from *. Pull the yarn through to form stitches of the same size as the knitted ones. To finish, darn in loose ends at the back of the work.

Knitting taken off the needles

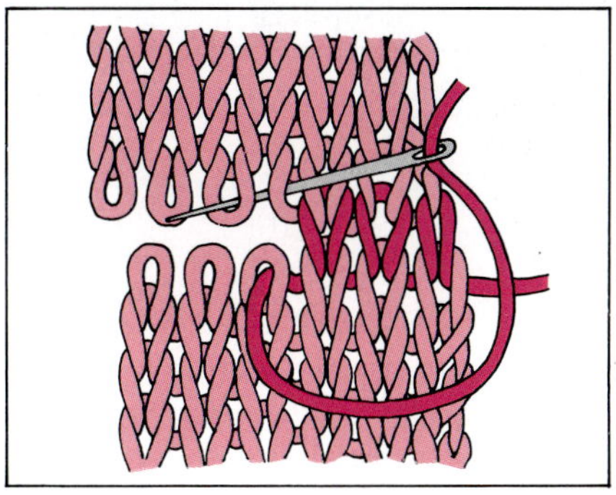

Carefully lay the pieces to be joined close together, with the stitches on each side corresponding to those opposite. Thread a wool or tapestry needle with the knitting yarn. Beginning on the right hand side, bring the needle up through the first stitch of the upper piece, bring it down through the first stitch of the lower piece and bring it up again through the next stitch to the left. *On the upper piece, pass the needle down through the same stitch it came up through before and bring it up through the next stitch to the left. On the lower piece, take the needle down through the stitch it came up through before and bring it up through the next stitch on the left. Repeat from *.

Knitting 2 sets of sts together

This is used when placing a pocket flap for example. On right side row work to position required, hold spare needle with pocket flap sts in front of left-hand needle, *insert right-hand needle through 1 st from each needle and knit them together as one stitch; repeat from * until all the sts have been worked off spare needle. Work to end of row.

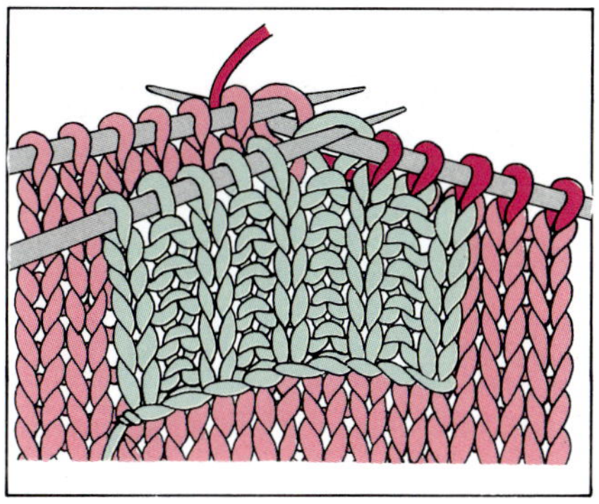

Casting off sts together

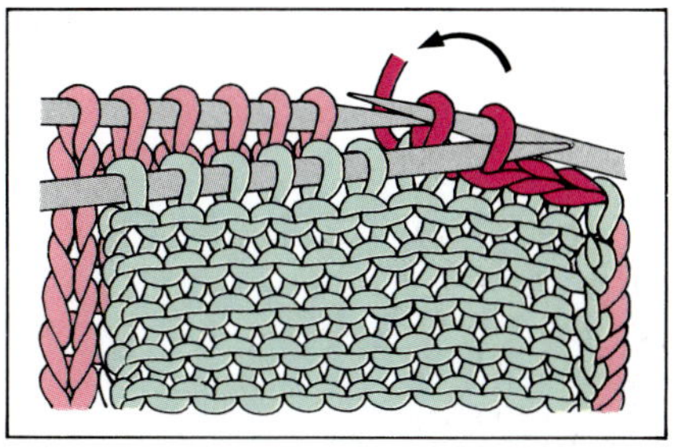

This is used when joining toe sts on a sock for example, to avoid a bulky seam. With sts to be cast off together on spare needles, place right sides together, *knit together 1 st from each needle, repeat from * once more (2 sts on right-hand needle), pass the first st over the 2nd to cast off. Continue in this way until all the sts have been cast off.

Extra Hints

Here are some ideas that will help to make your garment that little bit more individual, and also some slightly more advanced techniques.

Swiss Embroidery, Knitting Stitch Embroidery or Duplicate Stitch

Swiss embroidery (knitting stitch embroidery or duplicate stitch) is a form of embroidery on knitting that exactly covers the knitted stitches so that the finished embroidery looks as if it had been knitted in. It is a useful and versatile technique best used on areas of stocking stitch. When a pattern calls for very small or widely spaced colour motifs, or for a very thin vertical stripe as in many plaids, it is often much easier to darn in after-

For more obviously decorative effects, any suitable knitting or embroidery yarn can be used.

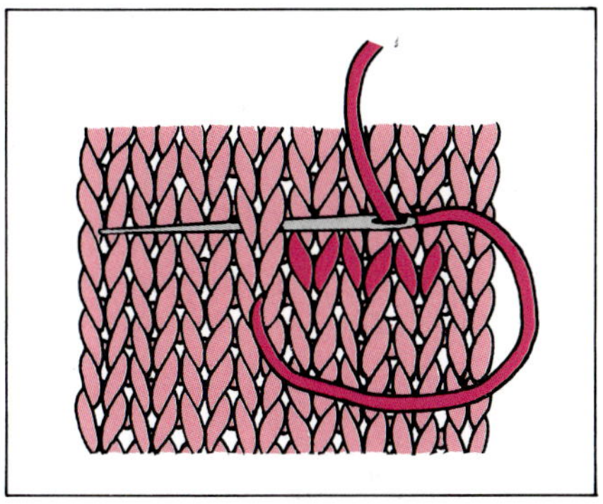

(a) To work duplicate stitch horizontally, work from right to left. Darn in the yarn invisibly at the back. Bring the needle out in the centre of a stitch, take it up and around the head of the stitch (under the stitch above). Take the needle back

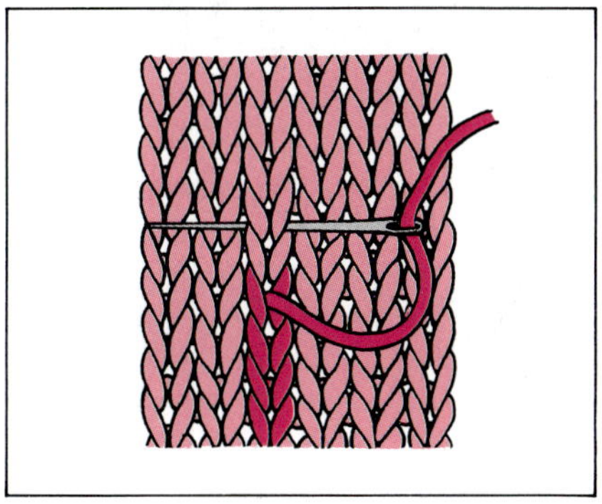

(b) To work the embroidery vertically (from bottom to top) work in the same way but take needle up through centre of stitch **above** at end.

Embroidery

Stocking stitch garments are an ideal surface on which to work embroidery. This

and rows of the knitting as a guide to size will keep the embroidery neat and uniform.

Cross Stitch

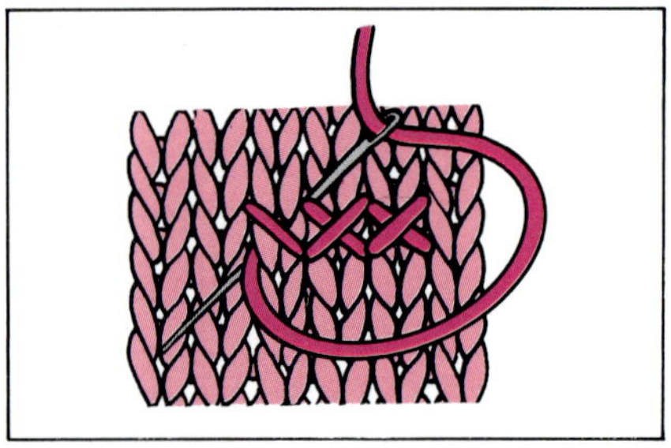

Insert needle as shown to avoid splitting threads.

Chain Stitch

Lazy Daisy

A slight variation on chain stitch gives this characteristic motif. The flower can be formed of 3, 4, 5 or more petals.

Blanket Stitch

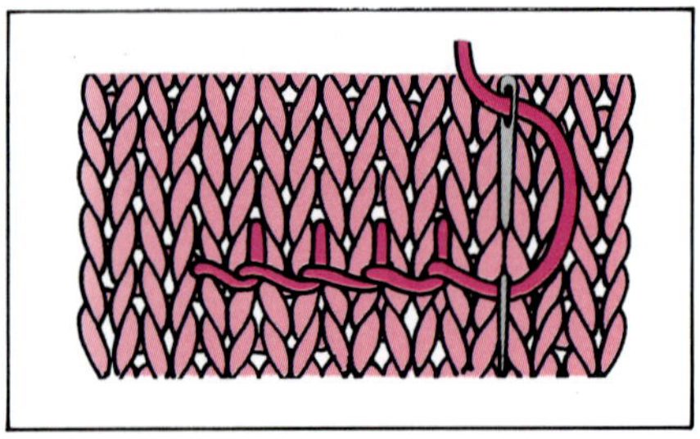

French Knot

Satin Stitch

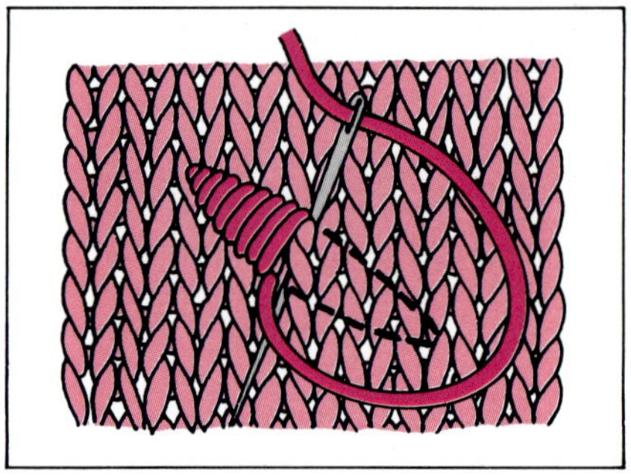

Stem Stitch

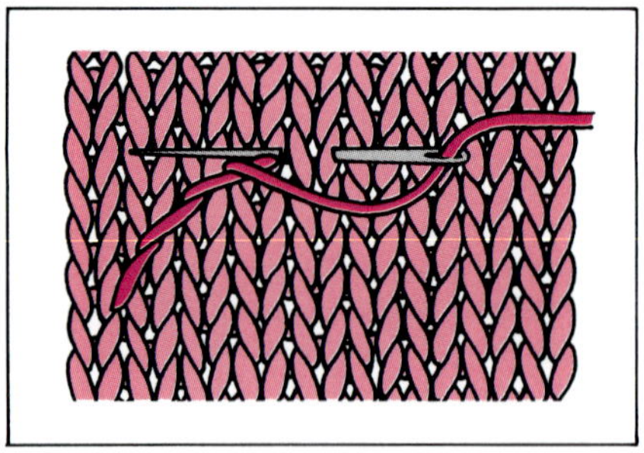

Beading or Sequins

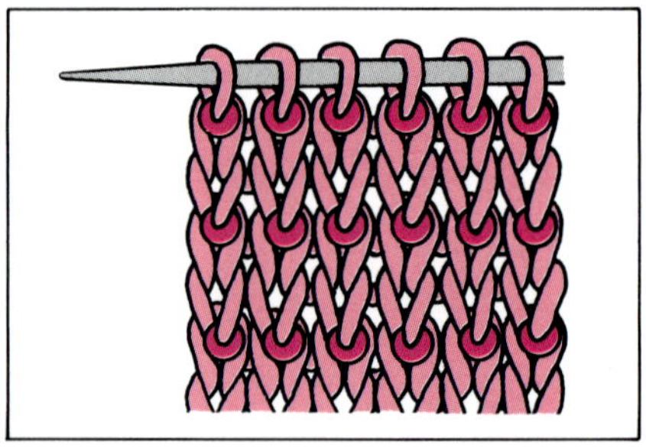

The beads or sequins are threaded onto the yarn before knitting commences, then as the position for each bead or sequin is reached, the next one is pulled up along the yarn close to the needles and the next stitch is knitted, thus fixing the bead or sequin into position.

Fringing

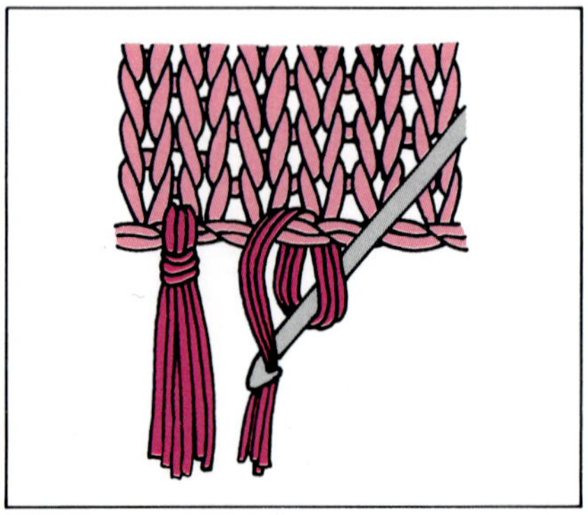

Fringes can be worked along the edge of knitted material as follows: Cut 1 or more lengths of yarn (just over twice the required finished length of the fringe). Fold in half and draw a loop through the edge stitch using a crochet hook. Now draw the loose ends of strands through the loop and pull down tightly to form a knot. Repeat as required at intervals along edge. Trim ends.

Pompons

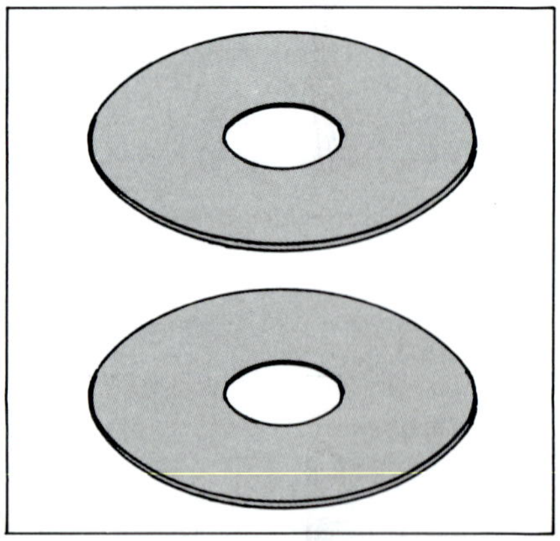

(a) Cut 2 rings of card. The finished diameter of the ring will indicate the approximate finished size of the pompon. Mark and cut a smaller circle at the centre of each piece to thread the wool through.

The larger the centre hole, the fuller and more compact the pompon will be.

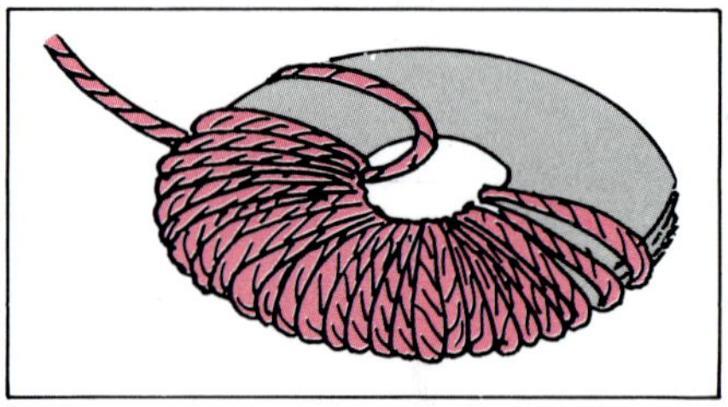

(b) Hold the 2 pieces of card together and wind the yarn round the ring until the card is covered. It is quicker to wind several strands at the same time.

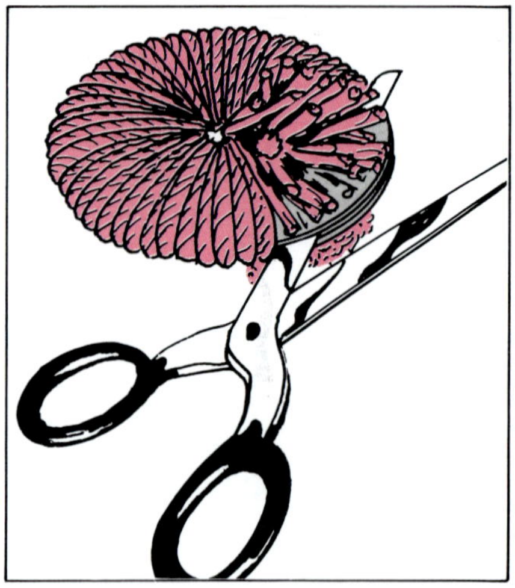

(c) Using a pair of sharp scissors cut between the 2 pieces of card, through all the yarn around the outside edge, until the full circle has been separated.

(d) Before taking the pieces of card away, thread a piece of yarn between the 2 rings and tie into a tight knot, securing the centre of the pompon and leaving enough yarn to attach the pompon where required.

Now pull the 2 pieces of card away and

fluff out the ball. Trim the ends until the required shape and size is achieved.

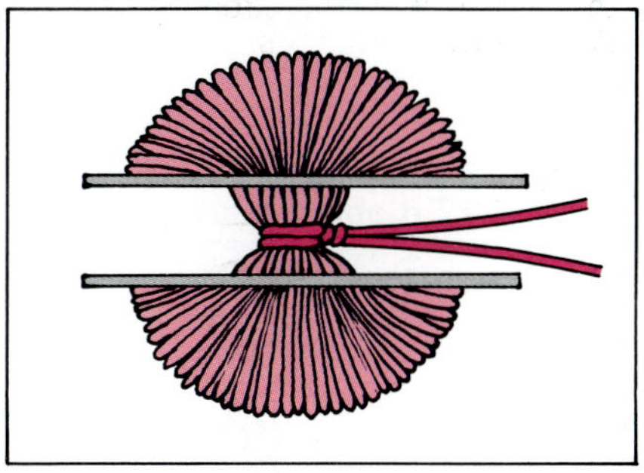

Tassel

(a) Cut a piece of card as wide as required length of tassel, and wind yarn round card to thickness of tassel required. Break yarn leaving a long end and thread through a darning needle. Slip needle through all loops.

(b) Tie this thread tightly round loops.

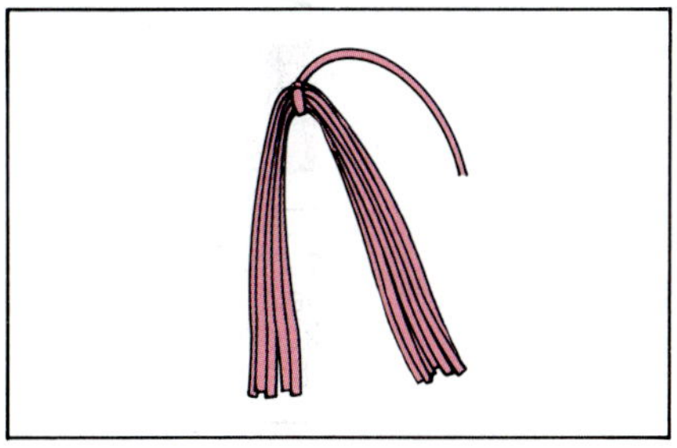

Remove card and cut through loops at other end.

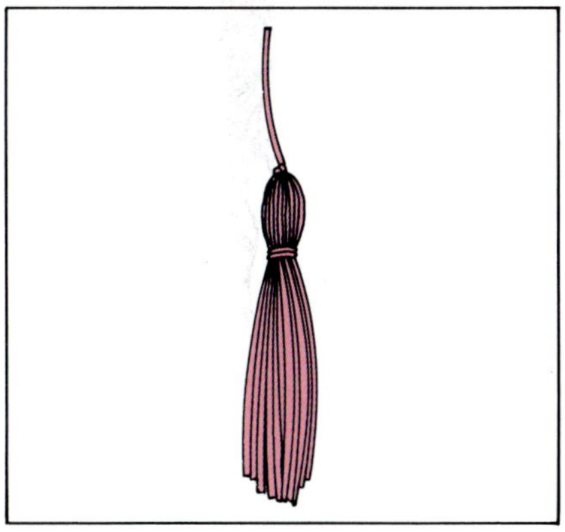

(c) Wind yarn around all loops below fold, make a stitch and fasten. Draw needle through top and attach firmly where required. Trim ends.

Knitting in the Round,

fabric with no seams to be joined. It can be worked on one long flexible needle with points at both ends, or on sets of double pointed needles.

Knitting with a Circular Needle

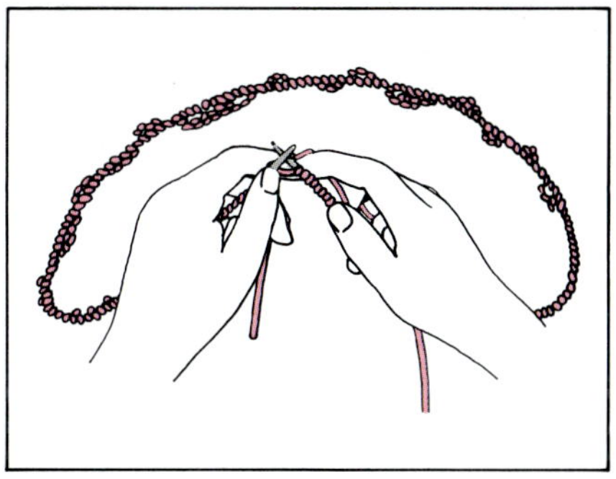

This is the best method to use if you are making a very large piece of circular knitting, such as a skirt. Simply cast on to one of the points the number of stitches required, then spread the stitches evenly along the whole length of needle and join them into a ring. It cannot be stressed how important it is to make sure that the cast on edge is not twisted, otherwise your piece of knitting will be twisted irrevocably, and you will be unable to use it!

Hints and Tips

If your circular needle has become bent, simply dip into a bowl of warm water to smooth out any kinks.

Knitting with a set of 4 double pointed needles

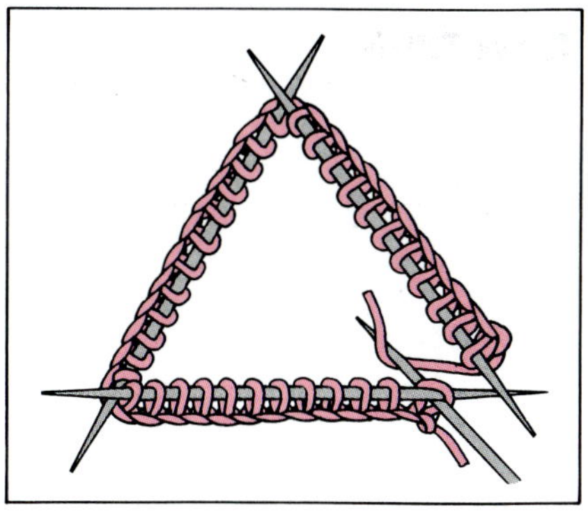

This is the best method to use if you are making smaller items such as socks, because of the relatively small number of sts that can be used. Simply divide the required number of stitches into 3, cast that number onto each of 3 of the needles, draw up the last stitch to meet first stitch on first needle, and use the 4th needle to start knitting. As each needle is emptied, it then becomes the next needle that you use to knit the stitches with.

Brushing Mohair Garments

To enhance the appearance of mohair or other fluffy yarns, brush **gently** to raise the pile or lift out the mohair fibres. This is particularly effective after washing. Great care must be taken as overbrushing will cause the garment to look matted.

Twisted Cord

A twisted cord requires several strands of yarn each about 2½-3 times the required finished length. 4 strands will give you a finished cord 8 strands thick.

(a) Cut the strands of yarn as indicated and knot together at each end making sure that the lengths are even.

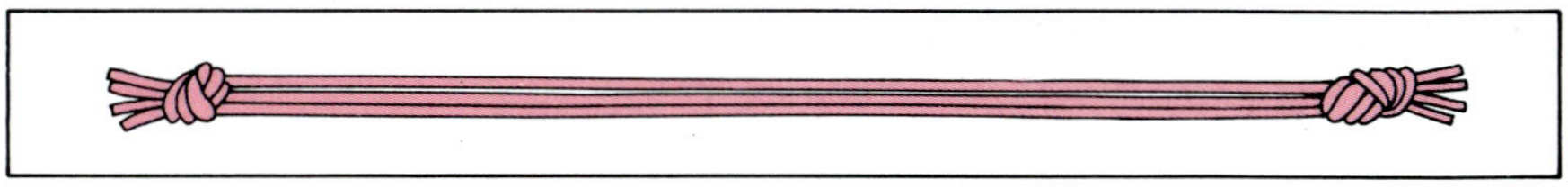

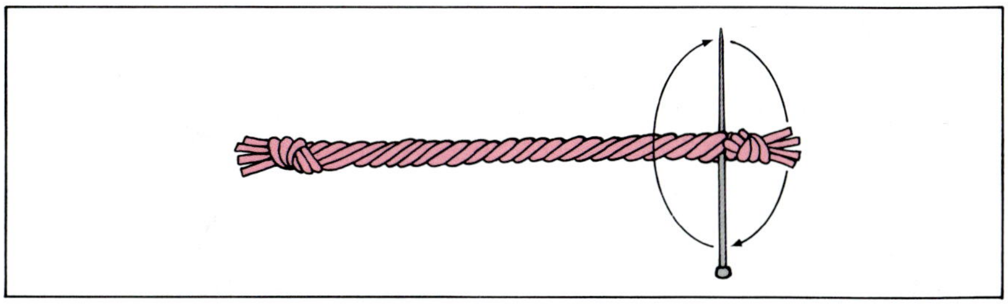

(b) Attach one end to a pin, hook or door handle. Insert a knitting needle through the other end. Twist the knitting needle clockwise until the strands are tightly twisted together. Holding the centre of the cord, place the needle end and the hook end together, keeping the cord taut to avoid tangling.

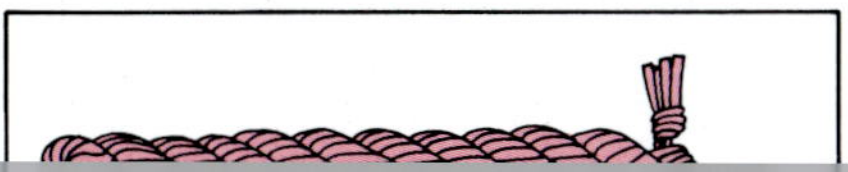

(c) Release the centre of the cord at short

Sample Knitting Stitches

Here is a selection of sample stitches to help you get used to pattern stitches, and also to give you ideas for creating your own designs.

Multiples

Each pattern stitch starts with the 'multiple' or number of sts required to be able to knit a complete and balanced sample. For example:

A multiple of 4 means that you would need to cast on 4, 8, 12 or 16 sts, and so on.

A multiple of 4 + 1 means that you would need to cast on 5, 9, 13 or 17 sts, and so on.

1. Lattice Stitch

Cast on a multiple of 6 sts + 1.

1st row (right side): K3, *P1, K5; rep from * to last 4 sts, P1, K3.

2nd row: P2, *K1, P1, K1, P3; rep from * to last 5 sts, K1, P1, K1, P2.

3rd row: K1, *P1, K3, P1, K1; rep from * to end.

4th row: K1, *P5, K1; rep from * to end.

5th row: As 3rd row.

6th row: As 2nd row.

Rep these 6 rows.

2. Diagonal Rib

Cast on a multiple of 4 sts.

1st row (right side): *K2, P2; rep from * to end.

2nd row: As 1st row.

3rd row: K1, *P2, K2; rep from * to last 3 sts, P2, K1.

4th row: P1, *K2, P2; rep from * to last 3 sts, K2, P1.

5th row: *P2, K2; rep from * to end.

6th row: As 5th row.

7th row: As 4th row.

8th row: As 3rd row.

Rep these 8 rows.

3. Basket Weave

Cast on a multiple of 6 sts + 2.

1st row (right side): Knit.

2nd row: Purl.

3rd row: K2, *P4, K2; rep from * to end.

4th row: P2, *K4, P2; rep from * to end.

Rep 3rd and 4th rows once more.

7th row: Knit.

8th row: Purl.

9th row: P3, *K2, P4; rep from * to last 5 sts, K2, P3.

10th row: K3, *P2, K4; rep from * to last 5 sts, P2, K3.

Rep 9th and 10th rows once more.

Rep these 12 rows.

4. 9-Stitch Plait

Down **Up**

Worked over 9 sts, shown on a background of reverse stocking st.

Special Abbreviations

C6B or C6F (Cable 6 Back or Cable 6 Front) = slip next 3 sts onto cable needle and leave at back (or front) of work, knit next 3 sts from left-hand needle, then knit sts from cable needle.

Up

1st row (right side): Knit.

2nd and every alt row: Purl.

3rd row: C6B, K3.

5th row: Knit.

7th row: K3, C6F.

8th row: Purl.

Rep these 8 rows.

For **'Down'** plait work C6F in place of C6B and vice versa.

5. Blackberry Stitch

Cast on a multiple of 4 sts + 2.

1st row (right side): Purl.

2nd row: K1, *(K1, P1, K1) into next st, p3tog; rep from * to last st, K1.

3rd row: Purl.

4th row: K1, *P3tog, (K1, P1, K1) into next st; rep from * to last st, K1.

Rep these 4 rows.

6. Lace Panel

Worked over 10 sts, shown on a background of stocking st.

1st row (right side): K2, K2tog, yfwd, K2tog but do not slip from needle, knit the first of these 2 sts again, then slip both sts from needle together, yfwd, sL 1K, K1, psso, K2.

2nd row: Purl.

3rd row: K1, K2tog, yfwd, K4, yfwd, sL 1K, K1, psso, K1.

4th row: Purl.

5th row: K2tog, yfwd, K1, K2tog, [yfwd] twice, sL 1K, K1, psso, K1, yfwd, sL 1K, K1, psso.

6th row: P4, K1 into first yfwd, P1 into 2nd yfwd, P4.

7th row: K2, yfwd, sL 1K, K1, psso, K2, K2tog, yfwd, K2.

8th row: Purl.

9th row: K3, yfwd, sL 1K, K1, psso, K2tog, yfwd, K3.

10th row: Purl.

Rep these 10 rows.

7. Bobble Cable

Worked over 13 sts, shown on a background of reverse stocking st.

Special Abbreviations

T3B (Twist 3 Back) = slip next st onto cable needle and leave at back of work, knit next 2 sts from left-hand needle, then purl sts from cable needle.

T3F (Twist 3 Front) = slip next 2 sts onto cable needle and leave at front of work, purl next st from left-hand needle, then knit sts from cable needle.

C5B (Cross 5 Back) = slip next 3 sts onto cable needle and leave at back of work, knit next 2 sts from left-hand needle, slip the purl st from point of cable needle back onto left-hand needle, purl this st, then K2 from cable needle.

1st row (wrong side): K4, P2, K1, P2, K4.

2nd row: P3, T3B, K1, T3F, P3.

5th row: K2, P2, [K1, P1] twice, K1, P2, K2.

6th row: P1, T3B, [K1, P1] twice, K1, T3F, P1.

7th row: K1, P2, [K1, P1] 3 times, K1, P2, K1.

8th row: T3B, [K1, P1] 3 times, K1, T3F.

9th row: P2, [K1, P1] 4 times, K1, P2.

10th row: T3F, [P1, K1] 3 times, P1, T3B.

11th row: K1, P2, [K1, P1] 3 times, K1, P2, K1.

12th row: P1, T3F, [P1, K1] twice, P1, T3B, P1.

13th row: As 5th row.

14th row: P2, T3F, P1, K1, P1, T3B, P2.

15th row: As 3rd row.

16th row: P3, T3F, P1, T3B, P3.

17th row: As 1st row.

18th row: P4, C5B, P4.

19th row: As 1st row.

20th row: P3, T3B, P1, T3F, P3.

21st row: [K3, P2] twice, K3.

22nd row: P2, T3B, P3, T3F, P2.

23rd row: K2, P2, K5, P2, K2.

24th row: P2, K2, P2, make bobble (MB) as follows: [K1, yfwd, K1, yfwd, K1] into next st, turn, P5, turn, K5, turn, P2tog, P1, P2tog, turn, sL 1K, K2tog, psso (bobble completed), P2, K2, P2.

25th row: As 23rd row.

26th row: P2, T3F, P3, T3B, P2.

27th row: As 21st row.

28th row: P3, T3F, P1, T3B, P3.

29th row: As 1st row.

30th row: As 18th row.

Rep these 30 rows.

8. Eyelet Diamonds

Cast on a multiple of 16 sts + 11.

1st row (right side): K10, yfwd, sL 1K, K1, psso, K3, K2tog, yfwd, *K9, yfwd, sL 1K, K1, psso, K3, K2tog, yfwd; rep from * to last 10 sts, K10.

2nd and every alt row: Purl.

3rd row: K3, K2tog, yfwd, K1, yfwd, sL 1K, K1, psso, *K3, yfwd, sL 1K, K1, psso, K1, K2tog, yfwd, K3, K2tog, yfwd, K1, yfwd, sL 1K, K1, psso; rep from * to last 3 sts, K3.

5th row: K2, K2tog, yfwd, K3, yfwd, sL 1K, K1, psso, *K3, yfwd, sL 1K,

7th row: K1, K2tog, yfwd, K5, yfwd, sL 1K, K1, psso, *K7, K2tog, yfwd, K5, yfwd, sL 1K, K1, psso; rep from * to last st, K1.

9th row: K2, yfwd, sL 1K, K1, psso, K3, K2tog, yfwd, *K9, yfwd, sL 1K, K1, psso, K3, K2tog, yfwd; rep from * to last 2 sts, K2.

11th row: K3, yfwd, sL 1K, K1, psso, K1, K2tog, yfwd, K3, *K2tog, yfwd, K1, yfwd, sL 1K, K1, psso, K3, yfwd, sL 1K, K1, psso, K1, K2tog, yfwd, K3; rep from * to end.

13th row: K4, yfwd, sL 1K, K2tog, psso, yfwd, *K3, K2tog, yfwd, K3, yfwd, sL 1K, K1, psso, K3, yfwd, sL 1K, K2tog, psso, yfwd; rep from * to last 4 sts, K4.

15th row: K9, K2tog, yfwd, K5, yfwd, sL 1K, K1, psso, *K7, K2tog, yfwd, K5, yfwd, sL 1K, K1, psso; rep from * to last 9 sts, K9.

16th row: Purl.

Rep these 16 rows.

9. Noughts and Crosses Cable

Worked over 12 sts, shown on a background of reverse stocking st.

Special Abbreviations

C6B or C6F (Cable 6 Back or Cable 6 Front) = slip next 3 sts onto cable needle and leave at back (or front) of work, knit next 3 sts from left-hand needle, then knit sts from cable needle.

Work 4 rows in stocking st, starting knit.

5th row: C6B, C6F.

6th row: Purl.

Rep these 6 rows once more.

Work 4 rows in stocking st, starting knit.

17th row: C6F, C6B.

18th row: Purl.

10. Fishermans's Rib

Cast on a multiple of 2 sts + 1.

Special Abbreviation

K1B = insert needle through centre of st below next st on needle and knit this in the usual way, slipping the st above off needle at the same time.

1st row (right side): SL 1K, knit to end.

2nd row: SL 1K, *K1B, P1; rep from * to end.

Rep these 2 rows.

11. Fern Diamonds

Cast on a multiple of 10 sts + 1.

1st row (right side): K3, *k2tog, yfwd, K1, yfwd, sL 1K, K1, psso, K5; rep from * to last 8 sts, K2tog, yfwd, K1, yfwd, sL 1K, K1, psso, K3.

2nd and every alt row: Purl.

3rd row: K2, *K2tog, [K1, yfwd] twice, K1, sL 1K, K1, psso, K3; rep from * to last 9 sts, K2tog, [K1, yfwd] twice, K1, sL 1K, K1, psso, K2.

5th row: K1, *K2tog, K2, yfwd, K1, yfwd, K2, sL 1K , K1, psso, K1; rep from * to end.

7th row: K2tog, *K3, yfwd, K1, yfwd, K3, sL 1K, K2tog, psso; rep from * to last 9 sts, K3, yfwd, K1, yfwd, K3, sL 1K, K1, psso.

9th row: K1, *yfwd, sL 1K, K1, psso, K5, K2tog, yfwd, K1; rep from * to end.

11th row: K1, *yfwd, K1, sL 1K, K1, psso, K3, K2tog, K1, yfwd, K1; rep from * to end.

13th row: K1, *yfwd, K2, sL 1K, K1, psso, K1, K2tog, K2, yfwd, K1; rep from * to end.

15th row: K1, *yfwd, K3, sL 1K, K2tog, psso, K3, yfwd, K1; rep from * to end.

16th row: Purl.

Rep these 16 rows.

12. Feather and Fan

Cast on a multiple of 17 sts + 2.

1st row (right side): Using A knit.

2nd row: Using A purl.

3rd row: Using A K1, *[K2tog] 3 times, [yfwd, K1] 5 times, yfwd, [K2tog] 3 times; rep from * to last st, K1.

4th row: Using A knit.

Rep the last 4 rows once more using B.

Rep these 8 rows.

13. Bubble Pattern

Cast on a multiple of 4 sts + 3.

Special Abbreviation

K5B (Knit 5th St Below) = slip next st off left-hand needle and drop 4 rows down. Insert point of right-hand needle under strands and into the st on the 5th row down, insert left-hand needle under the strands and into the stitch. Knit the st normally catching the strands at the same time.

Cast on and knit 1 row in A.

Commence Pattern

Using B work 4 rows in stocking st, starting knit.

5th row: Using A K3, *K5B, K3; rep from * to end.

6th row: Using A knit.

Using C work 4 rows in stocking st, starting knit.

11th row: Using A K1, *K5B, K3; rep from * to last 2 sts, K5B, K1.

12th row: Using A knit.

Rep the last 12 rows.

14. Trellis Pattern

Cast on a multiple of 12 sts (minimum 24 sts).

Note: Sts should be cast on **loosely.**

Base Triangles: Using A *P2 (wrong side of work), turn and K2, turn and P3, turn and K3, turn and P4, turn and K4, continue in this way working 1 more st on every wrong side row until the row 'turn and P12' has been worked; rep from * to end. Break off A.

1st row of Rectangles: Using B K2, turn and P2, turn, inc in first st (by knitting into front and back of st), sL 1K , K1, psso, turn and P3, turn, inc in first st, K1, sL 1K, K1, psso, turn and P4, turn, inc in first st, K2, sL 1K, K1, psso, turn and P5, turn, inc in first st, K3, sL 1K, K1, psso, turn and P6, continue in this way working 1 more st on every right side row until the row 'inc in first st, K9, sL 1K, K1, psso' has been worked (1 edge triangle complete), then continue as follows: *pick up and K12 sts evenly along edge of next triangle, [turn and P12, turn and K11, sL 1K, K1, psso] 12 times (1 rectangle complete); rep from * to edge of last triangle, pick up and K12 sts evenly along edge of last triangle, turn and P2tog, P10, turn and K11, turn and P2tog, P9, turn and K10, turn and P2tog, P8, turn and K9, continue in this way until the row 'turn and K2' has been worked, turn and P2tog (1 st remains on right-hand needle and edge triangle is complete). Break off B.

2nd row of Rectangles: Using A and continuing on from st on right-hand needle, pick up and P11 sts evenly along edge of triangle just worked, [turn and K12, turn and P11, P2tog] 12 times, then continue as follows: *pick up and P12 sts evenly along side of next rectangle, [turn and K12, turn and P11, P2tog] 12 times; rep from * to end. Break off A.

3rd row of Rectangles: As 1st row but picking sts up along side edge of rectangles instead of triangles.

Rep 2nd and 3rd rows for pattern.

Final row of Triangles: Using A *continuing on from st on right-hand needle, pick up and P11 sts evenly along edge of triangle just worked, turn and K12, turn and P2tog, P9, P2tog, turn and K11, turn and P2tog, P8, P2tog, turn and K10, turn and P2tog, P7, P2tog, continue in this way working 1 st less on every wrong side row until the row 'turn and K3' has been worked, turn and [P2tog] twice, turn and K2, turn and P1, P2tog, P1, turn and K3, turn and P3tog; rep from * but picking up sts along side of rectangle instead of triangle. Fasten off last st.

---

15. Cables with Eyelets

Cast on a multiple of 16 sts + 10.

Special Abbreviation

C6F (Cable 6 Front) = slip next 3 sts onto cable needle and leave at front of work, knit next 3 sts from left-hand needle, then knit sts from cable needle.

Note: Sts should only be counted after the 1st, 14th, 15th and 28th rows.

1st row (wrong side): K2, *P6, K2; rep from * to end.

2nd row: P2, [K2tog, yfwd] twice, K2tog, *P2, K6, P2, [K2tog, yfwd] twice, K2tog; rep from * to last 2 sts, P2.

3rd row: K2, P5, K2, *P6, K2, P5, K2; rep from * to end.

4th row: P2, K1, [yfwd, K2tog] twice, P2, *C6F, P2, K1, [yfwd, K2tog] twice, P2; rep from * to end.

5th row: As 3rd row.

6th row: P2, K1, [yfwd, K2tog] twice, P2, *K6, P2, K1, [yfwd, K2tog] twice, P2; rep from * to end.

Rep the last 2 rows twice more, then 5th row again.

12th row: As 4th row.

13th row: As 3rd row.

P2; rep from * to end.

15th row: As 1st row.

16th row: P2, K6, P2, *ybk, sL 1K, K1, psso, [yfwd, sL 1K, K1, psso] twice, P2, K6, P2; rep from * to end.

17th row: K2, P6, K2, *P5, K2, P6, K2; rep from * to end.

18th row: P2, C6F, P2, *ybk, [sL 1K, K1, psso, yfwd] twice, K1, P2, C6F, P2; rep from * to end.

19th row: As 17th row.

20th row: P2, K6, P2, *ybk, [sL 1K, K1, psso, yfwd] twice, K1, P2, K6, P2; rep from * to end.

Rep the last 2 rows twice more, then 19th row again.

26th row: As 18th row.

27th row: As 17th row.

28th row: P2, K6, P2, *K2, yfwd, sL 1K, K1, psso, yfwd, K1, P2, K6, P2; rep from * to end.

Rep these 28 rows.

---

16. Rosebud Garden

Cast on a multiple of 14 sts + 5.

Special Abbreviations

T2B (Twist 2 Back) = slip next st onto cable needle and leave at back of work, knit next st from left-hand needle, then purl st from cable needle.

T2F (Twist 2 Front) = slip next st onto cable needle and leave at front of work, purl next st from left-hand needle, then knit st from cable needle.

Note: Count each M5 and sts resulting from M5 on following rows as 1 st.

1st row (wrong side): K7, [P1, K1] twice, P1, *K9, [P1, K1] twice, P1; rep from * to last 7 sts, K7.

2nd row: P7, [K1, P1] twice, K1, *P9

Rep the last 2 rows once more then the 1st row again.

6th row: P6, T2B, P1, K1, P1, T2F, *P7, T2B, P1, K1, P1, T2F; rep from * to last 6 sts, P6.

7th row: K6, [P1, K2] twice, P1, *K7, [P1, K2] twice, P1; rep from * to last 6 sts, K6.

8th row: P5, *T2B, P2, K1, P2, T2F, P5; rep from * to end.

9th row: K5, *[P1, K3] twice, P1, K5; rep from * to end.

10th row: P5, *M5 as follows: [K1, yfwd, K1, yfwd, K1] into next st, P3, K1, P3, M5, P5; rep from * to end.

11th row: K5, *P5, K3, P1, K3, P5, K5; rep from * to end.

12th row: P5, *K5, P3, K1, P3, K5, P5; rep from * to end.

13th row: As 11th row.

14th row: P5, *K5, P3, M5, P3, K5, P5; rep from * to end.

15th row: K5, *[P5, K3] twice, P5, K5; rep from * to end.

16th row: P5, *D5 as follows: K2tog tbl, K3tog, pass K2tog st over K3tog st, P3, K5, P3, D5, P5; rep from * to end.

17th row: K9, P5, *K13, P5; rep from * to last 9 sts, K9.

18th row: P9, K5, *P13, K5; rep from * to last 9 sts, P9.

19th row: As 17th row.

20th row: P9, D5, *P13, D5; rep from * to last 9 sts, P9.

21st row: K2, P1, K1, P1, K9, *[P1, K1] twice, P1, K9; rep from * to last 5 sts, P1, K1, P1, K2.

22nd row: P2, K1, P1, K1, P9, *[K1, P1] twice, K1, P9; rep from * to last 5 sts, K1, P1, K1, P2.

Rep the last 2 rows once more then the 21st row again.

26th row: P2, K1, *P1, T2F, P7, T2B, P1, K1; rep from * to last 2 sts, P2.

27th row: [K2, P1] twice, K7, *[P1, K2] twice, P1, K7; rep from * to last 6 sts, [P1, K2] twice.

28th row: P2, K1, *P2, T2F, P5, T2B, P2, K1; rep from * to last 2 sts, P2.

29th row: K2, P1, K3, P1, K5, *[P1, K3] twice, P1, K5; rep from * to last 7 sts, P1, K3, P1, K2.

30th row: P2, K1, *P3, M5, P5, M5, P3, K1; rep from * to last 2 sts, P2.

31st row: K2, P1, *K3, P5, K5, P5, K3, P1; rep from * to last 2 sts, K2.

32nd row: P2, K1, *P3, K5, P5, K5, P3, K1; rep from * to last 2 sts, P2.

33rd row: As 31st row.

34th row: P2, M5, *P3, K5, P5, K5, P3, M5; rep from * to last 2 sts, P2.

35th row: K2, P5, *K3, P5, K5, P5, K3, P5; rep from * to last 2 sts, K2.

36th row: P2, K5, *P3, D5, P5, D5, P3, K5; rep from * to last 2 sts, P2.

37th row: K2, P5, *K13, P5; rep from * to last 2 sts, K2.

38th row: P2, K5, *P13, K5; rep from * to last 2 sts, P2.

39th row: As 37th row.

40th row: P2, D5, *P13, D5; rep from * to last 2 sts, P2.

How To Crochet

First of all you need a ball of any double knitting or 8 ply and a 4.50mm hook. We will start you actually crocheting first then explain in more detail about yarns and hooks in a later section (see pages 28 and 46).

Hints and Tips
Left-handed people may find it easier to prop the book up against a mirror to see the illustrations in mirror image, while still being able to read the text from the original page.

Holding the Hook and Yarn

Everyone has their own personal way of holding the hook and controlling the yarn in crochet.

Right-handers hold the hook in their right hand, usually in one of the two following ways.

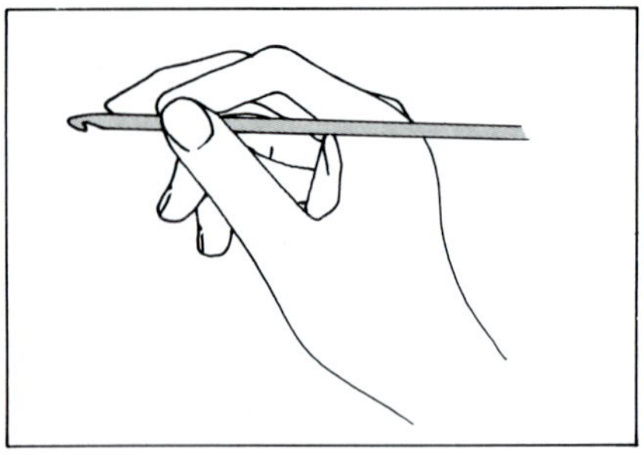

(a) As though it were a pencil.

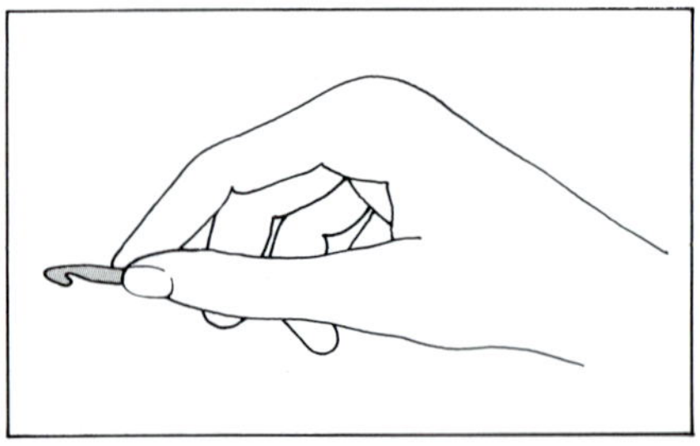

(b) In a firmer, overhand grip.

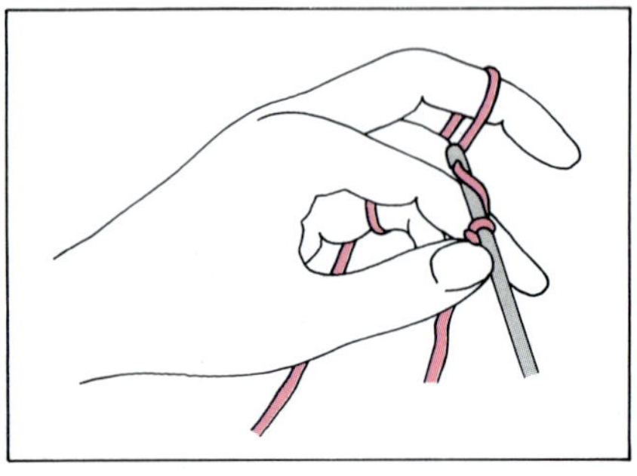

(c) The left hand holds the work and at the same time controls the yarn supply.

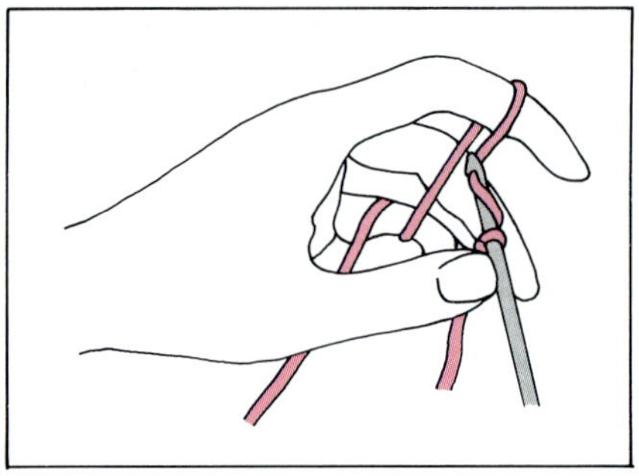

(d) If you prefer, the left hand index finger can be used to manipulate the yarn, while the middle finger holds onto the work.

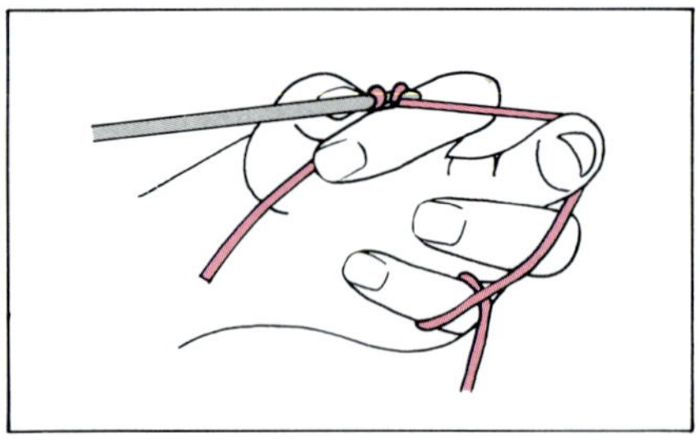

(e) To maintain the slight tension in the yarn necessary for easy, even working, it can help to arrange the yarn around the fingers of the left hand in this way.

The Foundation Chain

Almost all crochet starts with a foundation (or base) chain. This is the equivalent of 'casting on' in knitting. The foundation chain is a series of chain stitches which normally begin with a slip knot.

Slip knot

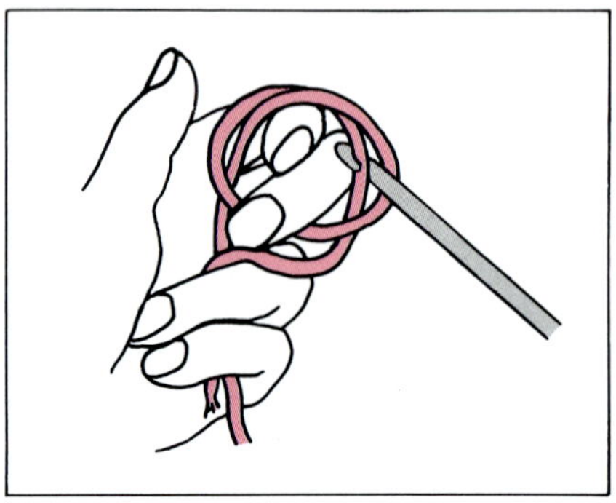

(a) Wind the yarn around two fingers and over the two fingers again to the left of the first thread. Pick up second thread through first loop.

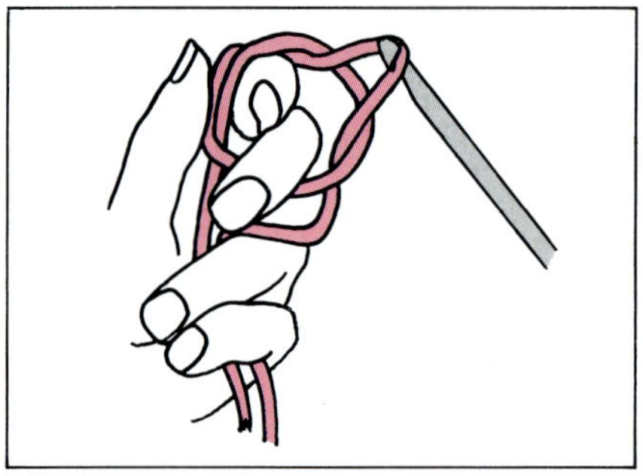

(b) Pull the second thread through the first one to form a loop.

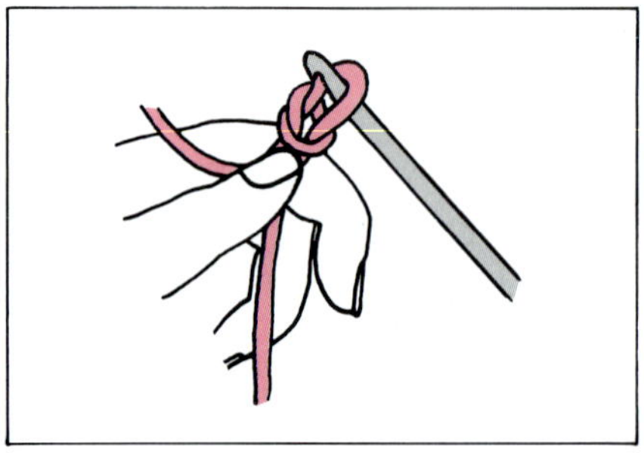

(c) Pull end to tighten the loop.

Chain Stitch (ch)

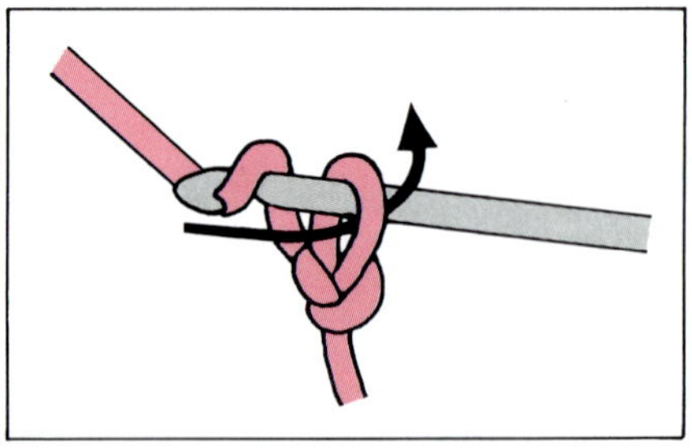

(a) Make a slip knot. *Wrap the yarn over the hook from back to front (or hold the yarn still and manoeuvre the hook).

Note: Unless otherwise specified, always wrap the yarn this way round. This may be written 'yarn over', 'yarn over hook' or 'yarn round hook' or abbreviated to 'yo', 'yoh' or 'yrh'.

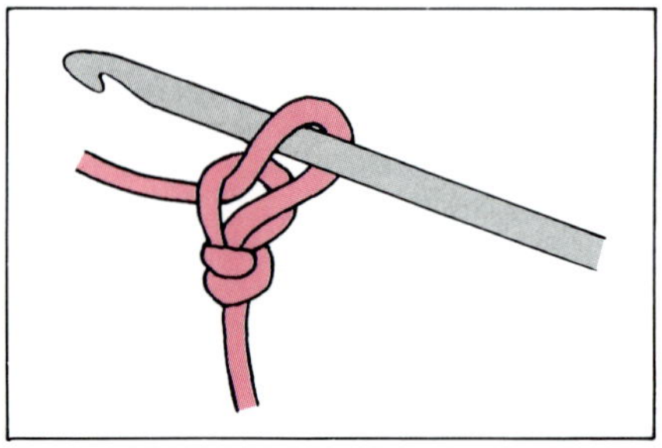

(b) Draw the yarn through to form a new loop without tightening up the previous one. Repeat from * until the required number of chains have been made.

Hints and Tips
Keep shifting your left hand position up close to the hook every couple of stitches or so by using a right hand finger tip to hold down the loop on the hook while you do so.

To count chains correctly **as you make them,** do not count the initial slip loop as a chain.

To count them **afterwards** first make sure that they are not twisted and that you are looking at the 'front', then count back,

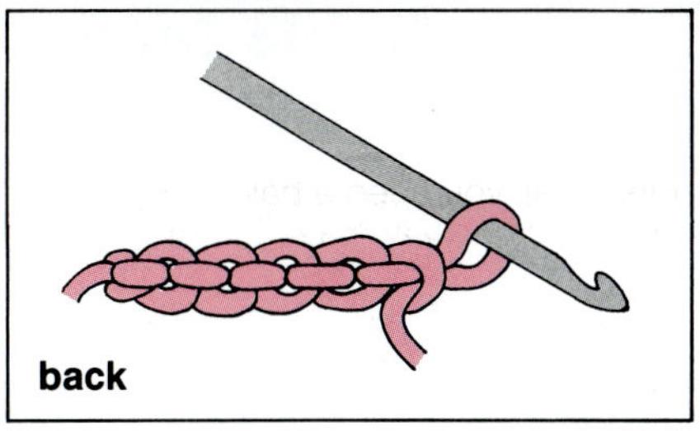

but ignore the loop still on the hook and now count the initial slip loop as a stitch.

The Basic Stitches

Note: Unless otherwise stated always insert hook under 2 loops of each stitch.

Slip Stitch (sl st)

This stitch is used during shaping. It does not create a fabric but is a means of working across existing material to a new position.

(a) Insert hook under one loop of 2nd chain from hook, yarn over, draw yarn through the work **and** loop on hook in one movement — one slip stitch made.

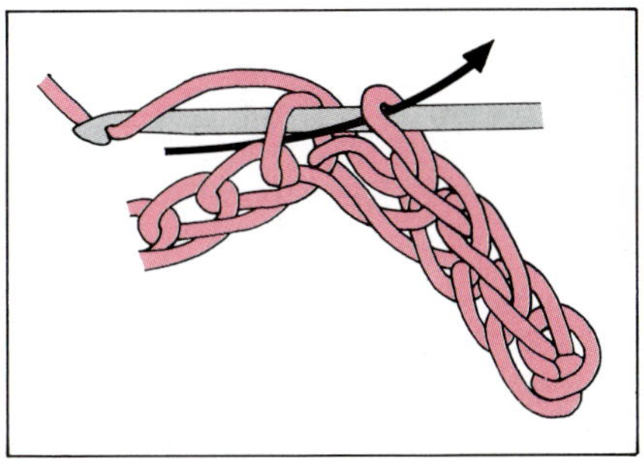

(b) Repeat this last step into each chain.

Double Crochet (dc)

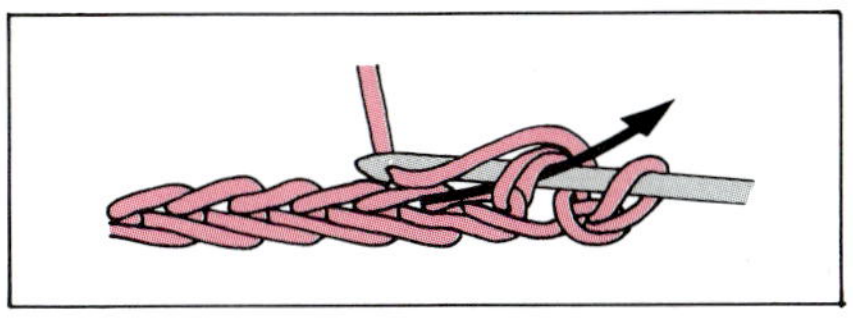

(a) Insert hook into 2nd chain from hook. *Yarn over hook and draw yarn through the work only.

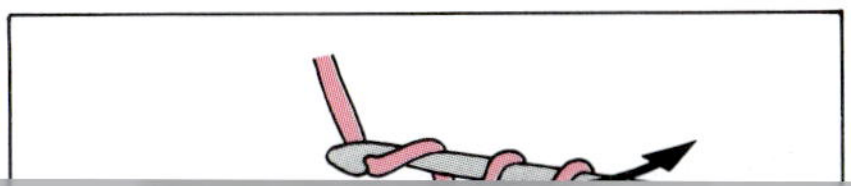

(b) Yarn over hook again and draw yarn through both loops on hook.

(c) 1 double crochet made. Insert hook into next chain. Repeat from *. into each chain to end.

Half Treble (htr)

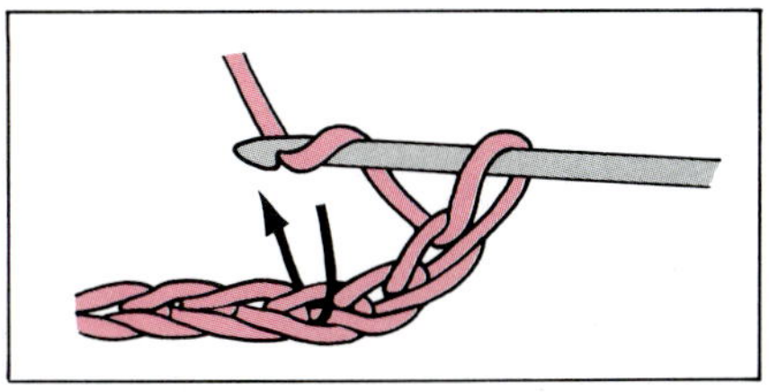

(a) Yarn over hook and insert hook into 3rd chain from hook. *Yarn over hook and draw through the work only.

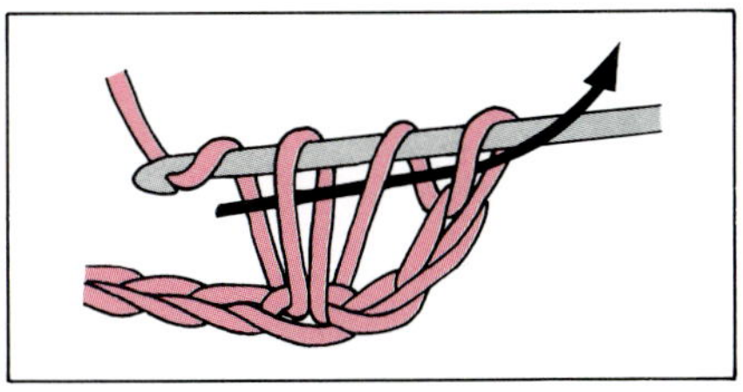

(b) Yarn over hook again and draw yarn through all 3 loops on hook.

Treble (tr)

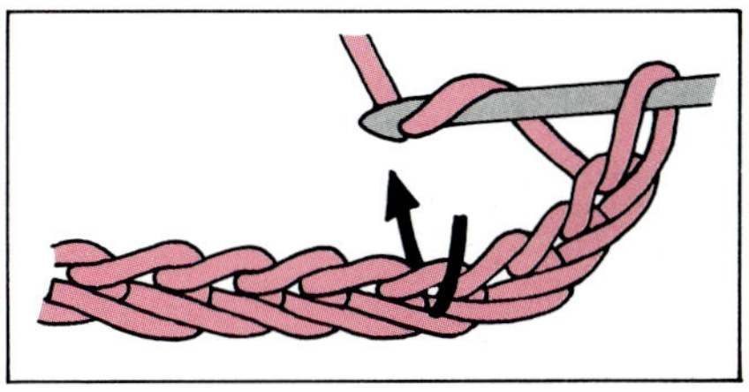

(a) Yarn over hook and insert hook into 4th chain from hook. *Yarn over hook and draw through the work only.

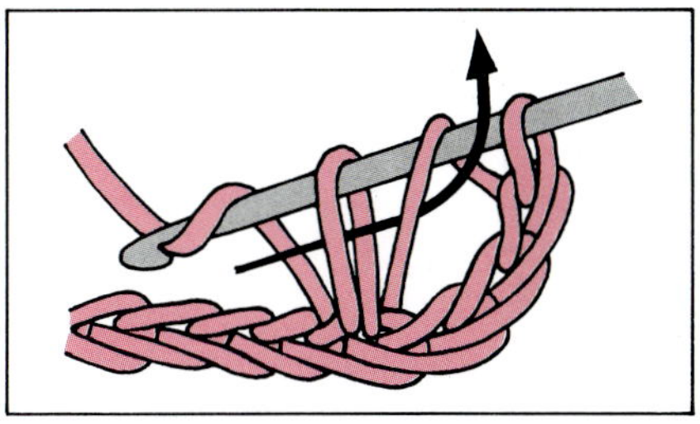

(b) Yarn over hook and draw through first 2 loops only.

(c) Yarn over hook and draw through remaining 2 loops on hook.

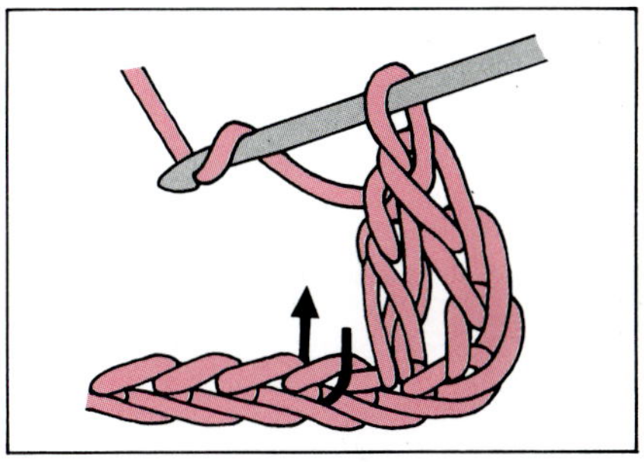

Double Treble (dtr)

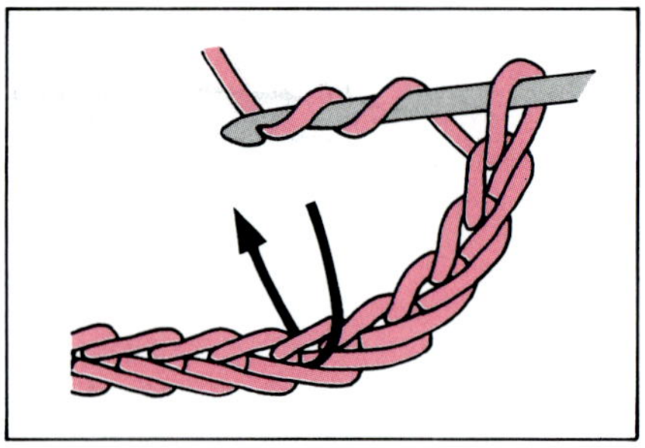

(a) Yarn over hook twice and insert hook into 5th chain from hook. *Yarn over hook and draw through the work only.

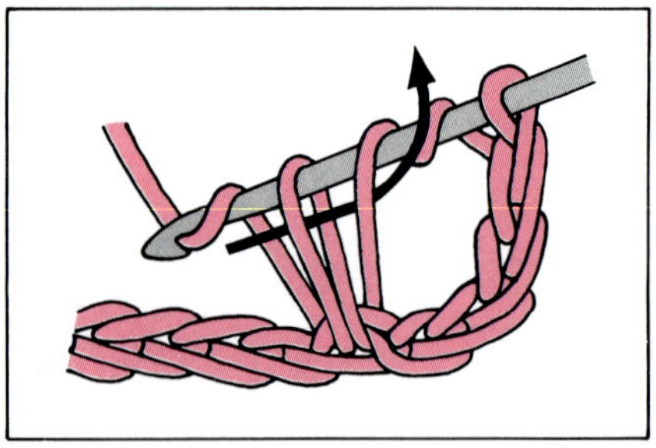

(b) Yarn over hook and draw through first 2 loops only.

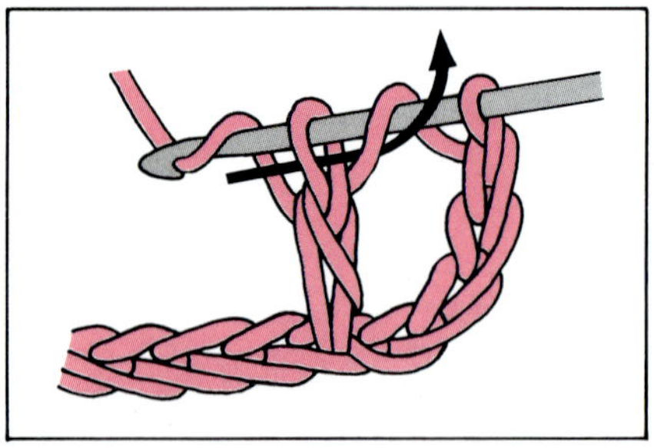

(c) Yarn over hook and draw through the next 2 loops only.

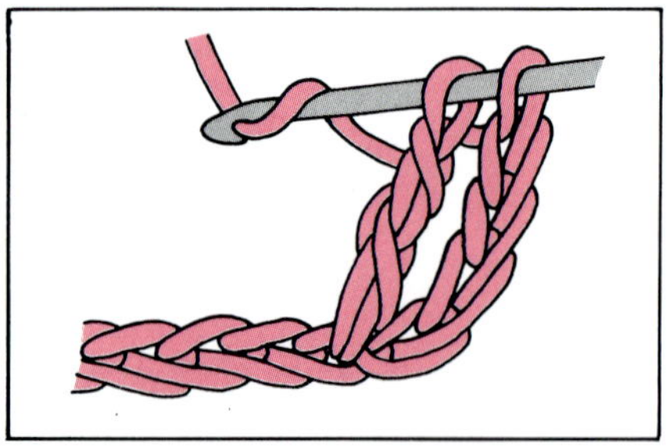

(d) Yarn over hook and draw through the last 2 loops on hook.

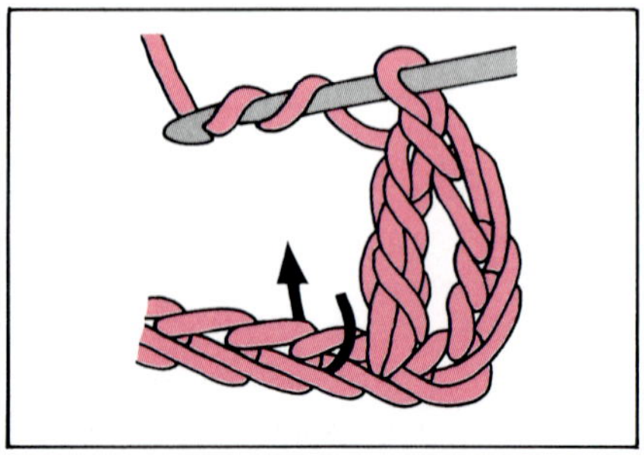

(e) 1 double treble made. Yarn over hook twice and insert into next chain. Repeat from * into each chain to end.

Triple Treble (trtr)

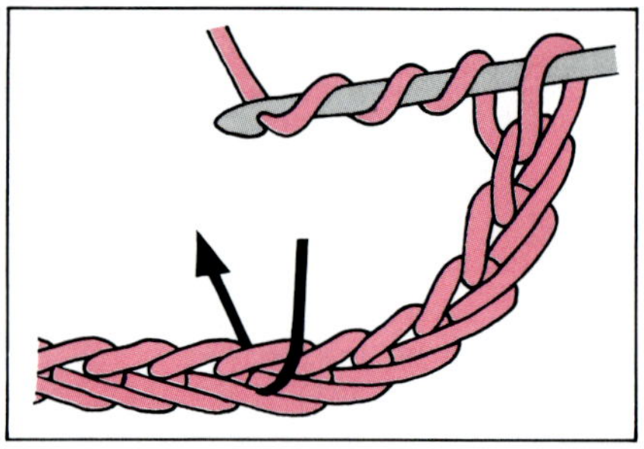

(a) Yarn over hook 3 times and insert hook into 6th chain from hook. *Yarn over hook and draw through the work only.

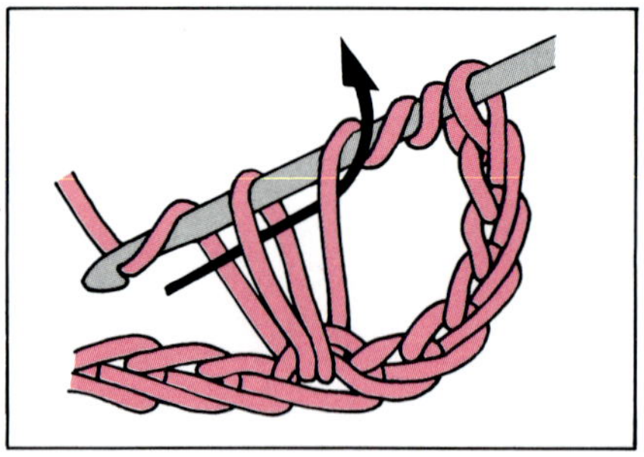

(b) Yarn over hook and draw through first 2 loops only.

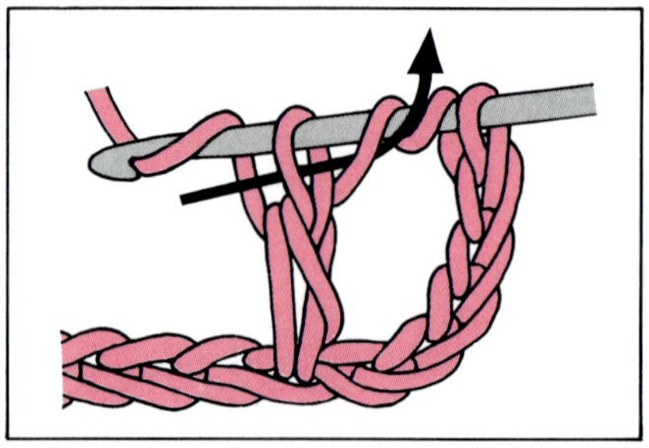

(c) Repeat this last step once more.

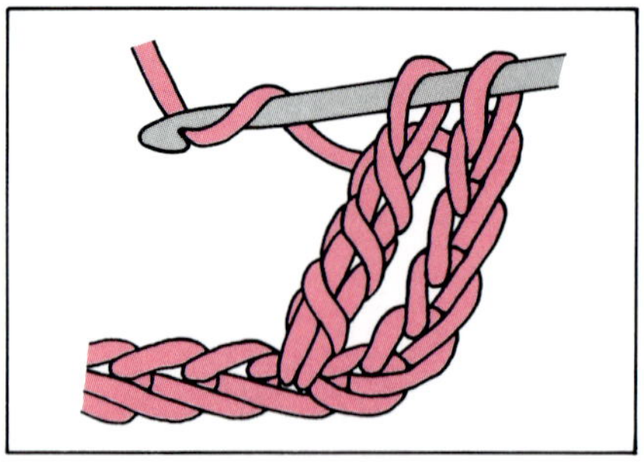

(d) Yarn over hook and draw through last 2 loops on hook.

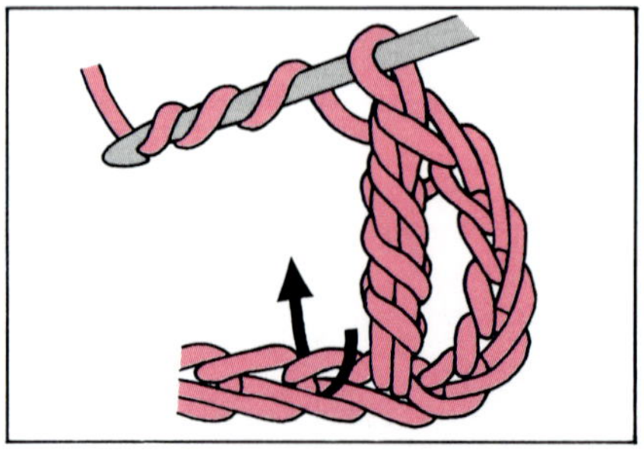

(e) 1 triple treble made. Yarn over hook 3 times and insert hook into next chain. Repeat from * into each chain to end.

Longer Basic Stitches

Longer basic stitches — usually called Quadruple Treble (quad tr), Quintuple Treble (quin tr), Sextuple Treble (sext tr), and so on, are made by wrapping the yarn 4, 5, 6, etc, times over hook at the beginning and by wrapping and drawing through 2 loops at a time more often to complete the stitch.

Fastening Off

To fasten off working yarn permanently, make one chain, cut yarn about 5 cm [2 ins] away (leave a longer length if you need to sew pieces together), draw end through the chain and tighten gently.

Making Crochet Fabric

These are the basic procedures for making crochet fabric — the things pattern instructions assume you know.

Working in rows

To work to and fro in rows make a foundation chain (see page 24) to begin.

At the very beginning of the first row, in order to give the first made stitch room to stand up to its proper height, one or more extra chains are added, which stand up alongside the made stitches. These extra chains look like and often 'count' as the first stitch in the row. The number of chains added depends upon the height of the stitch they are to match. Individual patterns will state how many chains to 'miss' at the beginning of the first row, and whether they count as a stitch or not.

On subsequent rows, a 'turning chain' (one or more single chains) must be worked to bring hook up to the height the row will be. Again individual patterns will state how many to work, and whether or not they count as a stitch.

In general the turning chains to match basic stitches are as follows: double crochet = 1 chain; half treble = 2 chains; treble = 3 chains; double treble = 4 chains, and so on. However, depending on your personal technique, the type of work you are doing, the thickness of yarn and size of hook you are using, you may find from time to time a larger or smaller number of chains gives better results.

Trebles

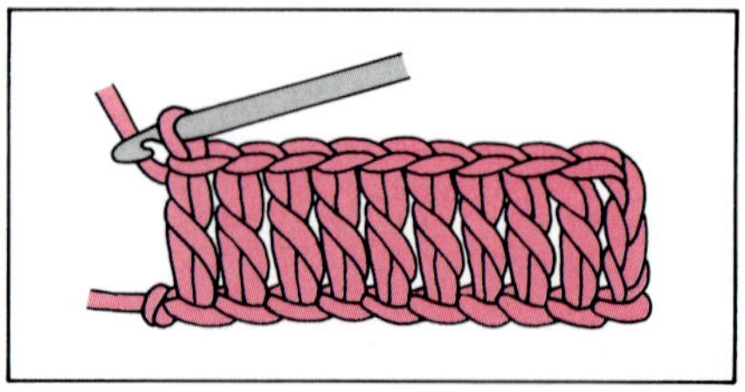

(a) The first row of fabric is made by working across foundation chain as shown on page 25. Right-handers work from right to left, left-handers work from left to right.

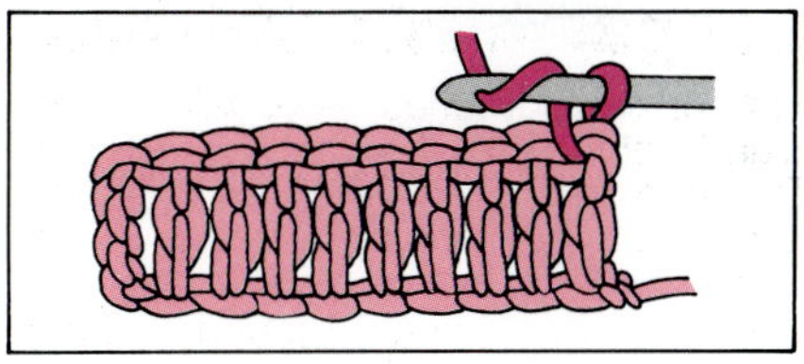

(b) At end of each row 'turn' work, so that another row can be worked across top of previous one again from right to left (left-handers from left to right).

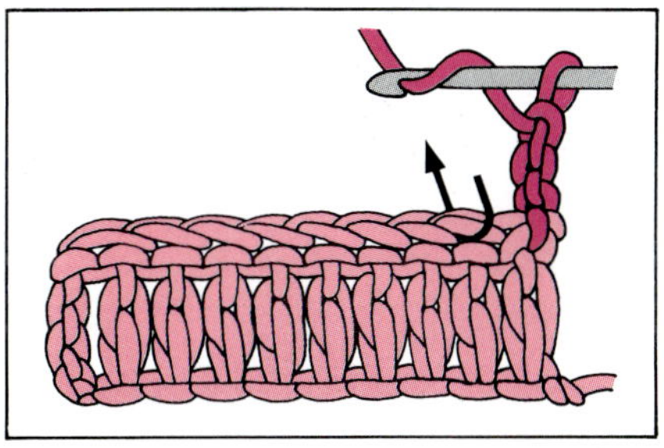

(c) Work 3 chains. The turning chain counts as first stitch in the new row, therefore miss first stitch in previous row and work into next stitch, inserting hook under the two loops lying on top.

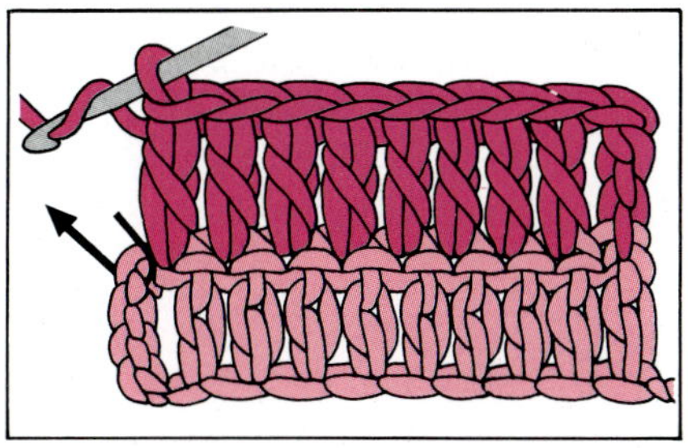

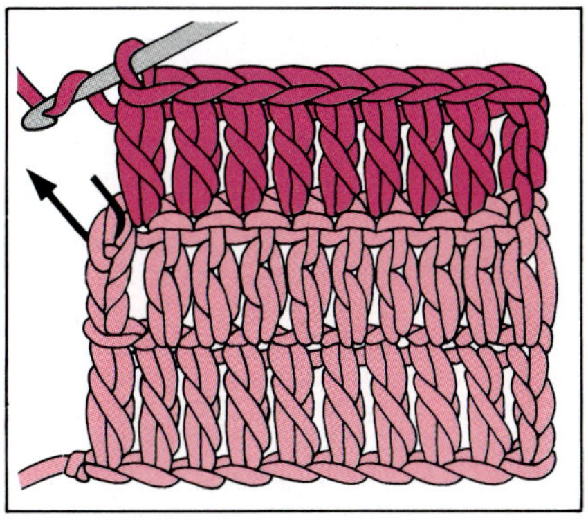

(d) and (e) When you reach end of row, the last stitch is worked into top of turning chain at beginning of previous row; 1 treble into top of 3 chain.

If, however, the turning chain does **not** count as a stitch, work into first stitch at beginning of row, but not into top of previous turning chain at end.

Hints and Tips

In order to gain a neater edge on trebles, some crocheters may prefer to work '1 dc in first st, 1 ch', which counts as first st and must be worked into at end of each row. Similarly, the first ch is replaced by 1 dc in first st on double trebles and triple trebles.

Working in rounds

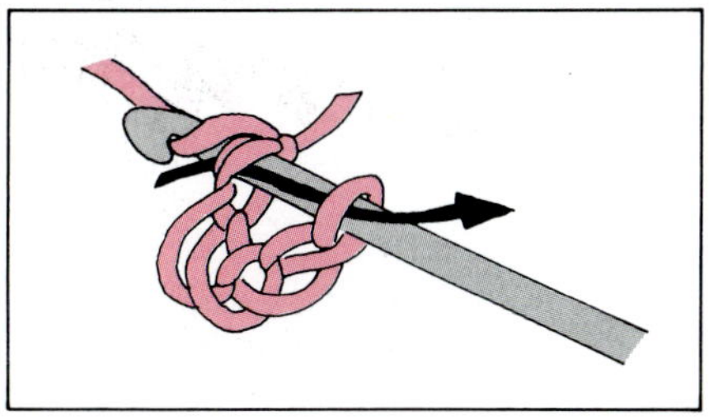

(a) To work in rounds make 3 or more chains (the exact number depends on the design) and join into a ring by inserting hook into the first of them and working a slip stitch.

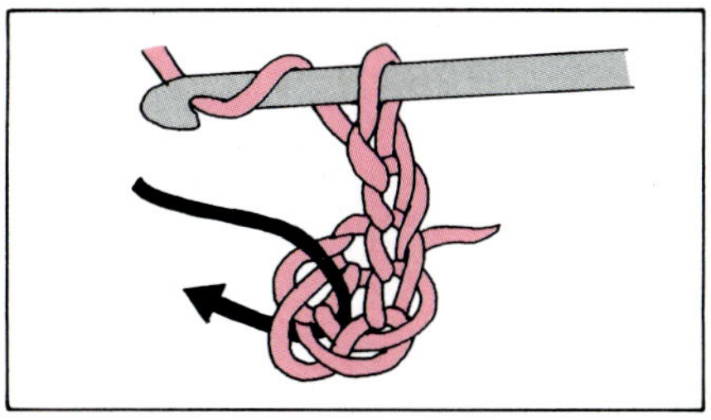

(b) To begin each round make a 'starting chain' (the equivalent of a 'turning chain' — see above) to match height of stitches of round. Insert hook always into **centre** of chain ring to work stitches of first round.

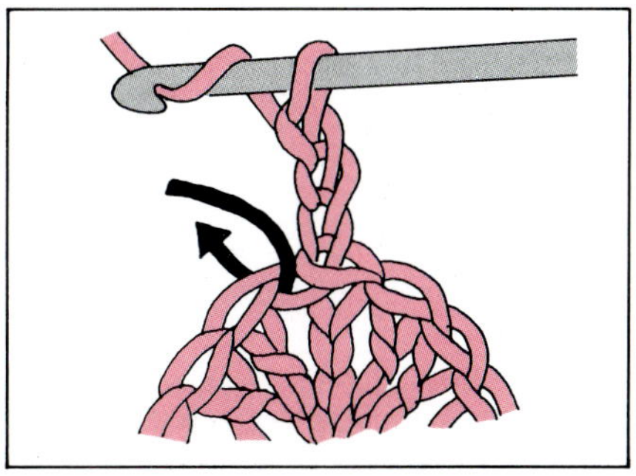

(c) From second round onwards insert hook under top 2 loops of stitches in previous round, unless otherwise directed.

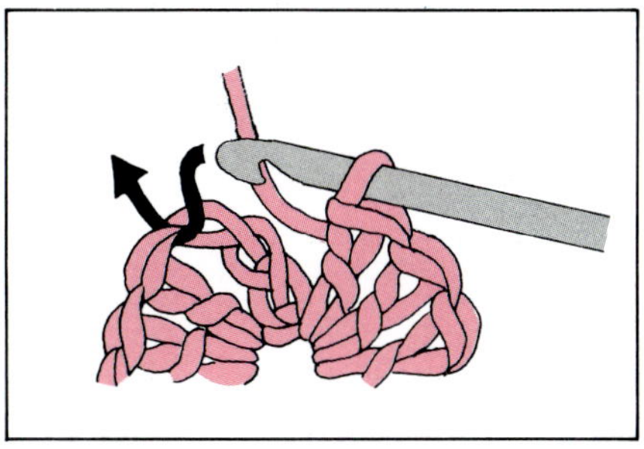

(d) When each round is complete insert hook into top of starting chain and make a slip stitch to join the round.

Note: Unless otherwise specified, do not turn work between rounds, but continue with same side facing and treat this as 'right side' of fabric.

To make an alternative starting ring —

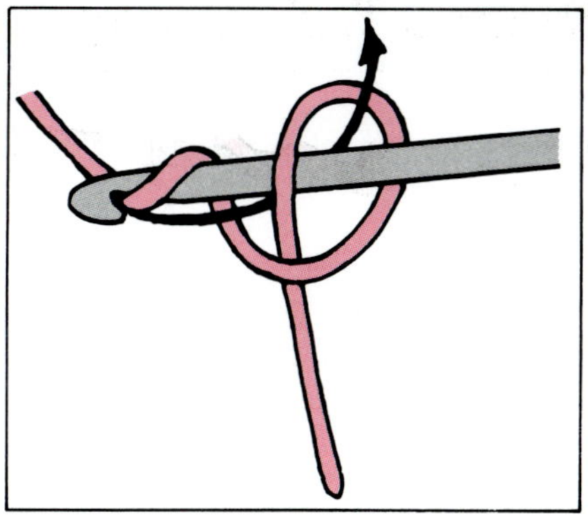

(e) Loop yarn once (or two or three times) round a finger, insert hook through loop and draw through a loop.

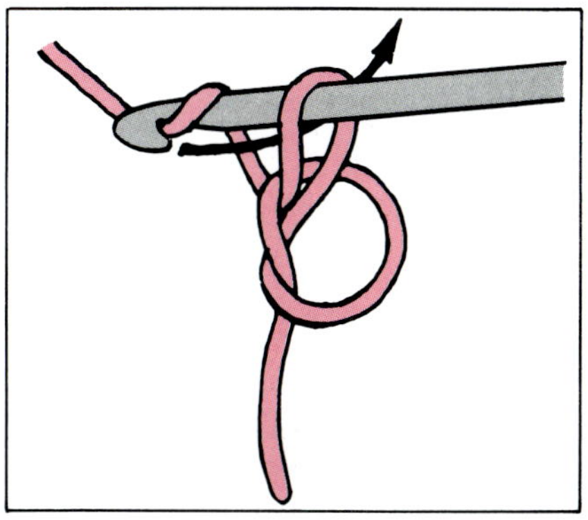

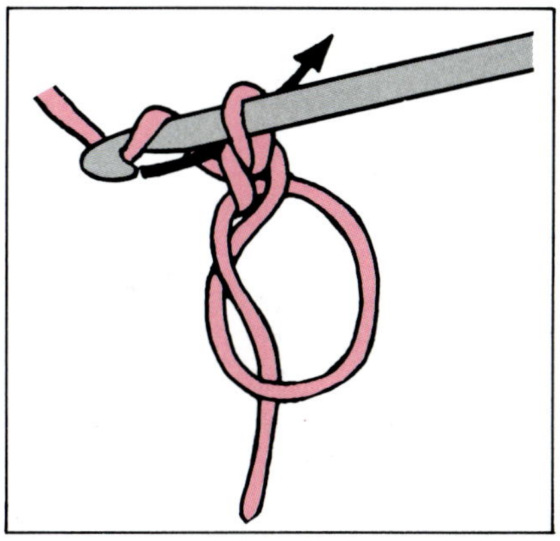

(f) and (g) Make a starting chain in the usual way.

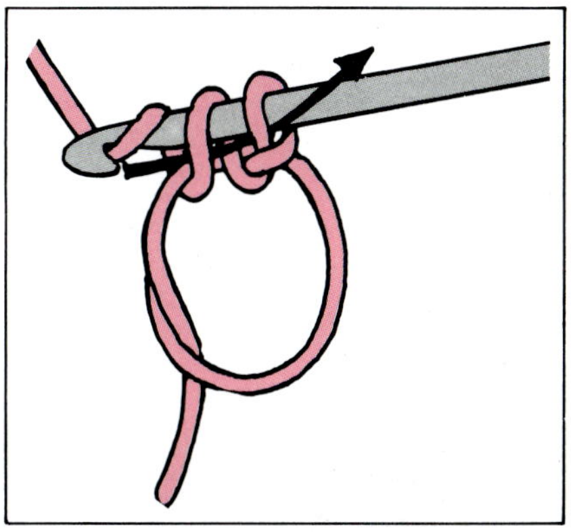

(h) Work into the centre of loop in the usual way.

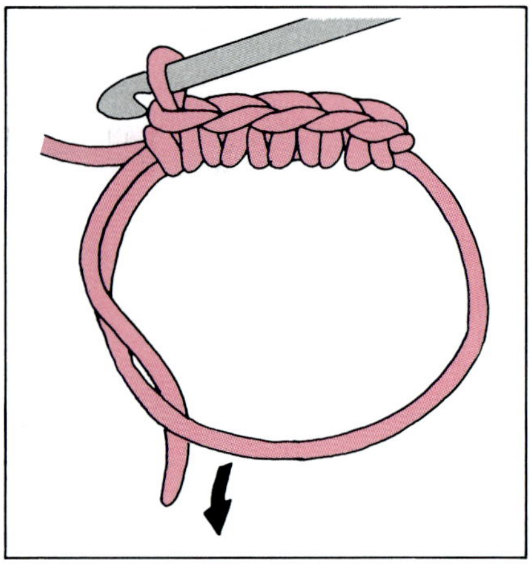

fabric, if necessary.

To fasten off after making the slip stitch which completes a round, do not make another chain.

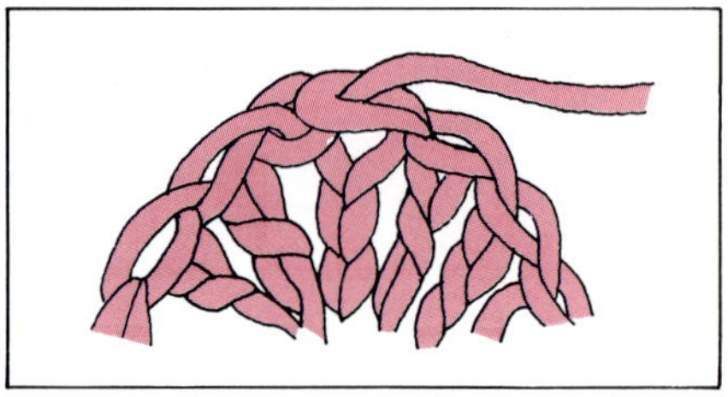

(a) Cut the yarn and draw the loose end through loop on hook.

(b) Insert hook again from the back through the place in the fabric where the slip stitch was worked (but not through the slip stitch loop itself) and draw the end of the yarn once again through to the back. Tighten gently.

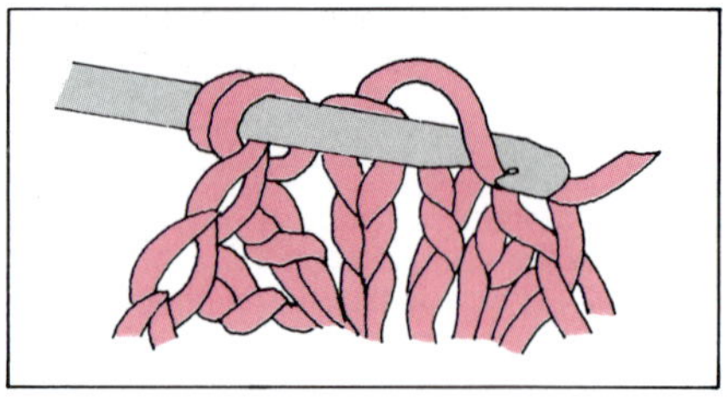

Congratulations! You have now discovered **how to crochet.** Now we will explain how to make sure that your first crochet project turns out to be the size and shape it was intended to be.

Crochet Accessories

The pattern will tell you what you need to complete the garment or item, but as well as the yarn you will also need to have a basic kit of accessories.

Crochet Hooks are generally made from steel or alloy and can range in size from 0.60mm to 8.00mm or even bigger for giant crochet. See page 48 for a complete hook conversion chart. It is a good idea to have the full range of sizes so that tension swatches can be made and compared. Keep them in a specially made case, so that you don't have to search through all of them to find the size you need.

A ruler and tape measure are essential for checking tension swatches and for measuring the length and width of completed fabric. For an accurate result, always lay work out on a flat, smooth surface before measuring it.

Pins (with coloured glass heads to make them more difficult to lose!) are used to measure the tension swatch, and also for picking up stitches evenly for an edging.

A row counter may be useful, but rows in crochet are generally much easier to count on the work than in knitting.

Wool sewing needles or knitters needles are used to sew completed pieces of work together. They are large with a broad eye for easy threading and a blunt point to avoid splitting the yarn. Do not use sharp pointed sewing needles. A tapestry needle is also suitable.

Reading Your Crochet Pattern (and understanding it!)

Now that you know the basics of crochet, you need to know how to read your pattern, and how to interpret the information given. At first glance it can all look like a foreign language, but read on.....

Measurements

Most crochet patterns for garments have an allowance for movement or ease over and above the actual bust or chest size. The amount of ease varies with the style of garment and fashions of the time. In other words a pattern may be 'To Fit' bust 85 cm [34 ins], with a 'finished measurement' of 95 cm [38 ins]. This garment has a 10 cm [4 inch] 'allowance' or ease. Generally jackets or cardigans have more allowance so that they can be worn over other bulky garments. The photograph will show the general appearance intended.

If in doubt about deciding what size to make, you may find the following tip helpful.

Choose one of your own sweaters that is a size you feel comfortable in, or is suitable for the style of garment that you are going to make.

Lay the garment out flat on a table and measure the width across the body. Double this measurement to find the finished size all round. Compare this with the actual size or finished measurement printed on your pattern. Make the size that has the nearest finished measurement to the one you want. Don't worry if the 'To Fit' size doesn't correspond with your actual size. These are only given as a guide.

There are of course exceptions to this general guideline, for example when a garment is influenced by thirties or forties styling, and is intended to have little or no allowance in order to fit closely to the figure. In this case, it would be best to follow the 'To Fit' size in order to achieve the appearance intended by the designer.

Tension

Whenever you are following crochet pattern instructions, whatever form they take, probably the most important single factor in your success is obtaining the 'tension' that the designer worked to. If you do not obtain the same tension as indicated, your work will not come to the measurement given.

The information given under this heading refers to the number of stitches and rows to fill a particular area; for example a tension indication may be '15 sts and 19 rows = 10 cm [4 ins] square measured over double crochet on 4.50mm hook'. This means that you should produce fabric made up of the proportion of stitches and rows as given in the tension paragraph in order to obtain the correct measurements for the garment or item that you intend to make, regardless of the hook size that **you** use. The hook size indicated in the pattern is the one which **most** crocheters will use to achieve this tension, but it is the tension itself that is important, not hook size.

Ensure that you do achieve the correct tension by working a tension piece before starting your garment. Although this may seem to be time wasting and a nuisance it can save time and aggravation in the long run. Nothing can be more annoying than finding that you have made your garment too big or too small!

Tension Piece

The instructions given in the tension paragraph of a crochet pattern may be either for working in dc, tr or pattern stitch. If they are given in pattern stitch is is necessary to work a multiple of stitches the same as the multiple required in the pattern. If in dc or tr any number of chains can be made but whichever method is used, there should always be enough to give at least 15 cm [6 ins] in width. Work in pattern, dc or tr according to the wording of the tension paragraph until the piece measures at least 15 cm [6 ins] in depth. Break the yarn about 5 cm [2 ins] from the work and thread this end through loop on hook.

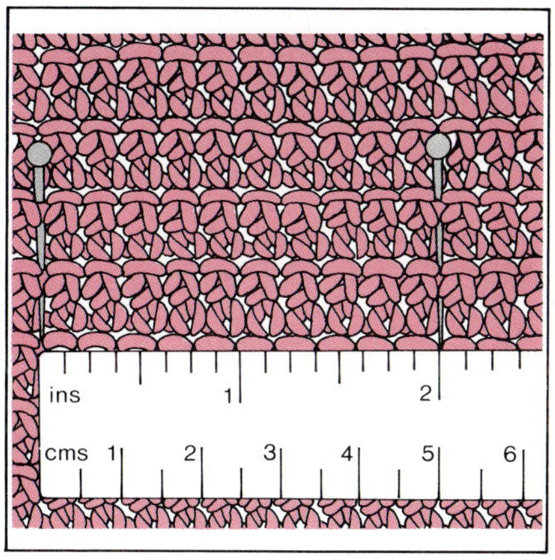

Place a pin vertically into the fabric a few stitches from the side edge. Measure 10 cm [4 ins] carefully and insert a second pin (Diagram illustrates 5 cm [2 ins]). Count the stitches. If the number of stitches between the pins is less than that specified in the pattern (even by half a stitch) your garment will be too wide. Use one size smaller hook to make another tension swatch. If there are more stitches over 10 cm [4 ins], the garment will be too small. Change to one size larger hook to make another swatch. Check the stitches again.

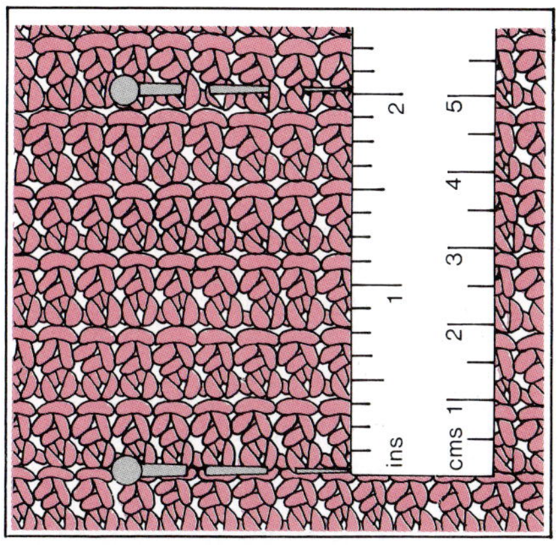

Row tension is also important, particularly on garments where the entire instructions are in rows. Place a pin horizontally in the fabric a few rows from the cast on edge. Measure 10 cm [4 ins] carefully and insert a second pin (Diagram illustrates 5 cm [2 ins]). Count the rows. If the number of rows between the pins is less than specified in the pattern your garment will be too long. If the number of rows between the pins is more than specified your garment will be too short.

It is possible to adjust the row tension by drawing the first loop of each stitch up a little higher or lower as necessary.

Your tension will become more even the more you practise crocheting. Experiment with different methods of holding yarn and hook. Once you have found the most comfortable method for **you** — stick to it. Everybody holds the yarn and hook

Hints and Tips

If you can't get tension exactly right on sts **and** rows, decide which is more important. Generally it is better to get the width measurement correct as lengths can usually be adjusted during the course of crocheting by adjusting the length to underarm or sleeve length, which are frequently given as a measurement and not in rows.

An exception to this would be when a garment is worked sideways from wrist to wrist, in which case the rows would be more important in order to get the correct width.

Standard Crochet Terms

Most crochet pattern instructions are written out in words although these days diagrams are becoming more popular. In order to follow both methods, you must first be able to understand the simple jargon, abbreviations and standard conventions. You are expected to know how to make the basic stitches and to be familiar with basic fabric-making procedures. Anything more advanced or specialised is always spelled out in individual pattern instructions.

Increasing and Decreasing

There are various methods of increasing and decreasing and they serve two purposes. The first is to make the work wider or narrower, to shape it. The second is to create decorative effects in lacy or textured patterns and is explained in detail below.

Using increasing and decreasing to shape

When working the various parts of a garment, increases or decreases are worked in pairs at each end of the row on the symmetrical pieces — (for example back or sleeves) to give a balanced shape. The fronts of a cardigan however are shaped differently on each side to give the correct shape for the armhole on one side and the neck shaping at the other.

It is very important to follow the instructions given in the pattern carefully. The designer will have worked out the various shapings to give the best possible results for each piece of material, and to ensure that the pieces fit together correctly when made up.

Increasing

Used when making fabric wider, or when adjusting for different stitch tensions.

In plain fabric such as trebles, working 2 or more stitches into one stitch at each end of the row is usually the best way of 'increasing' smoothly, for example when increasing up the sleeve seam from wrist

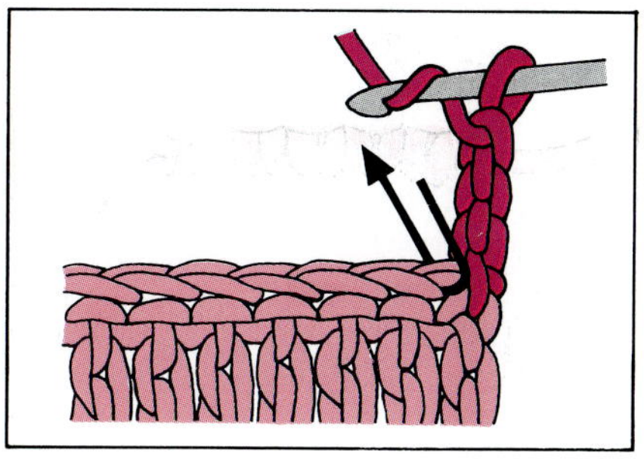

last stitch of previous row, instead of missing the first stitch. This would appear as follows: '3 ch (count as 1 tr), 1 tr into first stitch, work to end'.

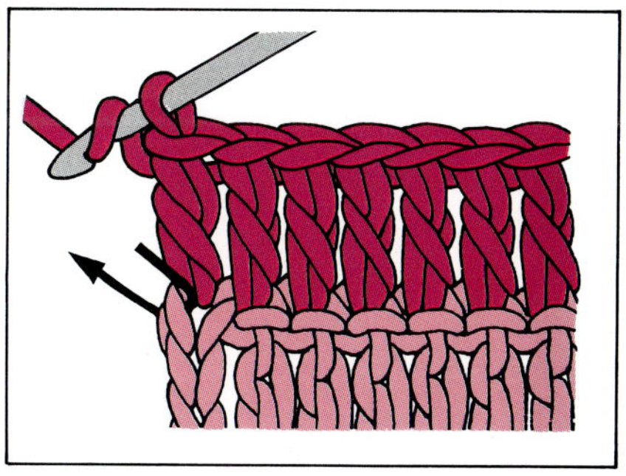

At the end of the row, the increase is made by working 2 stitches into the last stitch. This would appear as follows: 'work to last stitch, 2 tr into last stitch'.

An increase can be worked in the middle of a row in exactly the same way, simply by working 2 sts into the same place.

Decreasing

Used when making fabric narrower, or when adjusting for different stitch tensions.

In plain fabric such as double crochet or trebles, decreasing is generally done by working 2 or more stitches joined together at the top.

Dc2tog (double crochet 2 together — one stitch decreased)

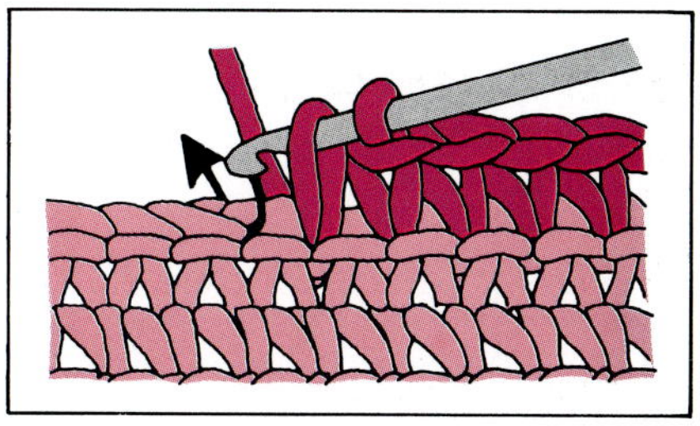

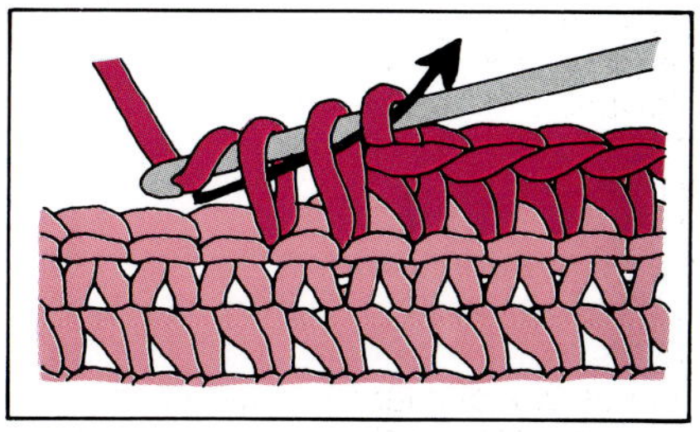

(a) and (b) Insert hook into next stitch (or as required), yarn over hook, draw a loop through. Repeat this step into next stitch

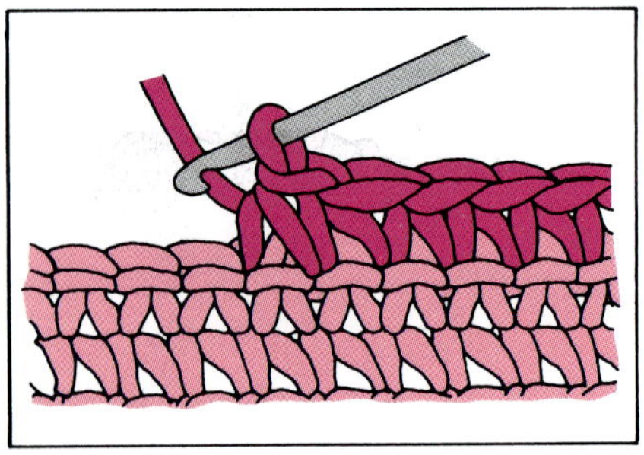

(c) 1 dc2tog completed.

Dc3tog (double crochet 3 together — 2 stitches decreased)
Work as for dc2tog until there are 3 loops on hook.

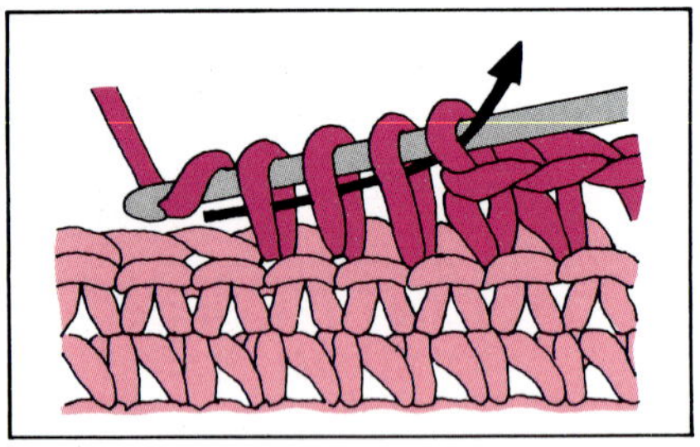

(a) Insert hook into third stitch, yarn over hook and draw through a loop (4 loops on hook). Yarn over hook and draw through all loops on hook to complete.

(b) 1 dc3tog completed.

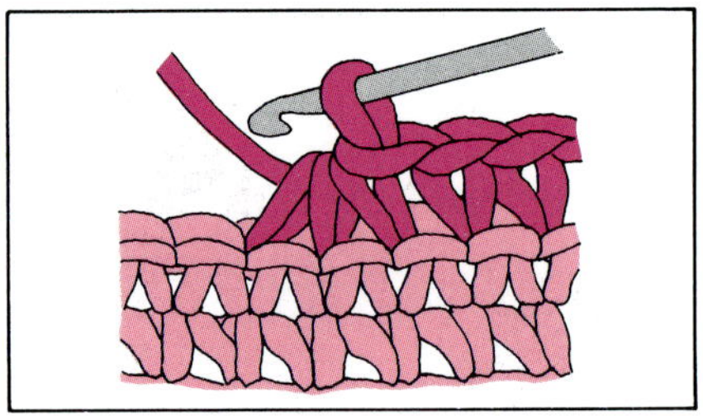

Tr2tog or Tr3tog (treble 2 or 3 together)

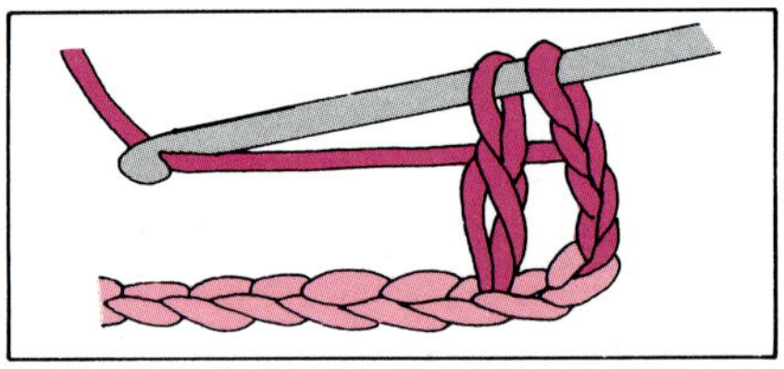

(a) Yarn over hook, insert hook into next stitch (or as required), yarn over hook, draw a loop through, yarn over hook and draw through 2 of the loops on hook (2 loops left on hook).

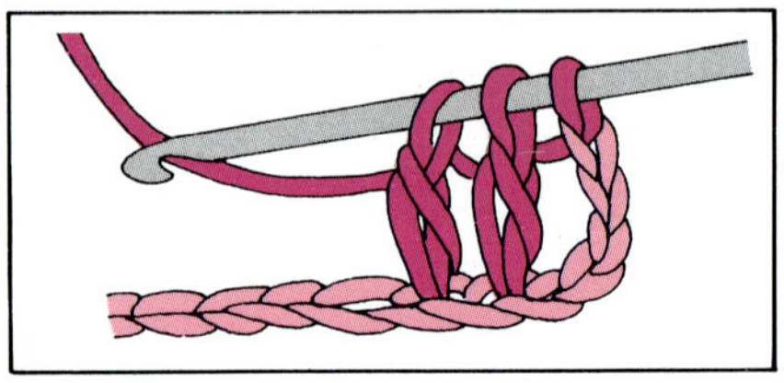

(b) Repeat this step into next stitch (3 loops on hook).

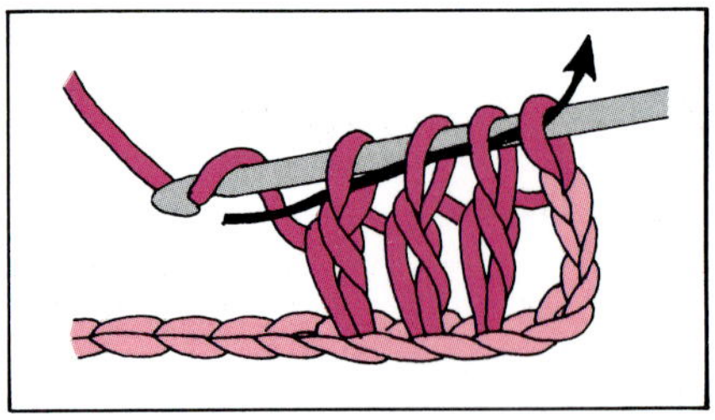

(c) For tr3tog only repeat once more into next stitch (4 loops on hook).

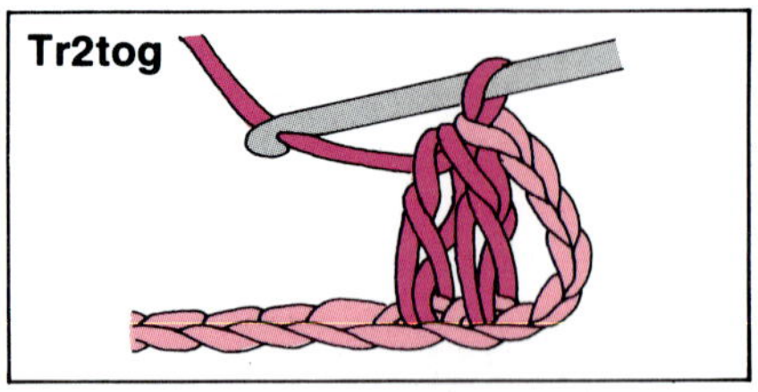

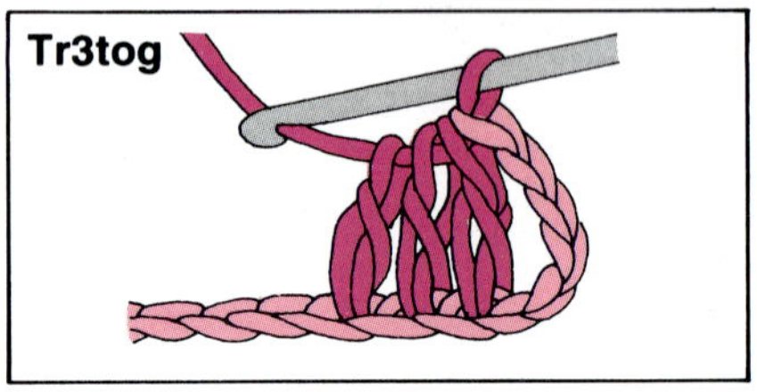

(d) Yarn over hook and draw through all loops on hook to complete.

Fancy Stitch Techniques

Hints and Tips
Always check the abbreviations given at the beginning of each pattern you work from, as there is not a fixed arrangement of stitches for such terms as 'shell', 'group', 'cluster', 'picot', and so on. Different patterns may have different sets of instructions for individual terms.

Groups

A group — several complete stitches worked into the same place — may consist of more than one kind of stitch.

(a) A group of 5 (or more) trebles is sometimes called a 'shell'.

Clusters

A cluster — 2 or more stitches joined together at the top — may consist of more than one kind of stitch. Any combination of stitches may be joined into a cluster by leaving the last loop of each temporarily on the hook until they are all worked off together.

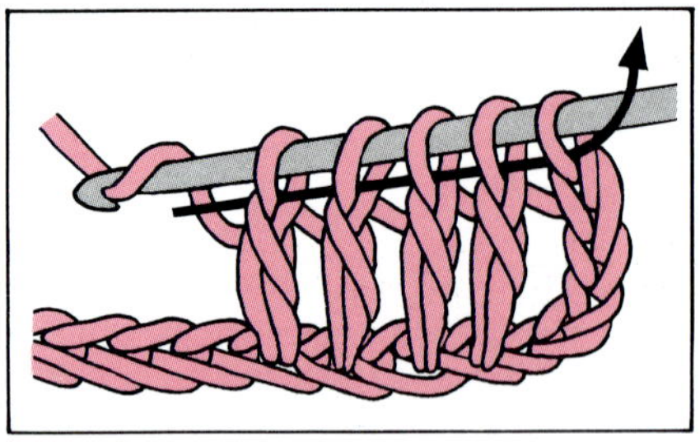

(a) A cluster of 4 trebles worked together.

Between Stitches

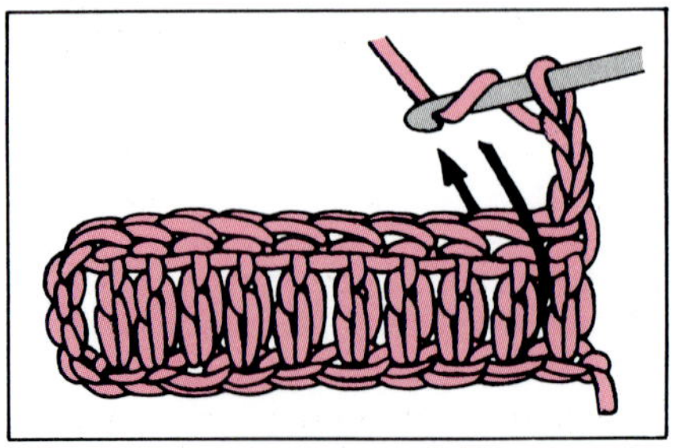

Inserting the hook between the stems of stitches and beneath the bundle of threads which joins them at the top will open up a solid fabric.

Under One Loop Only

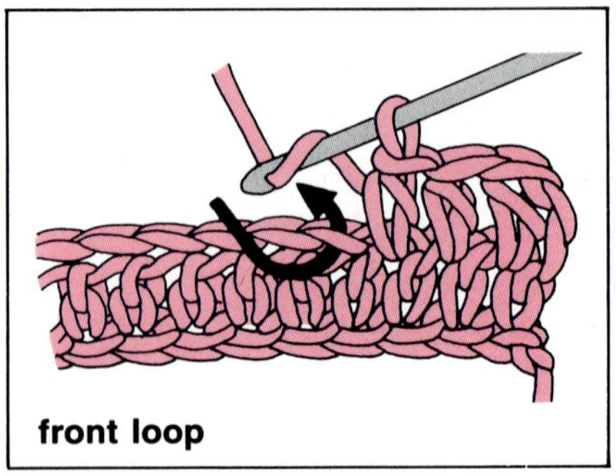

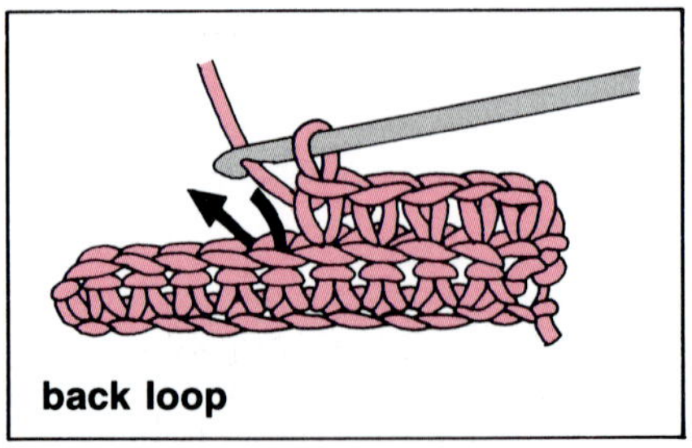

Inserting the hook under one loop only (either the back loop, or the front loop), leaves the other loop exposed as a horizontal bar. Depending upon which stitches are picked out in this way, horizontal ridges or 'woven' effects can be created. The fabric also tends to become more elastic.

Raised (Relief) Stitches

Inserting the hook round the whole stem of a stitch creates raised or relief effects. This can be worked from the front or back.

1 treble round front (1tr/F)

(a) Wrap yarn round hook, insert hook from front and from right to left round stem of appropriate stitch.

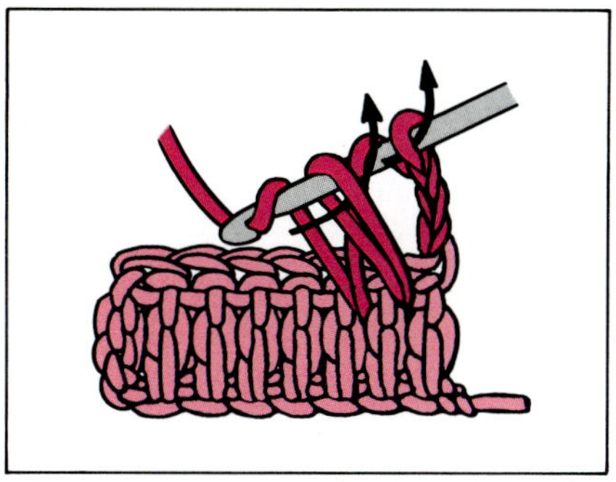

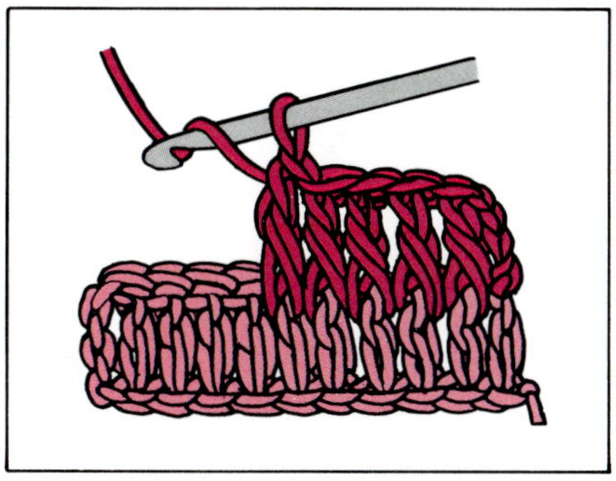

(b) and (c) Complete the stitch normally.

1 treble round back (1tr/B)

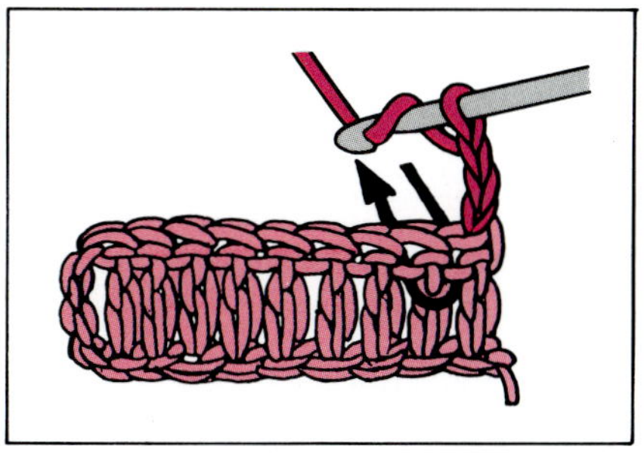

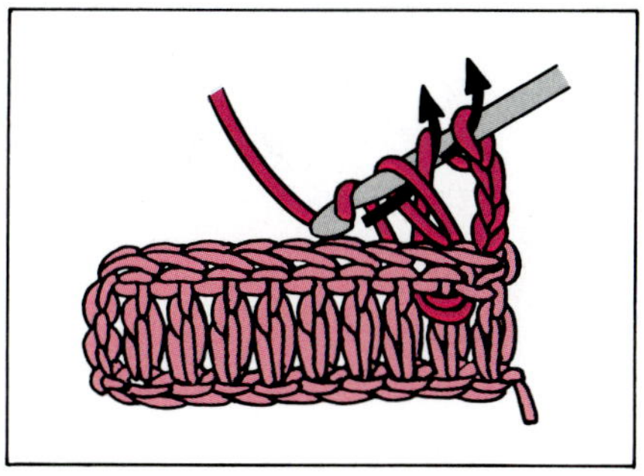

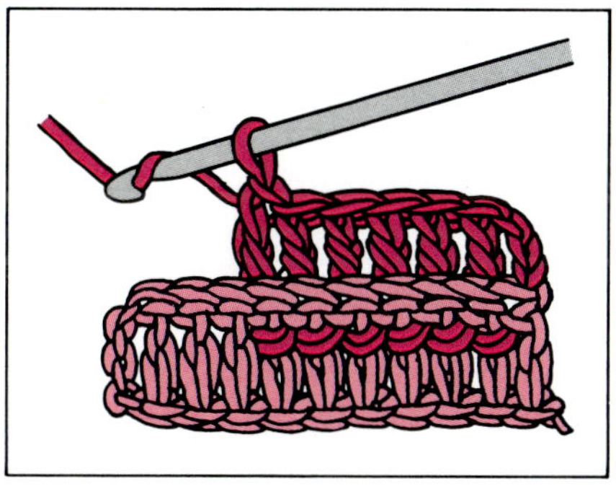

(e) and (f) Complete the stitch normally. Any stitch can be worked in this way, singly, or in a group, or cluster.

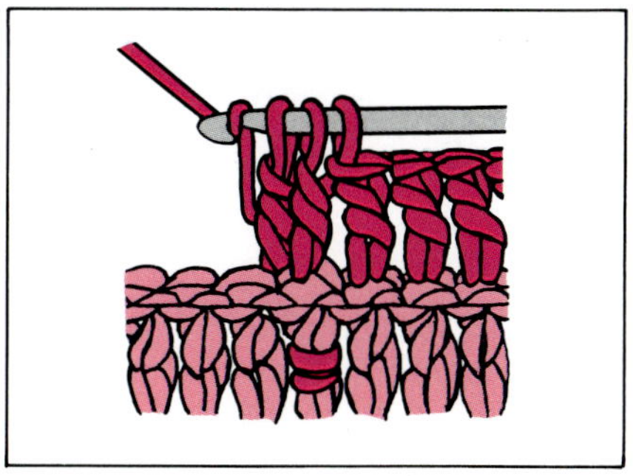

(g) A 'raised' stitch may also be worked as a 'twin' cluster together with a stitch worked normally under top 2 loops of stitch above.

Chain Spaces

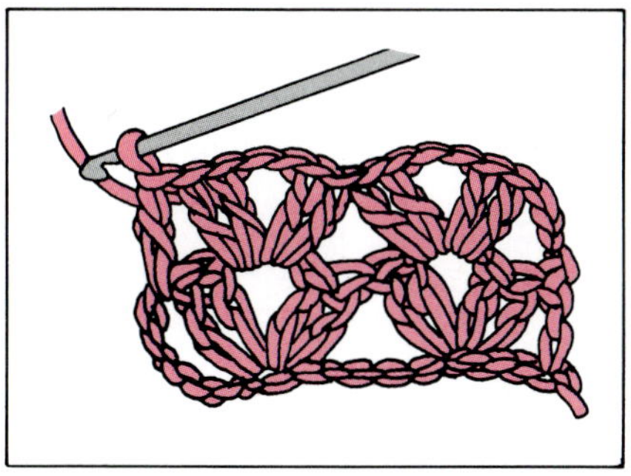

(a) When working a single stitch, or group, into a chain space, or chain loop, it is normal to insert hook into space beneath chain arch. This is quick and easy to do.

(b) It is important to note when pattern instructions tell you to work **into** a partic-ular chain, for example when working into

Spikes

Spikes are made by inserting the hook further down into the fabric than usual, either below the next stitch, or to one side of it.

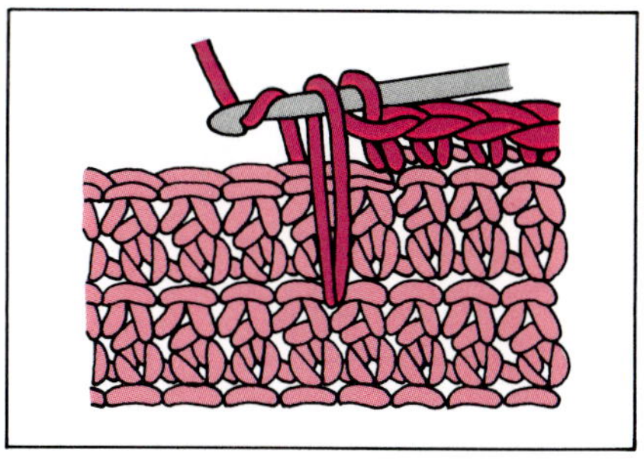

(a) A loop is drawn through and up to the height of the current row. The stitch is then completed normally.

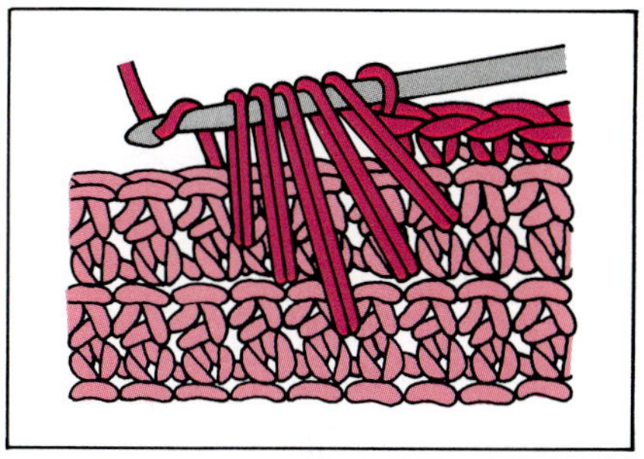

(b) Spikes can be worked singly, in sequences, or in clusters by inserting hook in different places, drawing a loop through each and finishing by drawing a loop through all loops so collected. They add interest to fabric texture, but are most dramatic when worked in contrasting colours.

It is important to work 'spike' loops loosely enough to avoid squashing the fabric, but with sufficient tension to maintain the stability of the fabric. When a whole sequence of stitches is 'spiked', it may help to work each one as a 'twin' cluster together with a stitch worked normally under the top 2 loops of the stitch above as follows:

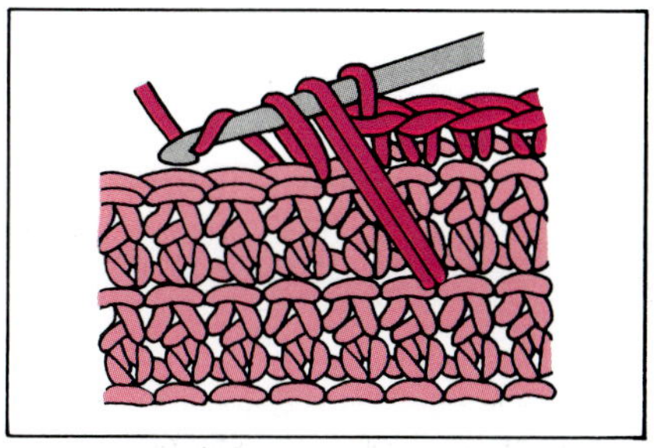

Insert hook under top 2 loops of next stitch, yarn over hook and draw a loop through (3 loops on hook). Yarn over hook and draw through all loops on hook to complete.

Stars (or Marguerites)

A popular form of 'spiked' cluster — often called a 'Star' or 'Marguerite' — is formed by inserting hook 3, 4, 5 or more times, partly into side of previous stitch and partly into next few stitches in previous row.

Star with 4 'Spikes'

1st Star

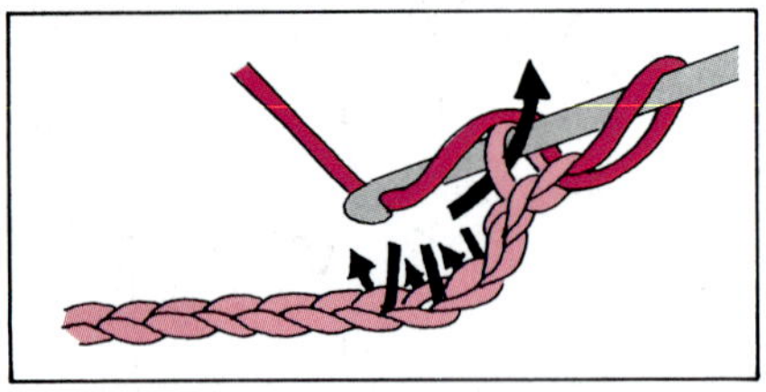

(a) Insert hook into 2nd chain from hook, yarn over hook and draw a loop through. Repeat this step 3 more times into 4th, 5th and 6th chains from hook (5 loops on hook).

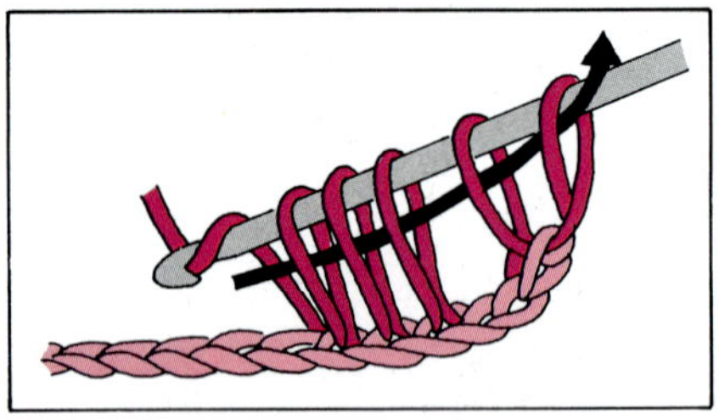

(b) Yarn over hook and draw through all loops.

(c) Make one chain firmly to close the Star.

2nd and subsequent Stars

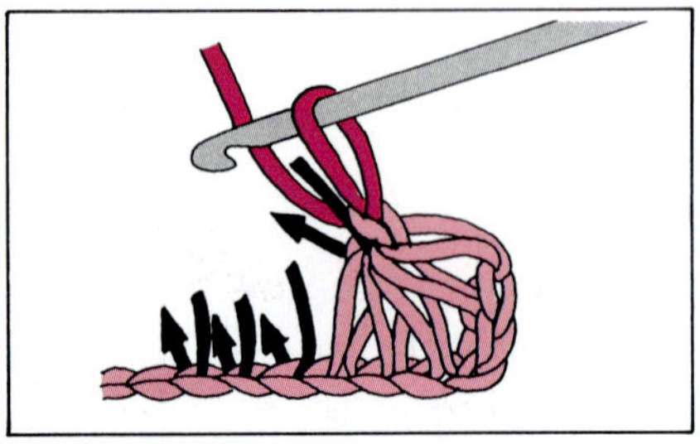

(d) Insert hook, yarn over hook and draw loops through as follows: into loop which closed previous star, into same place as previous Star completed, and into each of next 2 stitches (5 loops on hook).

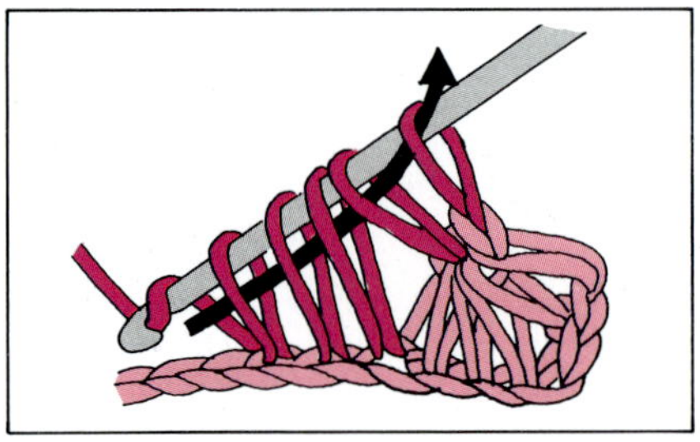

(e) Yarn over hook, draw through all loops on hook and make a chain firmly to close Star.

Picots

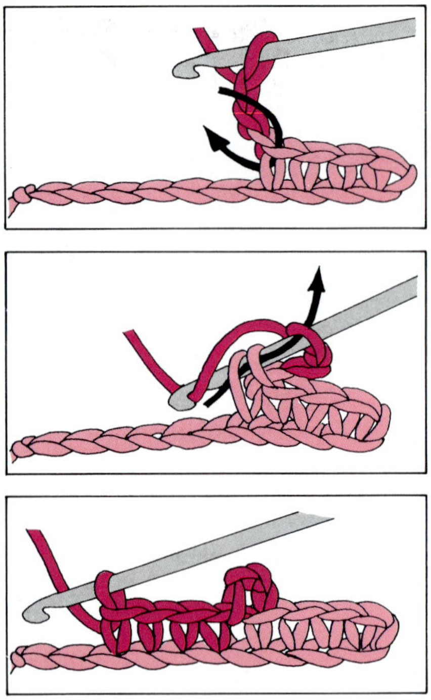

A picot is normally a chain loop made into a closed ring by a slip stitch, or double crochet. The number of chains in a picot varies. A common type of small picot shown here made with 3 chains is closed by inserting hook down through top of previous stitch, yarn over hook and drawing a loop through all loops on hook.

Crossed Stitches

Closed Cross

The simplest form of crossed stitch is made by inserting hook into a previously unworked stitch, yarn over hook and bringing a loop through and forward again in order to be able to complete stitch normally. The threads of new stitch thus made not only cross over, but also sandwich previous stitches.

(a) *Miss 1 stitch, then work 1 treble.

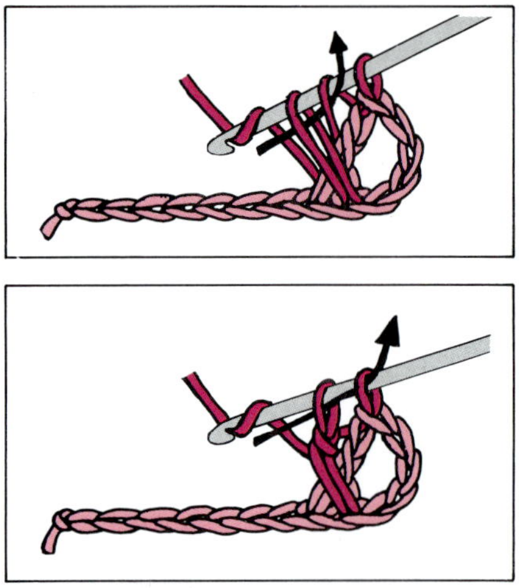

(b) and (c) Work 1 treble into stitch missed before first treble.

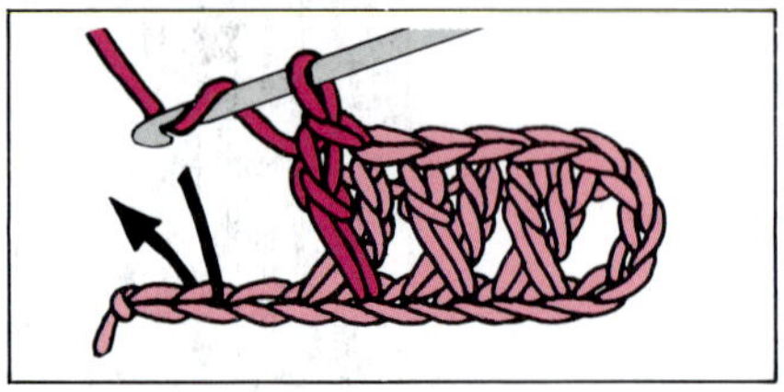

(d) Repeat from * to continue with pattern of crossed pairs of trebles.

Open Cross

To make stitches which, although crossed, are not entangled with each other and so maintain a clear 'X' shape, work as follows:

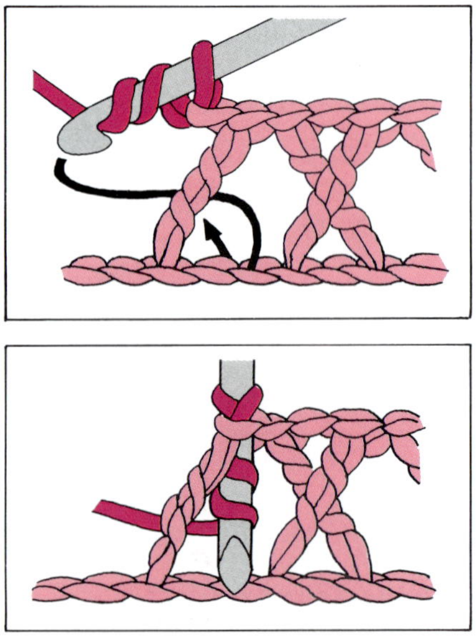

(a) and (b) Miss 2 stitches, work 1 treble into next stitch, 1 chain, taking hook behind (or in front of) first stitch work second treble.

'X', 'Y' and 'λ' Shapes

In lacy stitch patterns long stitches are sometimes made into 'X' and 'Y' shapes without crossing them.

Double Treble 'λ' and 'X' shape

(a) Yarn over hook twice, insert hook as required to make lower part of first 'leg'.

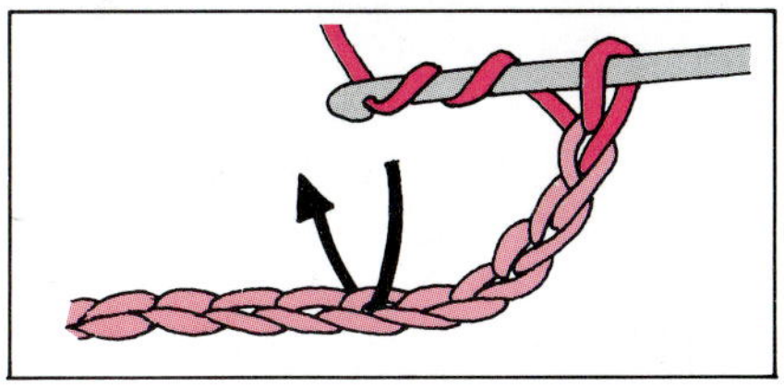

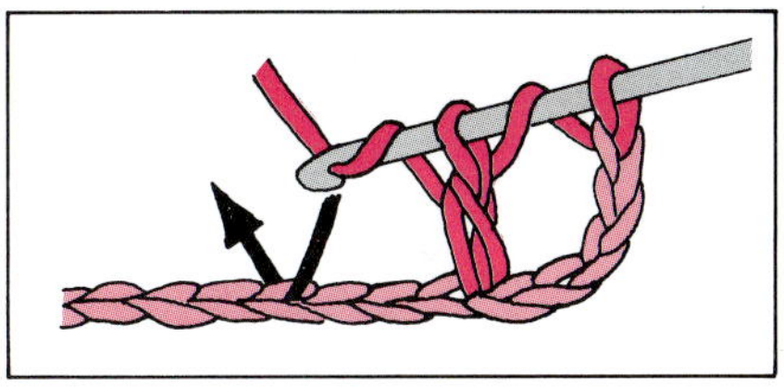

(b) Yarn over hook, draw a loop through, yarn over hook and draw through 2 loops (3 loops on hook). Yarn over hook once more and insert hook again as required to make lower part of second 'leg'.

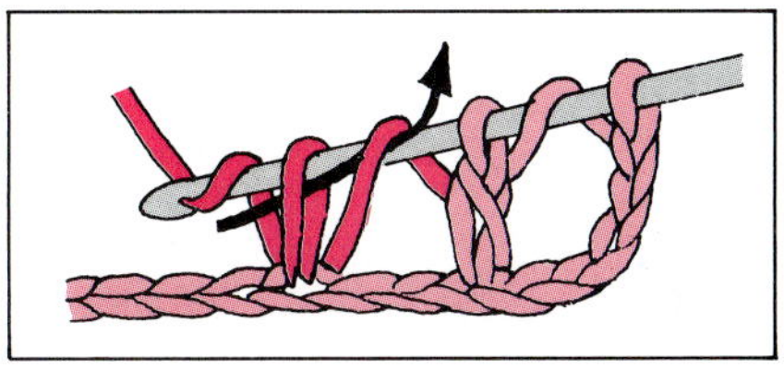

(c) Yarn over hook, draw a loop through, yarn over hook and draw through 2 loops to complete both lower 'legs'.

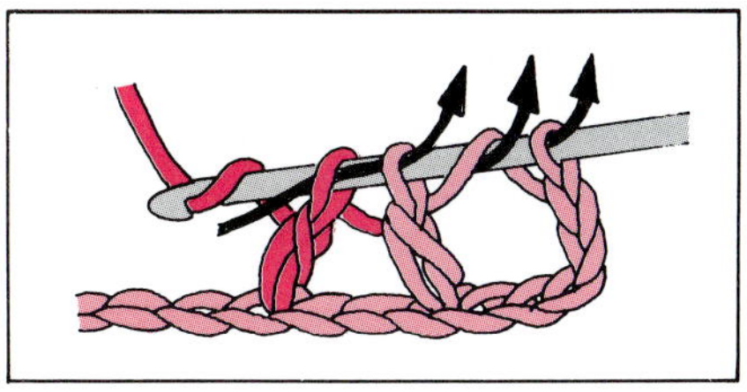

(d) Yarn over hook and draw through 2 loops. Repeat last step twice more to complete first 'arm' (note that at this stage you have completed a 'λ' shape).

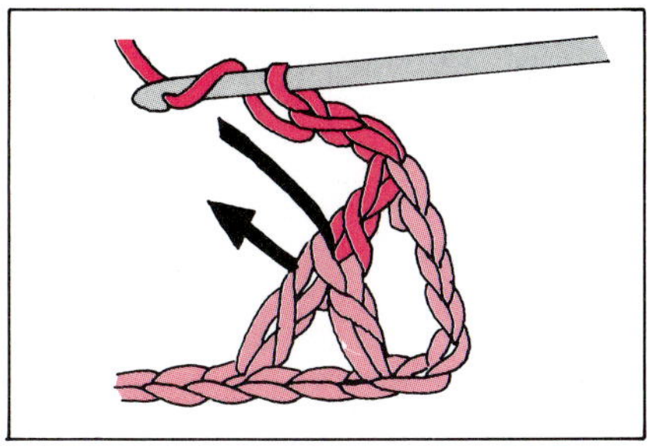

(e) Make chains as required to take hook to top of second 'arm', yarn over hook, insert hook into centre of cluster just completed, picking up 2 threads at left-hand side, and draw a loop through.

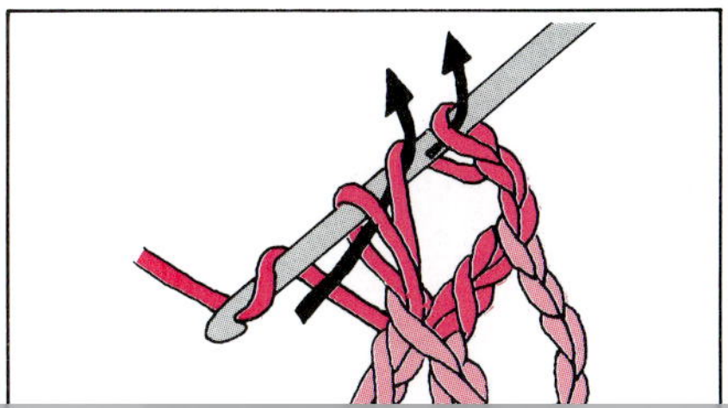

(f) Yarn over hook and draw through 2 loops.

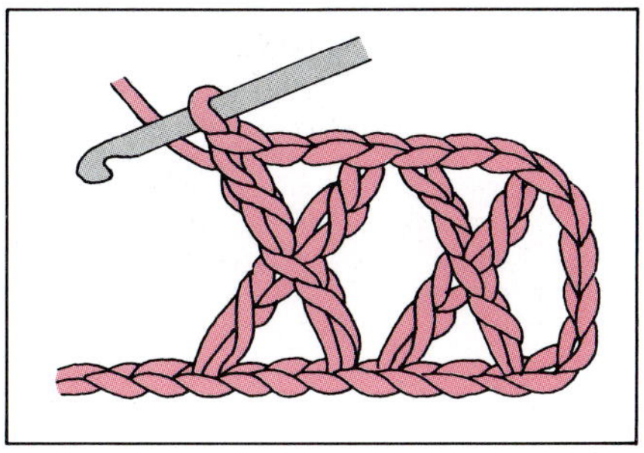

(g) Repeat last step to complete second 'arm' and whole 'X' shape.

Triple Treble 'Y' shape

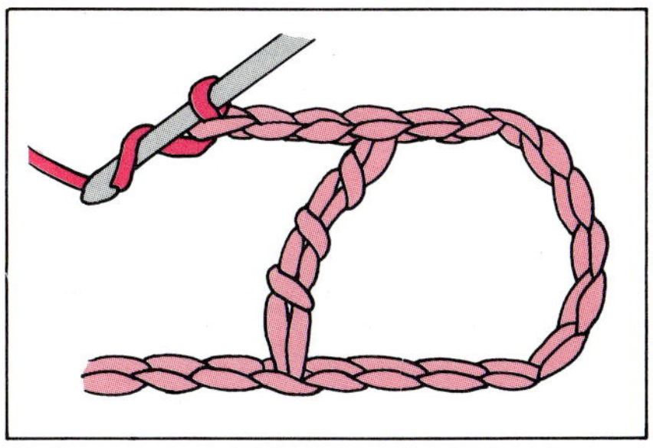

(a) Work one complete triple treble for lower 'leg' and first 'arm'.

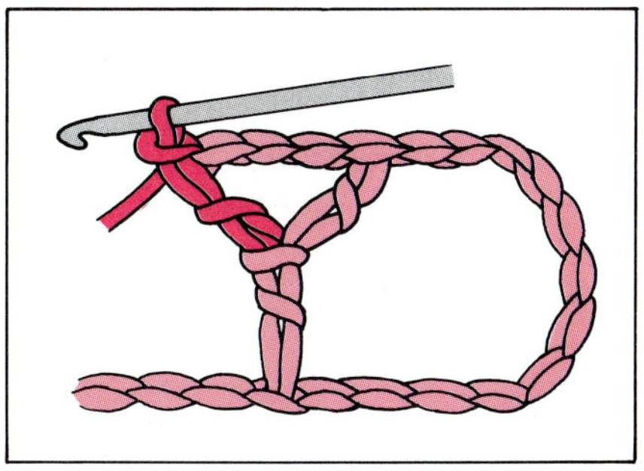

(b) Make chains as required to take hook to top of second 'arm' and work 1 treble into centre of triple treble to complete second 'arm' and whole 'Y' shape in same way as for 'X' shape above.

Puff Stitch

A puff stitch is a cluster of half trebles (usually 3 to 5), worked into the same place to make a soft puff effect.

Puff stitch of 3 half trebles

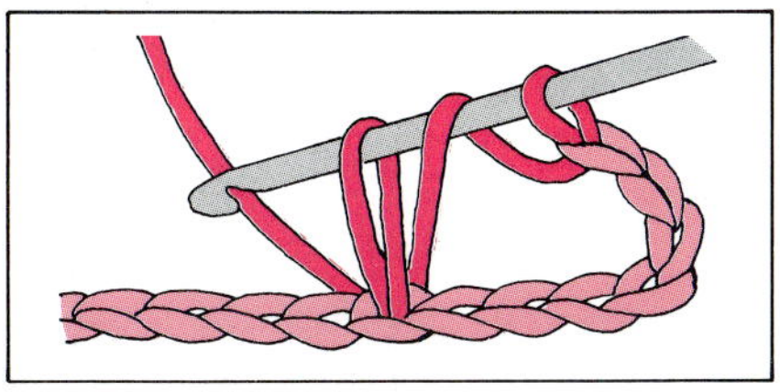

(a) *Yarn over hook, insert hook, yarn over hook and draw a loop through (3 loops on hook).

(b) Repeat from * twice more inserting

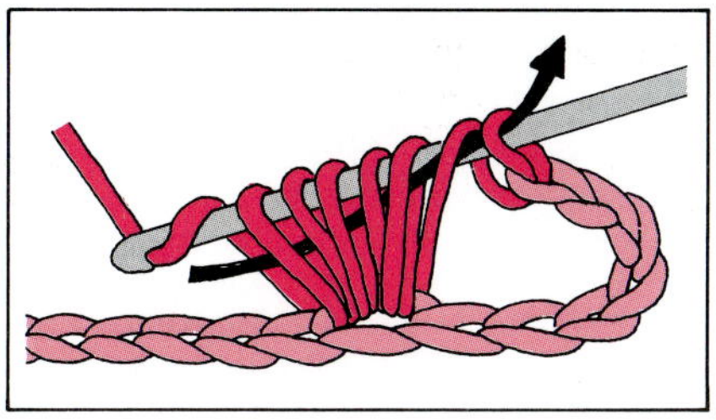

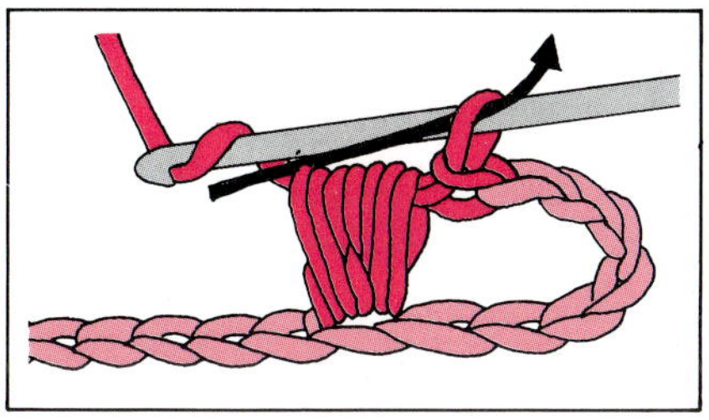

(c) Work 1 chain to close puff stitch firmly.

Popcorns

A popcorn is a group of complete stitches, usually worked into the same place, folded and closed at the top. The number and type of stitches included varies.

Popcorn with 4 trebles

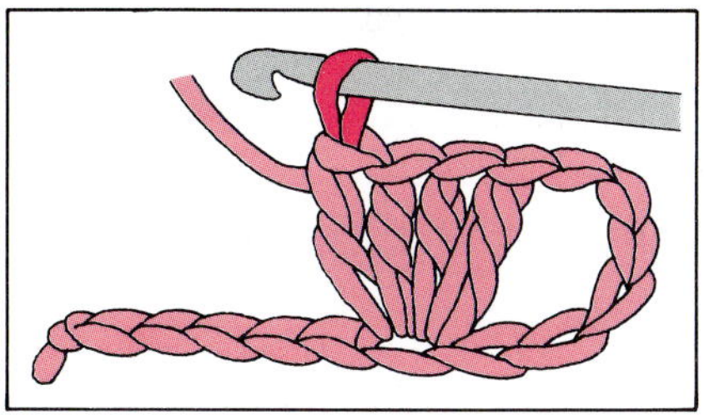

(a) Work 4 trebles into one stitch normally.

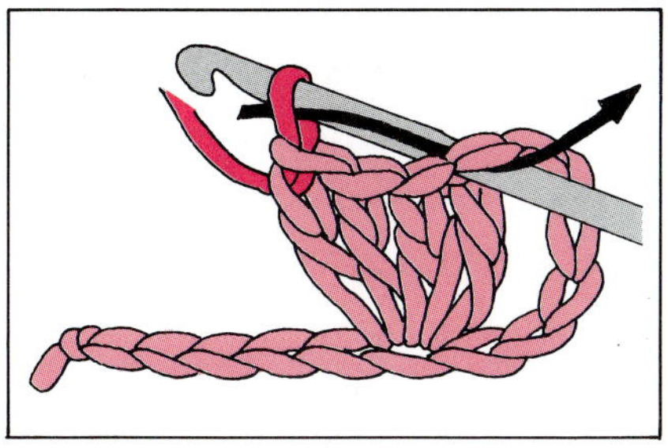

(b) Take hook out of working loop, insert under top 2 loops of first treble in group just made.

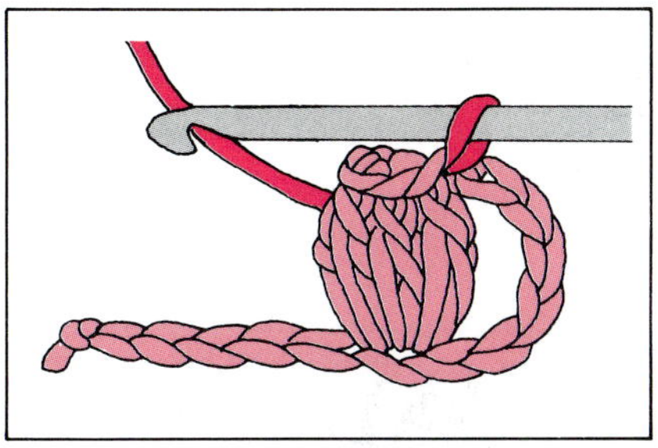

(c) Pick up working loop again and draw through to close group together and project it towards you.

Bobbles

A bobble is a cluster of stitches (usually 3 to 5) all worked into the same place and joined together at the top. Bobbles are thrown into relief most effectively when the stitches before and after them are shorter, and when they are worked on wrong side rows.

Bobble of 3 trebles

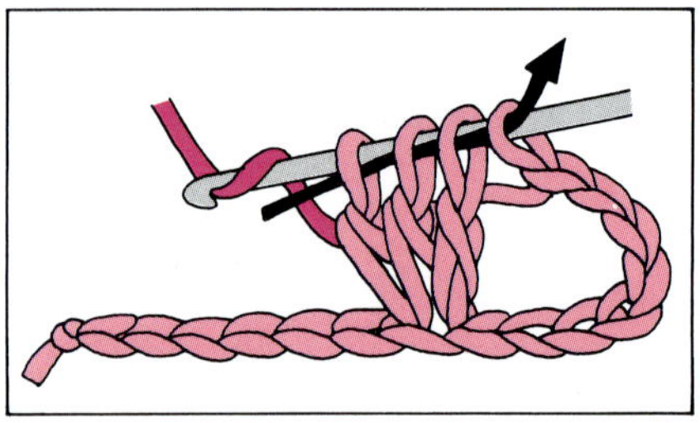

(a) Work 3 trebles always inserting hook into same stitch and leaving last loop of each on hook as for tr3tog (see page 30). Yarn over hook and draw through all loops on hook to complete.

(b) It often helps, particularly with bulkier bobble clusters, to work an extra chain to close them firmly.

Pineapple

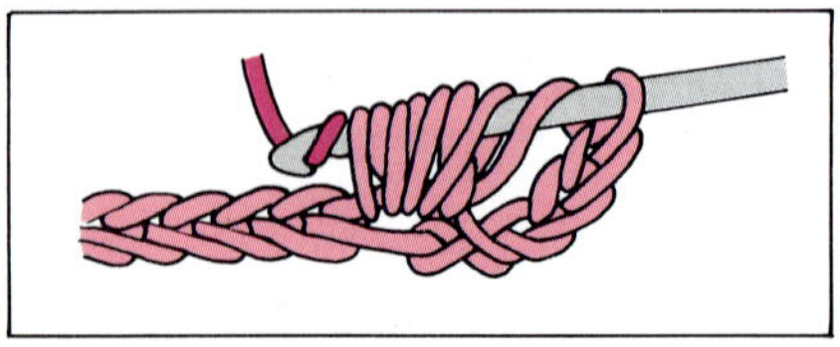

(a) *Yarn over hook, insert hook, yarn over hook and draw through a loop. Repeat from * 4 more times into same stitch (9 loops on hook).

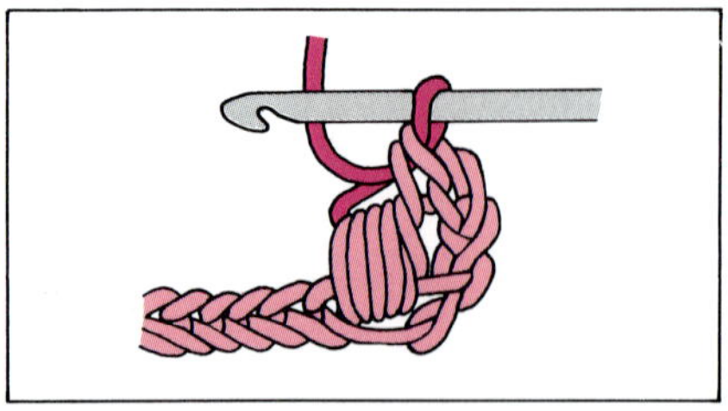

(b) Yarn over hook and draw through 8 loops, yarn over hook and through remaining 2 loops. 1 chain to close pineapple firmly.

Bullion Stitch

Yarn over hook as many times as specified (usually 7 to 10 times). Insert hook as required, yarn over hook and draw a loop through. Yarn over hook and draw

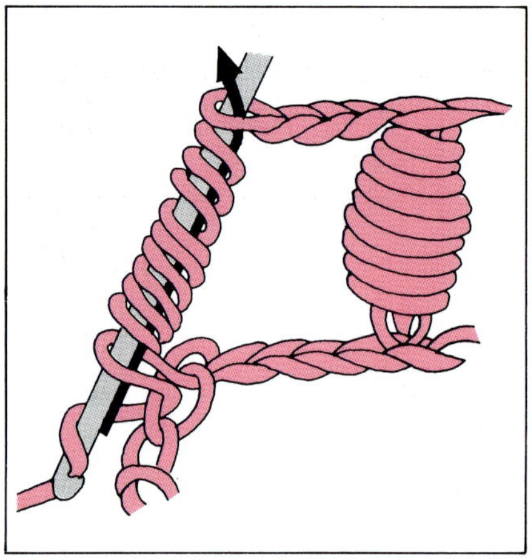

through all loops on hook, one at a time if necessary. Work 1 chain to complete the bullion stitch.

Fur or Loop Stitch

Loop stitch is a variation of double crochet and is usually worked on a wrong side row because the loops form at back of fabric.

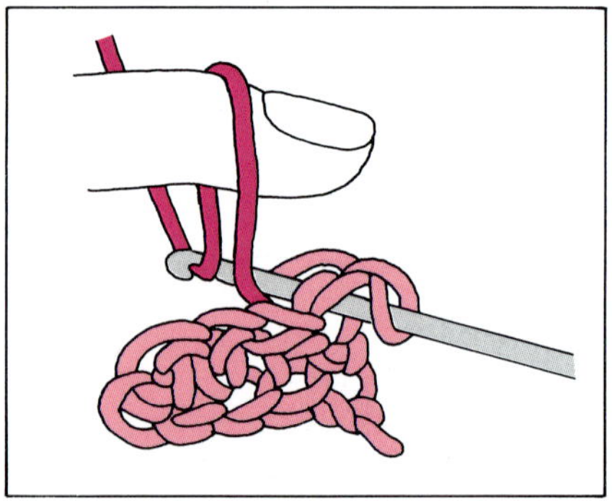

(a) Using the left-hand finger to control loop size insert hook, pick up both threads of loop and draw through.

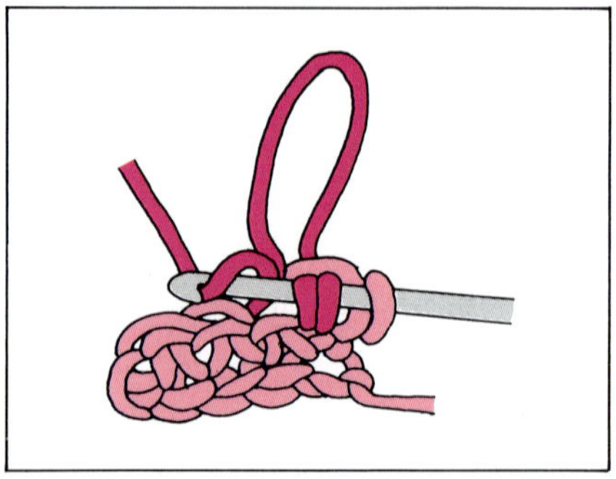

(b) Yarn over hook.

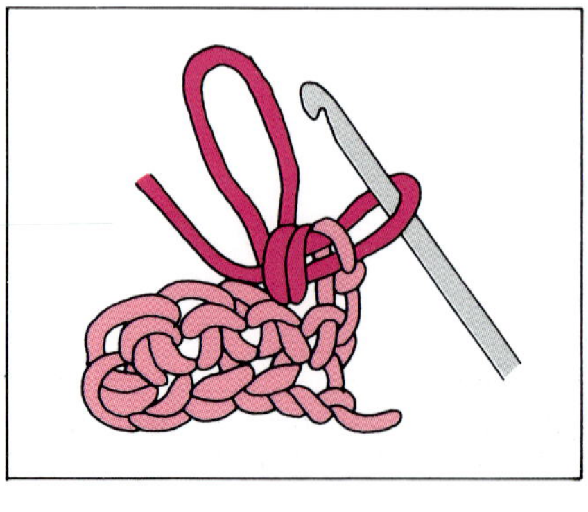

(c) Draw through all loops on hook to complete.

Note: You can either leave the loops, or cut through each one afterwards to produce a 'fur' fabric.

Crab Stitch or Reversed Double Crochet

Crab stitch can be used as a decorative texture (Corded Rib), or edging (Corded Edge). It consists of working double crochet stitches in the wrong direction, for example from left to right for right-handers. After a right side row do not turn.

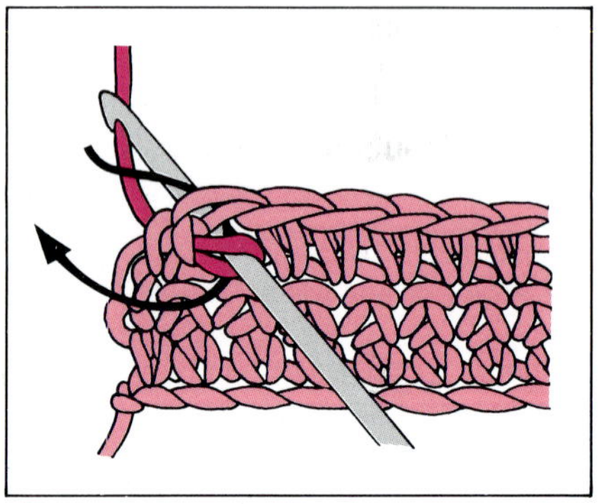

(a) Always starting with hook facing downwards insert hook back into next stitch to right. Draw a loop through twisting hook to face upwards at the same time.

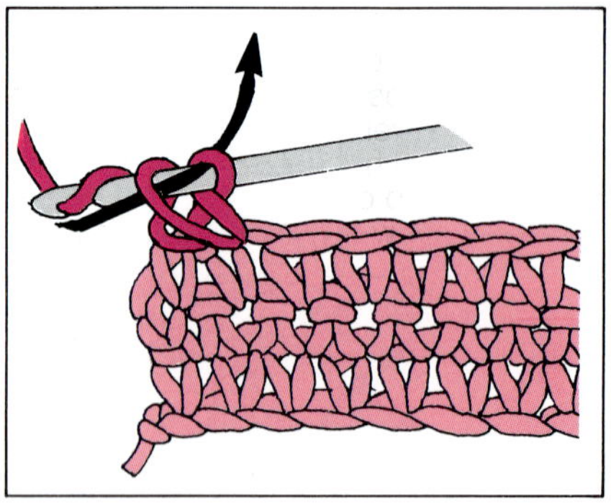

(b) Yarn over hook and draw through to finish off dc as usual.

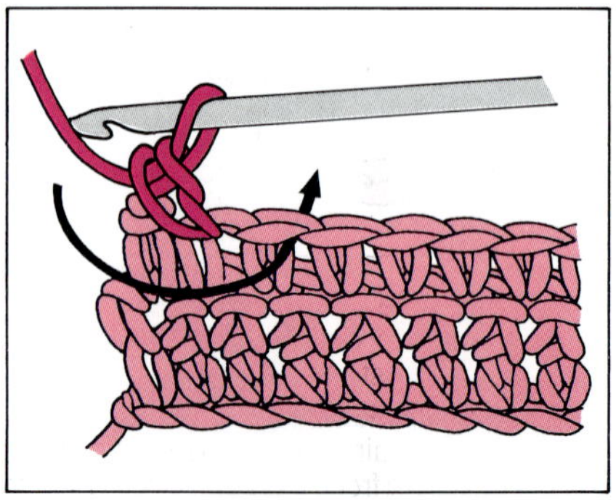

(c) Insert hook ready for next stitch.

(d) Direction of working causes the stitches to twist and create the decorative effect.

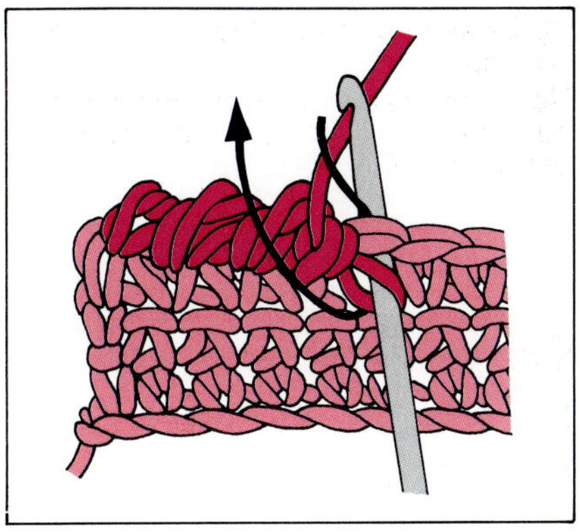

Linked Stitches

The stems of all basic stitches, except double crochet, may be linked to each other in the middle. This gives resulting fabric greater firmness and stability.

Linked Double Trebles

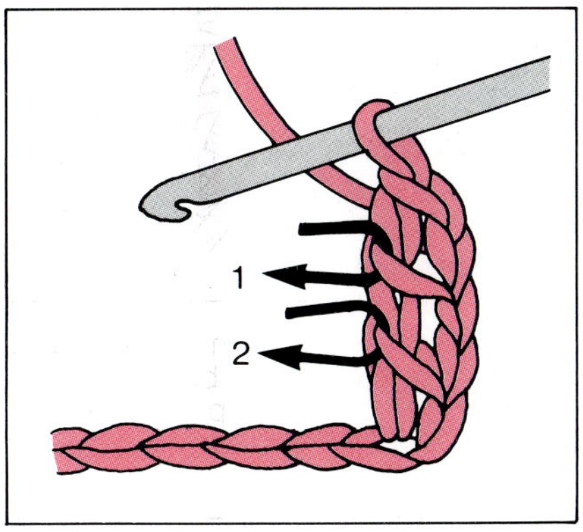

(a) Insert hook down through upper of 2 horizontal loops round stem of previous stitch, yarn over hook and draw a loop through. Insert hook down through lower horizontal loop of same stitch, yarn over hook and draw another loop through.

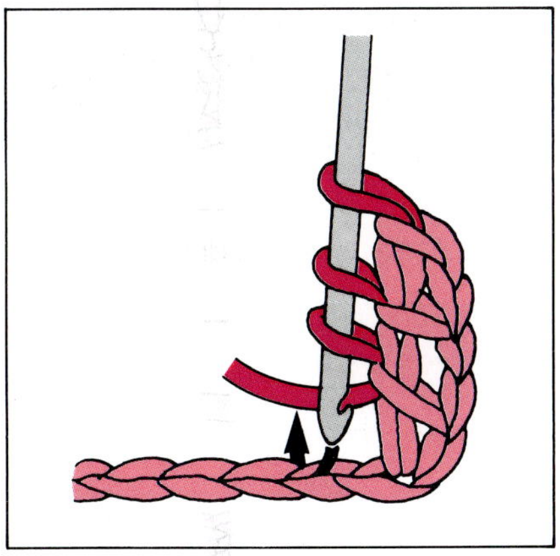

(b) Treat these 2 loops as yarn overs required for an ordinary double treble, and complete stitch in normal way.

To make first linked double treble following turning chain, insert hook into 2nd then 4th chains from hook in order to pick up the 2 preliminary loops.

Both trebles and longer stitches are made

Lace Loops

Lace loops are most often used either as a decorative edging or for the kind of fabric-making sometimes called 'broomstick' crochet.

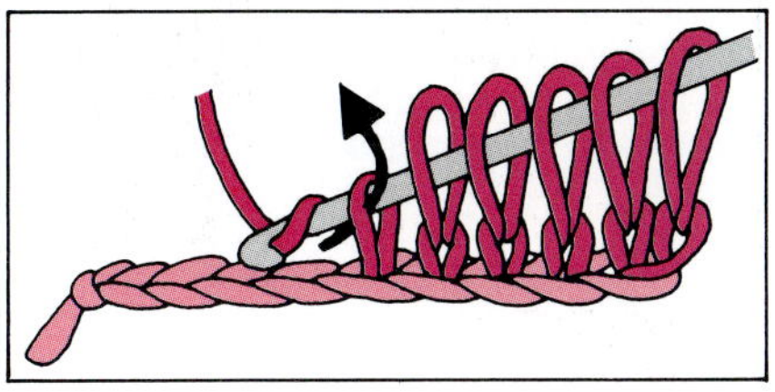

(a) *Insert hook, yarn over hook and draw a loop through. Yarn over hook, draw another loop through first loop and lengthen as required. Repeat from *, keeping each loop on hook.

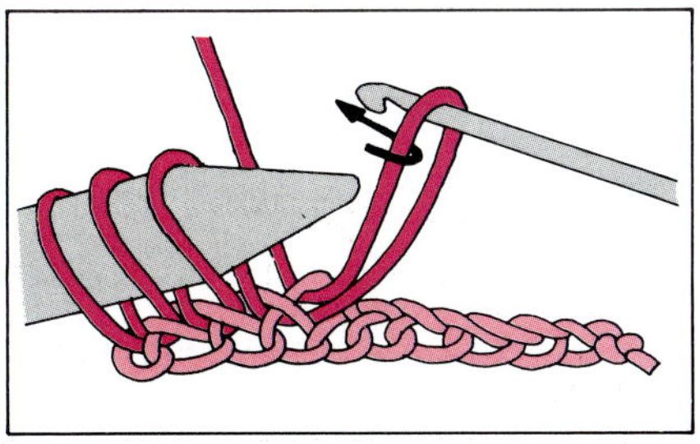

(b) To keep larger loops even in size, work from left to right and transfer each loop to a large size knitting needle (or 'broomstick').

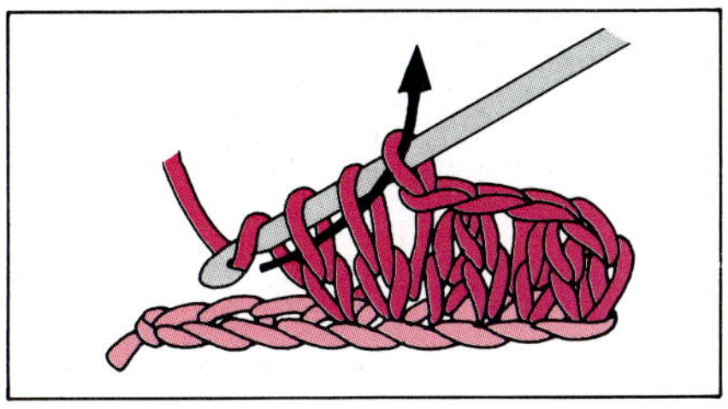

(c) 2 or more lace loops can be made into clusters in various ways as an alternative to basic stitches.

Solomon's Knot

Solomon's Knot is a lengthened chain locked with a double crochet worked into its back loop. Once you have mastered the technique, the stitch is quite easy to do!

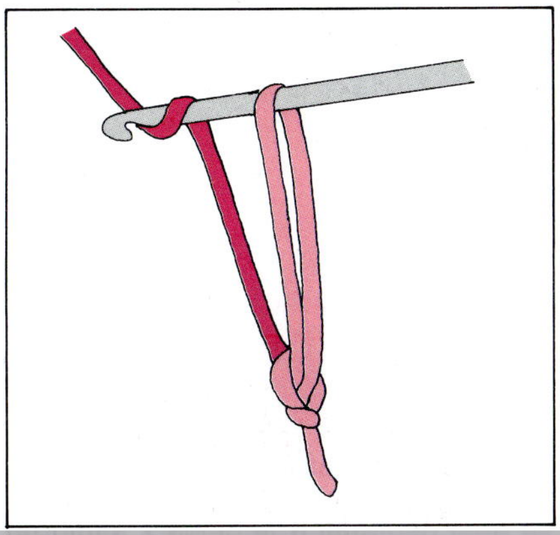

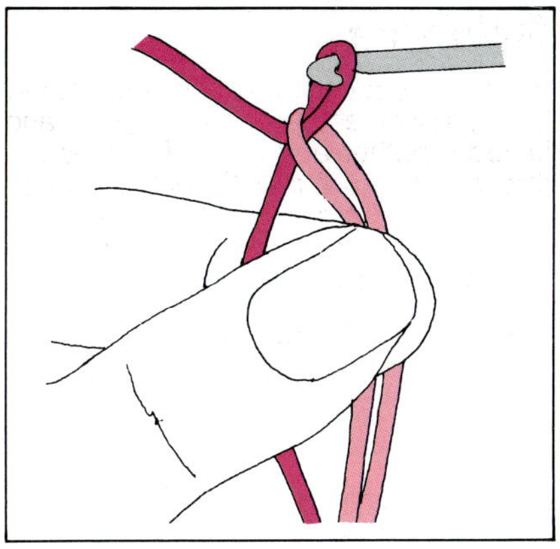

(b) Draw through loop on hook, keeping single back thread of this long chain separate from 2 front threads.

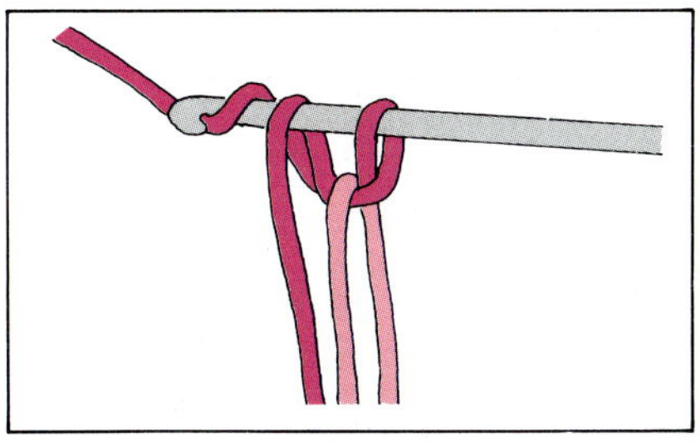

(c) Insert hook under this single back thread, yarn over hook.

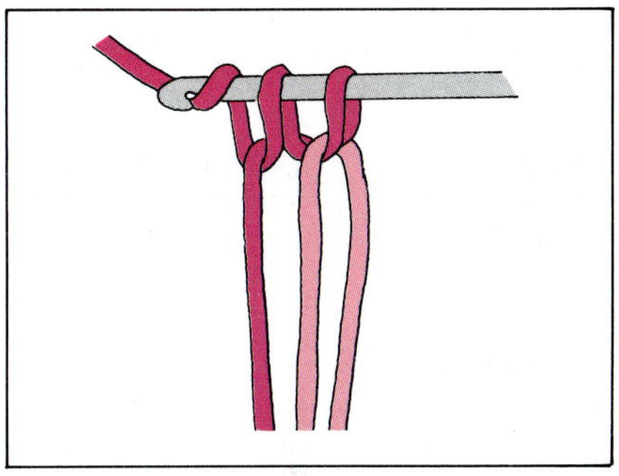

(d) Draw a loop through, yarn over hook.

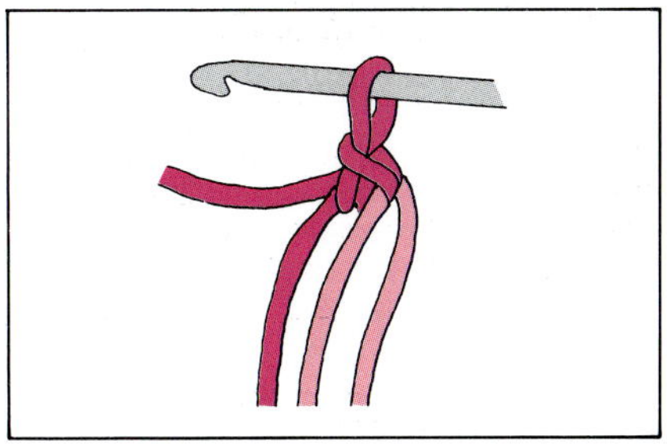

(e) Draw through both loops on hook to complete.

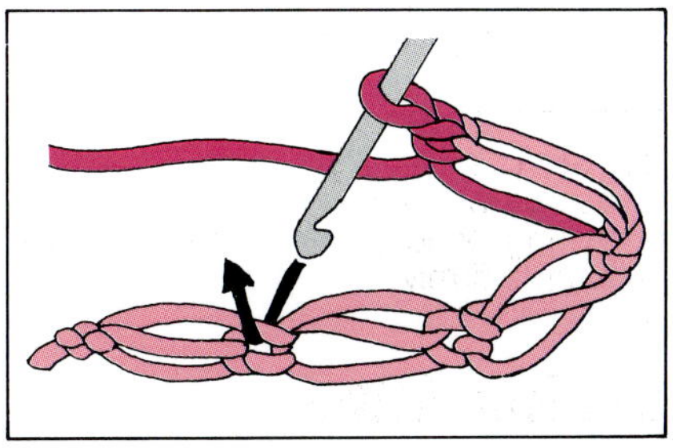

Working Notes

This section contains general information to help you while you are crocheting.

Following a Pattern

Crochet patterns are written in a language all of their own. Abbreviations are used for many of the repetitive words which occur in the instructions and although all manufacturers do not use exactly the same abbreviations, an experienced crocheter can follow the jargon.

Before starting to crochet any pattern, always read it right through. Even if you are not experienced, this will give you an idea of how the pattern is structured and you will know what to expect. After working one or two patterns you will understand how the pattern works.

Where imperial and metric measurements are given always work **either** in inches throughout **or** centimetres throughout, (for example when checking tension or measuring lengths).

Below is an explanation of general instructions found on most crochet patterns, and a brief resumé of common crochet terms.

Asterisks, *, and Brackets, ( ) [ ]

These are used to indicate repetition.

A sequence of stitches after an asterisk means that the whole sequence between that asterisk and next semi-colon is to be repeated as many times as necessary to reach the end of the row, for example: *1ch, miss 1ch, 1tr into next st; rep from * to end. This means you repeat '1ch, miss 1ch, 1tr into next st', to end of row.

If no further details are given, as in this case, the end of sequence will coincide exactly with end of row. If there are stitches remaining unworked after last complete repeat sequence, details of how to complete row are given. For example: 'rep from * to last 4 sts, 1ch, miss 1ch, 1tr into each of last 3 sts'.

Instructions are also often put inside brackets, and these are to be worked the number of times stated outside the brackets. For example: '[1ch, miss 1ch, 1tr into next st] 5 times'.

Work straight

Work over the existing row of stitches without increasing or decreasing, until fabric measures required length or a certain number of rows have been worked.

Yarn over hook

The stitch-making instruction to wrap yarn from the ball over hook (or manipulate hook round yarn) in order to make a new loop. Always done from back to front unless otherwise stated.

Front/back

Front and Back mean the front and back surfaces of a fabric for the time being as you hold and look at it. These change over every time you turn the work.

Hints and Tips

Crochet stitches are not the same back and front and so both sides of a fabric may well be quite different. Even when a stitch pattern has no particular right side, it is wise to make a positive decision in respect of all separate pieces of same article, so that the 'grain' of the rows can be matched exactly, when you join the pieces together.

Colour Note

Capital letters A, B, C, D, etc, are used to indicate different yarn colours. When only two colours are involved and one of these is intended to dominate, the terms 'main (M)' and 'contrast (C)' may be used instead.

General Abbreviations

Common abbreviations with which you should be familiar include:

Alt = alternate

For example: increase 1 stitch at beg of next and every **alt** row until there are X sts. This means that counting the next row as row 1, the increase is worked on rows 1, 3, 5, 7 and so on.

Beg = begin(ning)
Ch = chain
Ch sp = chain space
Cl = cluster
Cm = centimetres
Dc = double crochet
Dec = decrease
Dtr = double treble
Foll = following
Gr = group
Htr = half treble
Inc = increase
Ins = inches
Quad tr = quadruple treble
Quin tr = quintuple treble
Rem = remaining
Rep = repeat
Sext tr = sextuple treble
Sl st = slip stitch
St(s) = stitch(es)
Tog = together
Tr = treble
Ttr = triple treble
Yoh = yarn over hook

Stitch Diagrams

Many crochet patterns use stitch diagrams as well as, or instead of having the pattern rows written out. They are detailed 'maps' of the crochet fabric in a stylised form, illustrating right side of work. They show you at a glance what you are going to do before you start and also where you are at any moment. To follow them you must first be familiar with all the basic stitch and fabric making procedures needed for following written instructions.

The Stitches

As soon as you know the stitches themselves, it is easy to identify the symbols which represent them. From treble onwards the number of short angled strokes crossing the stems represents the number of times the yarn is wrapped before the hook is inserted.

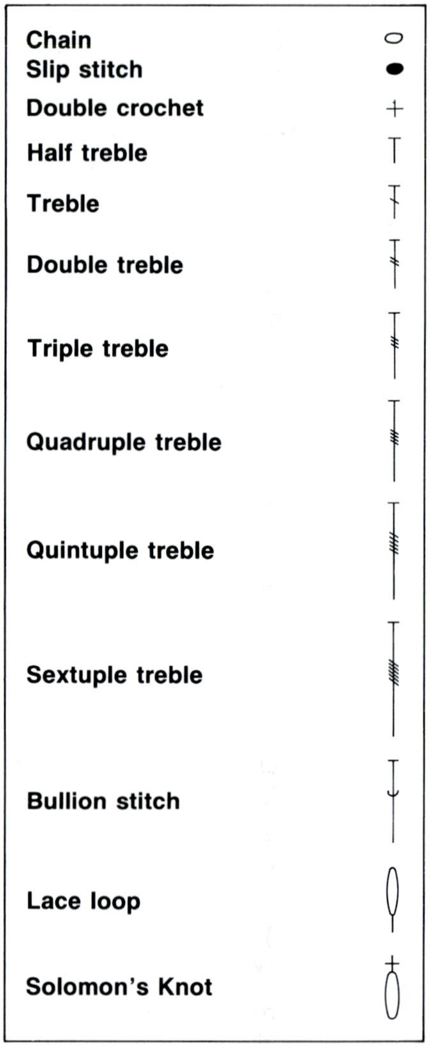

Groups, Clusters and Picots, and so on, are usually obvious although you may need to remind yourself exactly how to work a complex cluster combination.

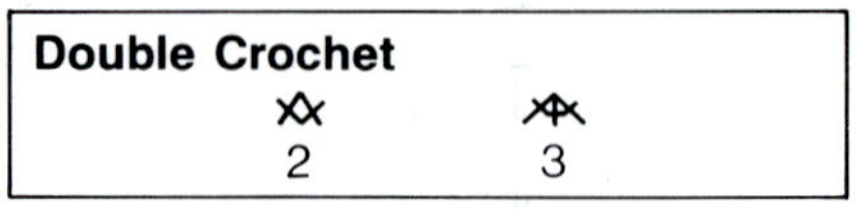

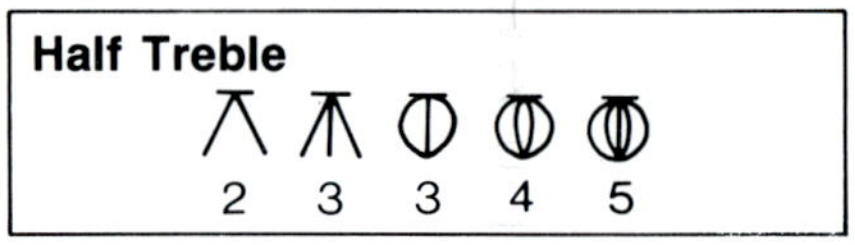

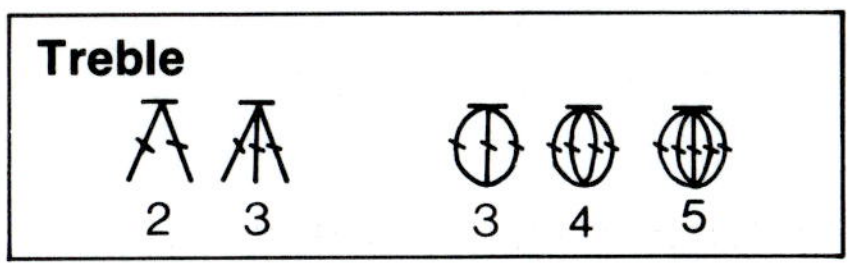

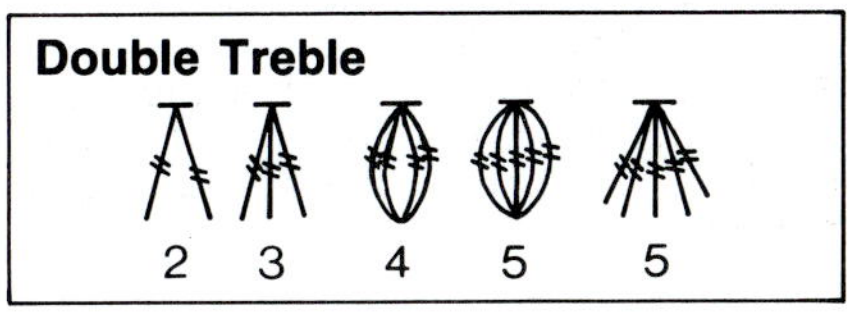

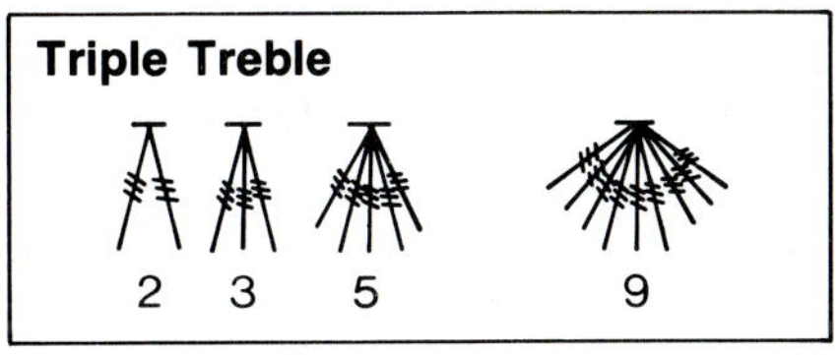

Spikes

The stitch symbol is extended downwards to show where hook is to go through fabric.

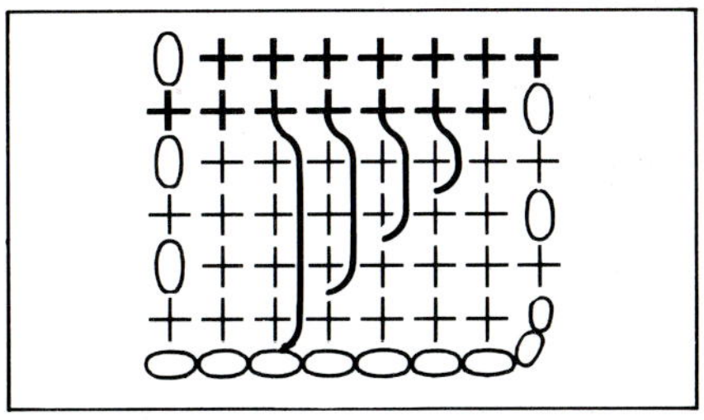

Popcorns

The tops of group of stitches forming popcorn are linked into an oval.

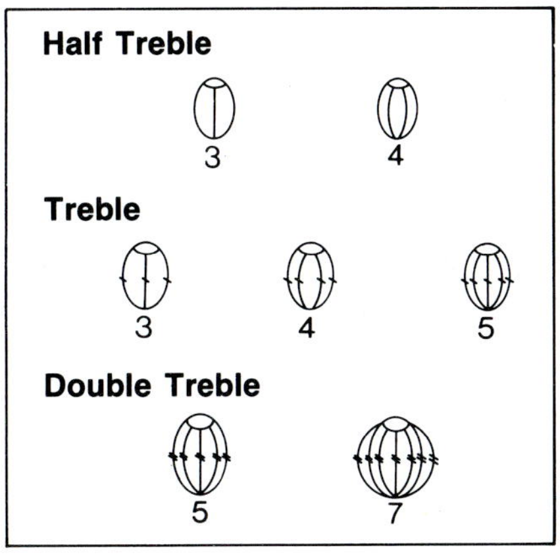

Raised (relief) stitches

When a stitch is worked by inserting hook behind a stem (instead of under top two loops), the stitch symbol ends in a 'crook' round appropriate stem. The direction of crook indicates which side of fabric hook is to be inserted. On right side rows work a raised stitch with right side crook at front, and wrong side crook at back (vice versa on wrong side rows).

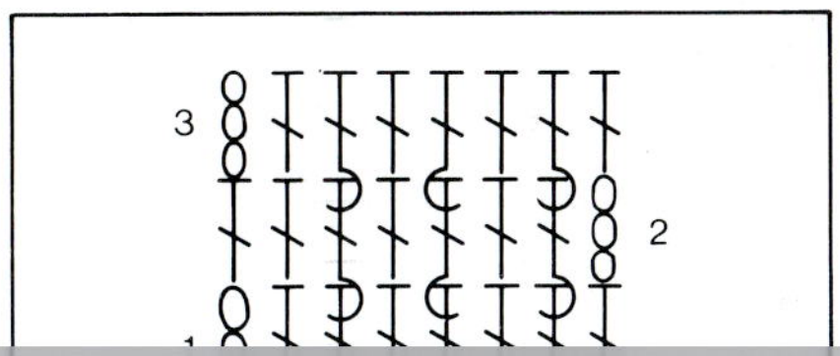

Crossed stitches

(a) When stitch symbols cross each other, work a Closed Cross.

(b) When a stitch is broken as shown take hook **behind** previous one and work an Open Cross.

(c) When crossbars are drawn both above and below crossing point of stitches work as for an 'X' shape (see page 32 for all 3 methods).

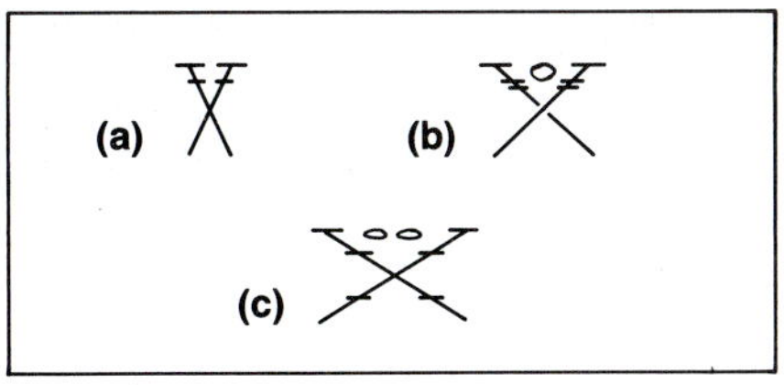

Picots

When a single picot loop occurs after a solid stitch, see page 32 for the usual method of working the closing slip stitch.

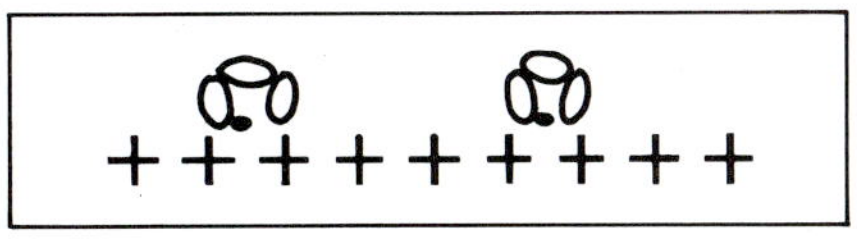

Figures

Figures indicate row (or round) numbers.

Colour

Light and heavy stitch symbols confirm changes of colour.

Note: Stitch symbols are drawn and laid out as realistically as possible with consistent relative length and width, but sometimes they have to be distorted for the sake of clarity. For example, chain stitches may look extra long on some of the diagrams. This is only to show clearly where they go and you should not try to make artificially long stitches.

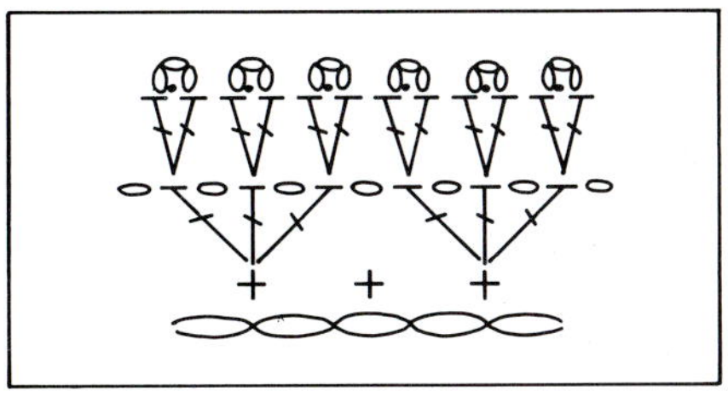

Changing colour

When joining in, or changing from one colour to another, for example in trebles, work as follows:

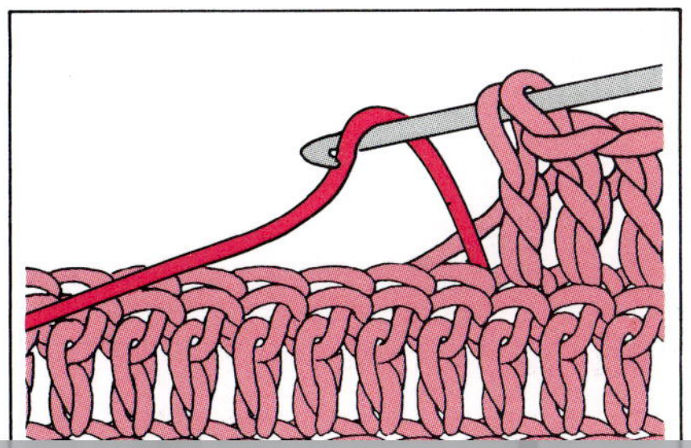

(a) Drop old colour and pick up new before completing last stitch in old colour.

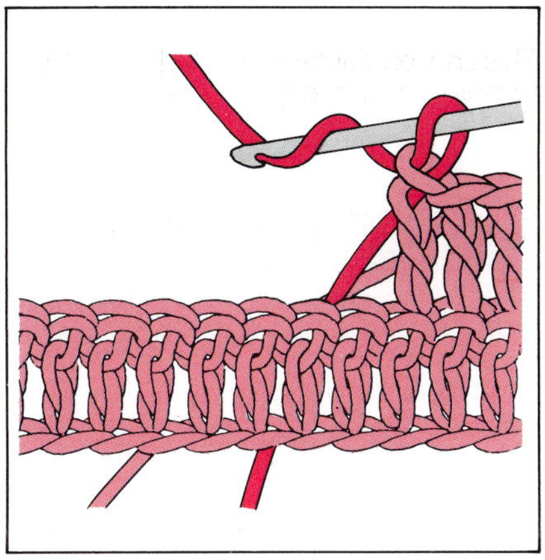

(b) Loop on hook afterwards is now in new colour.

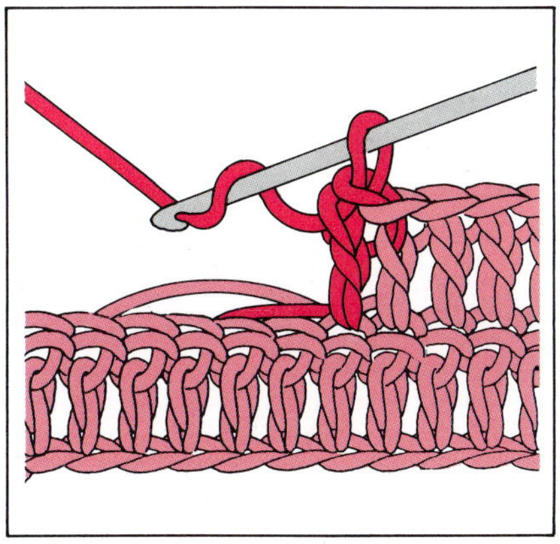

(c) One treble in new colour completed.

When working whole rows in different colours, make the change during last stitch in row, so new colour for next row is ready to work turning chain.

Do not cut off any yarns unless otherwise stated, in case they may be needed again later at the same edge. Rejoin as required, leaving an unbroken float thread up side edge of fabric.

You may find that a pattern requires you to return to beginning of row just worked without turning, and work another row in a different colour in same direction. In this case complete first row in old colour and fasten off by lengthening final loop on hook, passing whole ball through and gently tightening again. That yarn is now available if you need to rejoin it later at same edge (if not, cut it).

When changing colour during a row (for example when following a chart or other multi-colour pattern), it is important to change colour just before completing the previous stitch, and also to be constantly aware of which is the right and wrong side of your fabric at all times. After every colour change and before continuing, make sure all yarns which are not in use at the moment are taken to wrong side. When they are rejoined later, allow them to form loose floats on wrong side. In some cases such as solid stitch patterns on right side rows, you can avoid floats by working **over** any yarns you need to carry along, or by winding off short

precise treatment will depend upon stitch pattern, nature of article, character of yarn and (of course) your personal preferences!

Joining in new yarn

To join in new yarn where you have fastened off in one place and are going to rejoin in another, or to start an edging, work as follows:

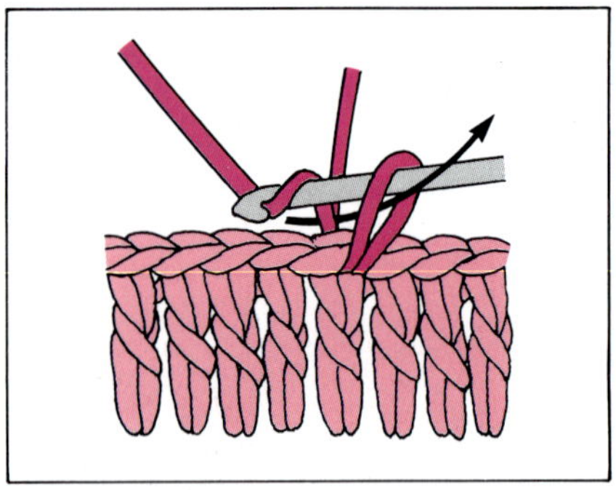

(a) Insert hook where required, yarn over hook, draw through and make 1 chain. If you feel it would be more secure, make first loop with a slip knot as though starting a base chain.

You will sometimes need to join a new ball in the middle of work, when the old ball runs out. Before making final 'yarn over' to complete last stitch, drop old yarn, make a loop with new yarn, pick this up and draw through to complete. Hold down both short ends temporarily until you have worked the next stitch. A knot or splice is unnecessary. The ends can be darned in afterwards.

If you are making a solid fabric such as double crochet, work as follows:

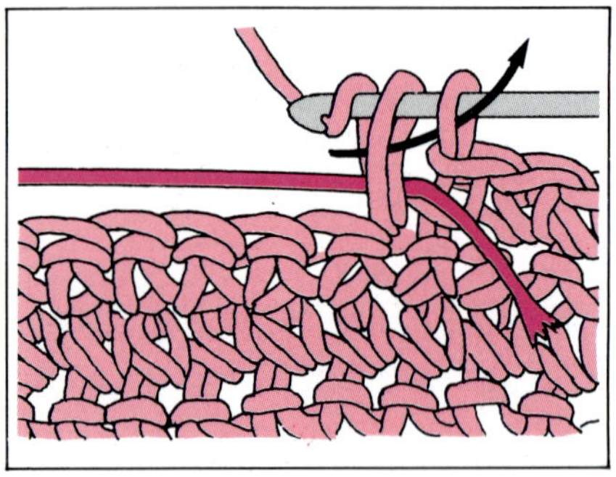

(a) Lay new yarn in advance across tops of stitches ahead and work over it.

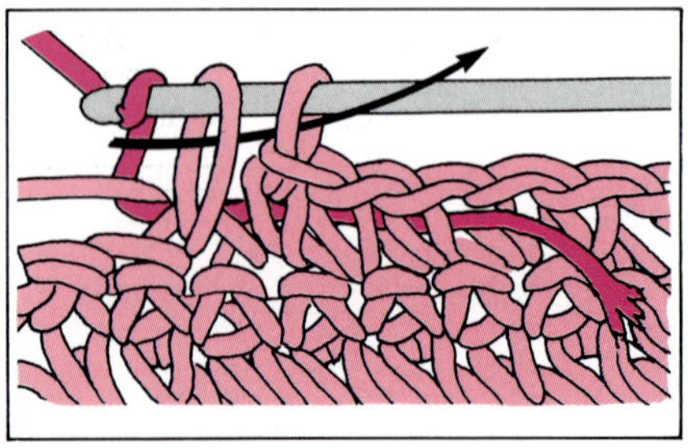

(b) After changing yarns, work over end of old yarn. This saves later 'darning in' time.

Colour work with charts

When squared charts are used for colour work they are to be read from the bottom upwards to and fro. It is the square spaces which represent the stitches. Usually double crochet stitches are used because they are small and compact.

In practice no crochet stitch works out 'square' — double crochet is too shallow; half treble too deep — and this should be born in mind before you begin. Treble stitches, which are even taller, are sometimes represented on squared charts by two squares per row.

The squares may be blocked or hatched in, numbered or coloured in different ways. A key is always given showing you what each square represents. For technical details of how to use several different colours on one row see page 37.

Filet Crochet

Filet crochet is based on a simple net background with a regular, square grid, made of treble and chain stitches. Pattern instructions are therefore usually in the form of squared charts, in which vertical lines represent trebles and horizontal lines (tops of rows) chain stitches. An endless variety of designs are created by filling in some of the squares or spaces with trebles instead of chains.

The chart represents a view of the finished fabric with the right side facing — you are to imagine having made it from the bottom upwards working to and fro. Odd number (right side) rows are read from right to left. Even number (wrong side) rows are read from left to right.

Each open square represents 2 treble stitches with a space between of 2 chains, or as specified. When a square is filled by a dot (or otherwise marked) the 2 chain space is replaced by 2 trebles, making a single 'block' of 4 trebles. 2 'blocks' together make 7 trebles and 3 make 10 trebles and so on.

The base row consists of a multiple of 3 stitches + 1, (multiply number of squares, □, by 3 and add 1).

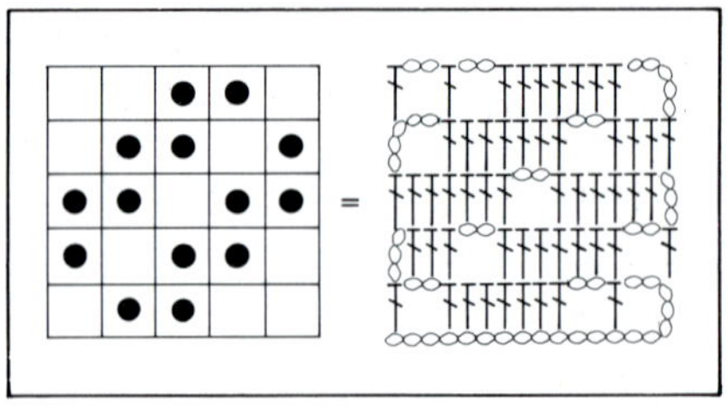

If first square to be worked is a 'space', add 4 extra chain to base chain and work first treble into 8th chain from hook.

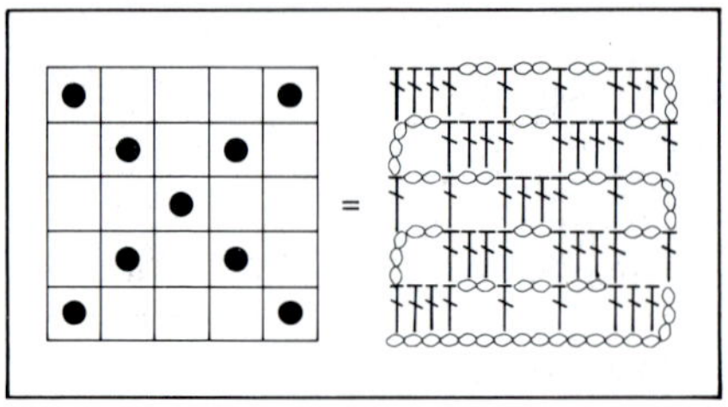

If first square is a solid 'block', add 2 extra chain to base chain, work first treble into 4th chain from hook, 1 treble into each of next 2 chains.

From 2nd row onwards work spaces and blocks as follows:

Space over a space

At beginning of row = '5ch (count as 1tr and 2ch sp), miss first st and 2ch, 1tr into next tr, ...'

At end of row = '. . . 1tr into last tr, 2ch, miss 2ch, 1tr into 3rd of 5ch.'

Space over a block

At beginning of row = '5ch (count as 1tr and 2ch sp), miss first 3 sts, 1tr into next tr, ...'

At end of row = '. . . to last 4 sts work 1tr into tr, 2ch, miss 2tr, 1tr into top of 3 ch.'

Block over a space

At beginning of row = '3ch (count as 1tr), miss first st, 1tr into each of next 2ch, 1tr into next tr, ...'

At end of row = '. . . 1tr into last tr, 1tr into each of next 3ch of 5ch.'

Block over a block

At beginning of row = '3ch (count as 1tr), miss first st, 1tr into each of next 3tr, ...'

At end of row = ' 1tr into each of last 3tr, 1 tr into top of 3 ch.'

Hints and Tips

Any squared chart can be adapted for filet crochet. Furthermore you can choose to work it upwards, downwards, or sideways according to your needs. Using plain graph paper it is quite easy to draw in and plot your own designs and compositions, but note that your basic network is not likely to work out exactly square, whatever combination of chain spaces and stitch lengths you use.

Measuring Lengths

Always measure at centre of work, never at side edge which is usually looser than the main work. Place a marker (a safety pin or piece of yarn) at centre of last row before start of armhole shaping. This makes it easier to measure the armhole length when you come to it.

Counting rows

You will achieve a much more professional finish if you work the same number of rows on similar pieces, particularly when they are to be joined together at the side edges — for example the back and front. It is helpful either to make a note of rows in the margin of your pattern for each section, or the number of times a pattern is repeated.

Finishing and Making Up

Once all the separate pieces for a garment or item have been crocheted, and before they are joined together or edgings added, the pieces may need to be pressed or blocked to the correct size and shape. For general instructions see page 46.

Joining Seams

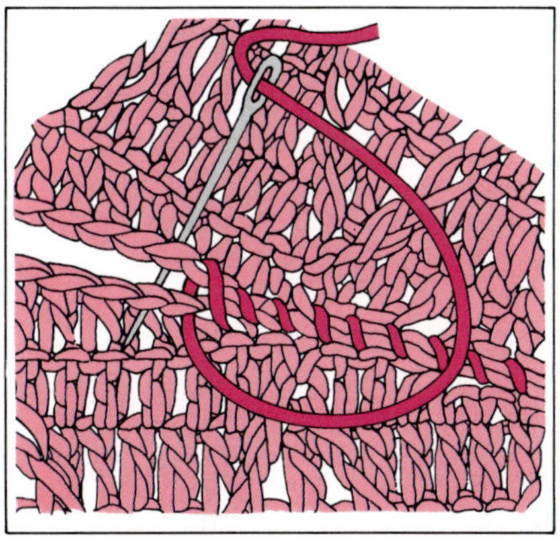

(a) Whipped seam worked with a sewing needle, shown on a shoulder seam.

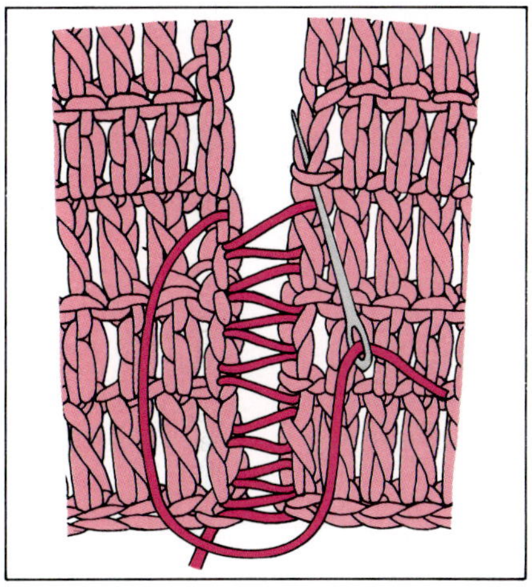

(b) Invisible or flat seam woven with a sewing needle shown worked on a side seam (similar to running stitch seam on knitting, see page 14).

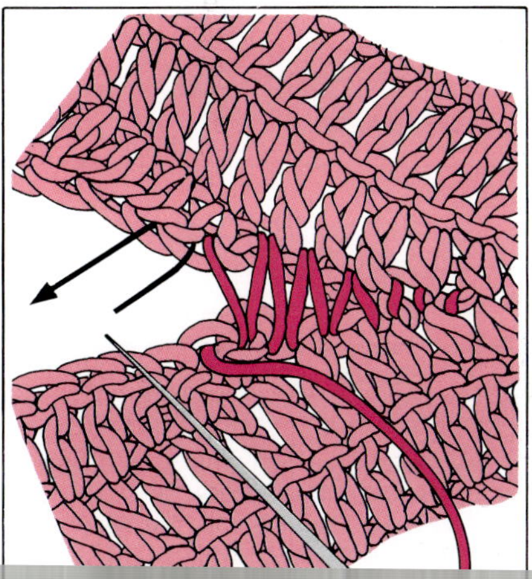

(c) Invisible method worked on a shoulder seam.

Joining Motifs

For joining motifs together you may prefer to use one of the following methods with the crochet hook, as this is usually quicker.

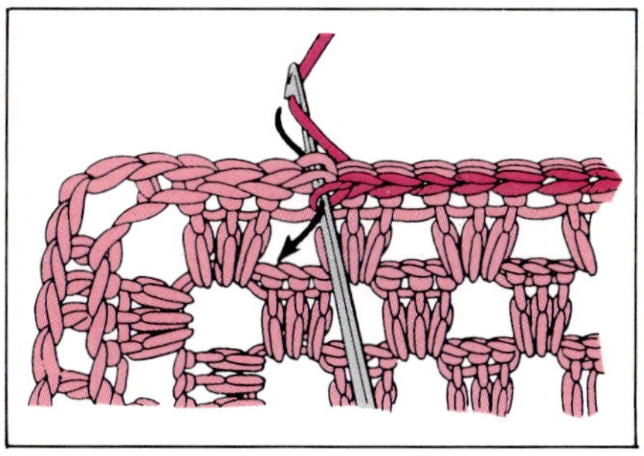

(a) Slip stitch.

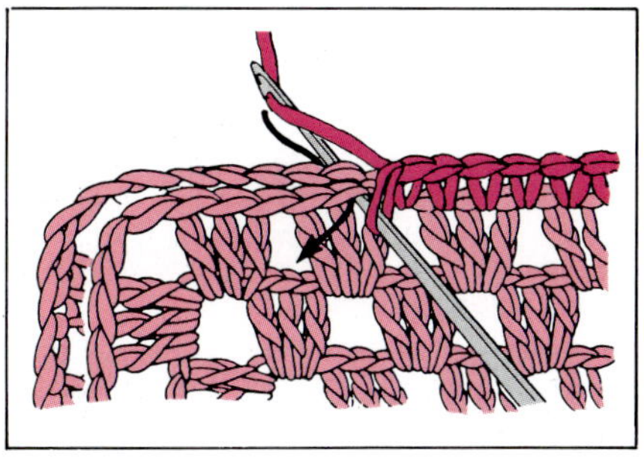

(b) Double crochet through both edges at once.

To be invisible crochet seams should be done on wrong side of work, with right sides of work together. Both (a) and (b) above create a certain bulk and it may be more suitable to pick up just the single loop of each pair of stitches.

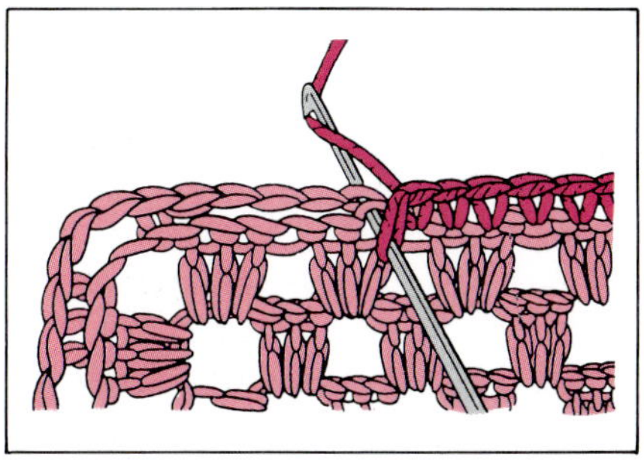

(c) Outer loop.

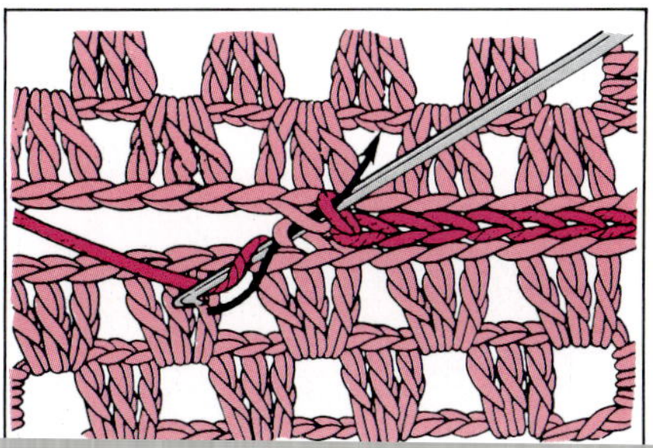

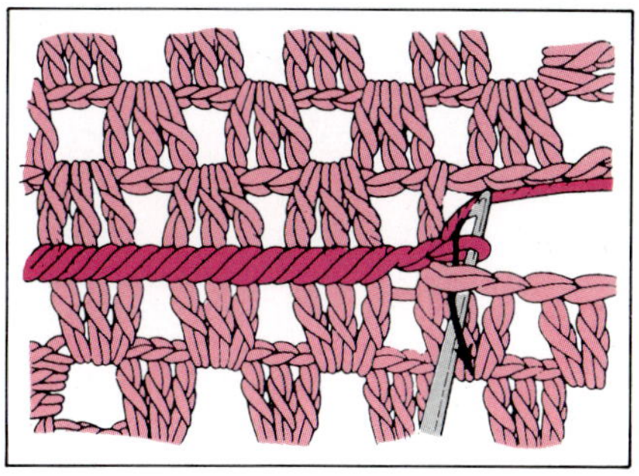

(e) Corded Double Crochet makes a ridge which can be used as a deliberate, decorative feature when worked on right side.

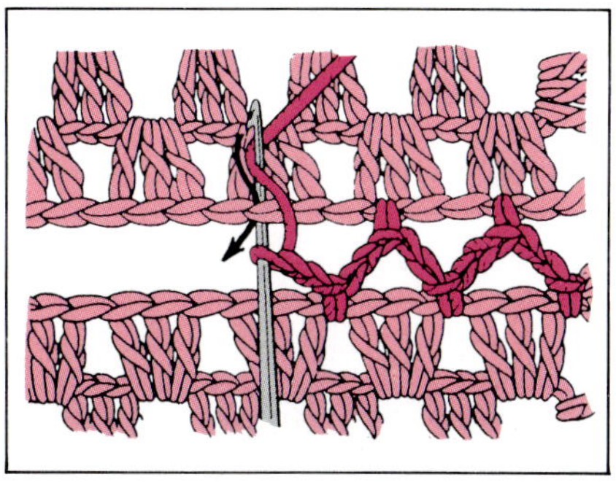

(f) Fancy or openwork motifs, or those which leave space between them, may be joined indirectly with a suitable series of chain arches and bridges anchored with slip stitches or double crochets.

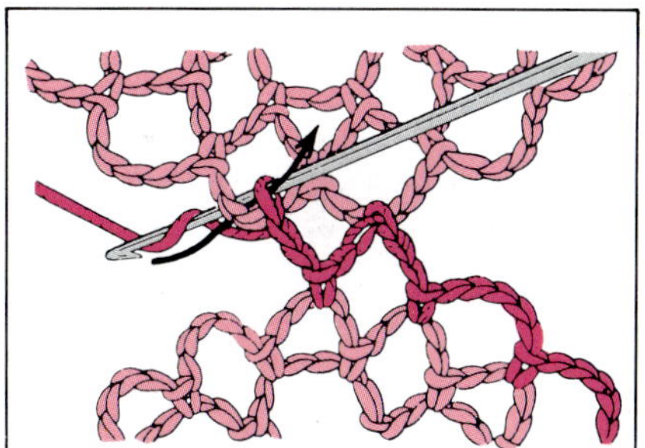

(g) Some designs, particularly those with picots or chain arches round their edges, can be joined to previous motifs during the course of their final rounds. This is done by interrupting picots or arches midway through and slip stitching to corresponding places on adjacent motifs. Instructions for this would be detailed in the pattern.

(h) — (j) Depending upon their shape some motifs, such as squares, triangles, hexagons, etc, fit together exactly.

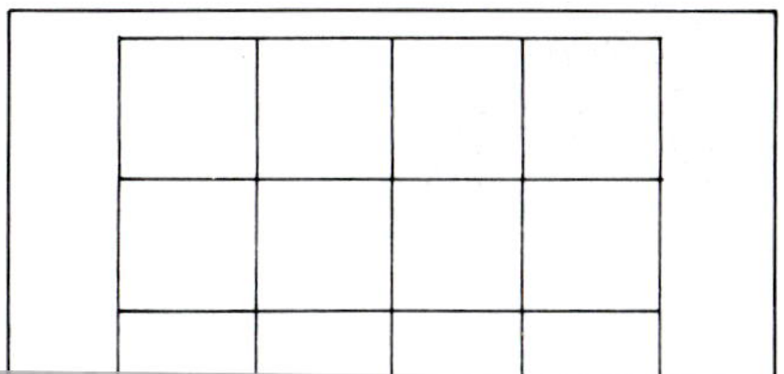

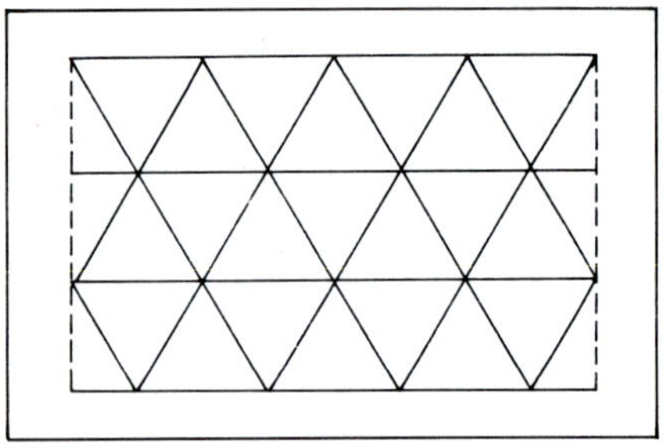

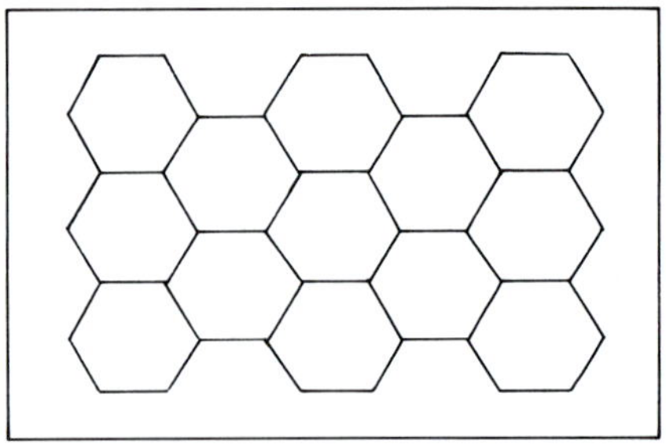

(k) Others leave interesting spaces which may be joined along the edges that touch by sewing or crochet.

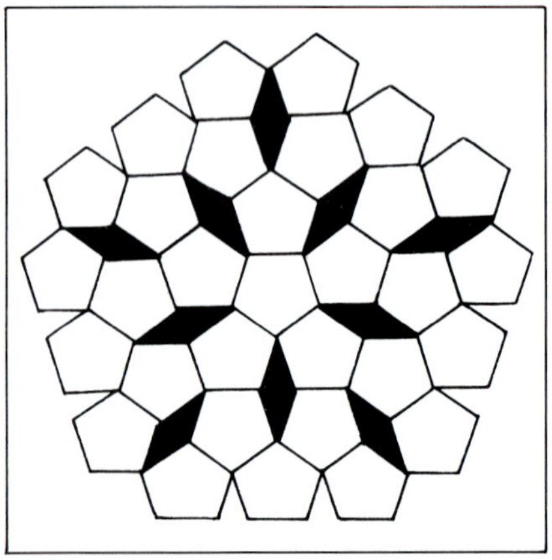

Spaces between motifs are sometimes filled with small single round motifs, made and joined in at the same time as they are worked. Again, specific instructions would be included in the pattern.

Working Edgings

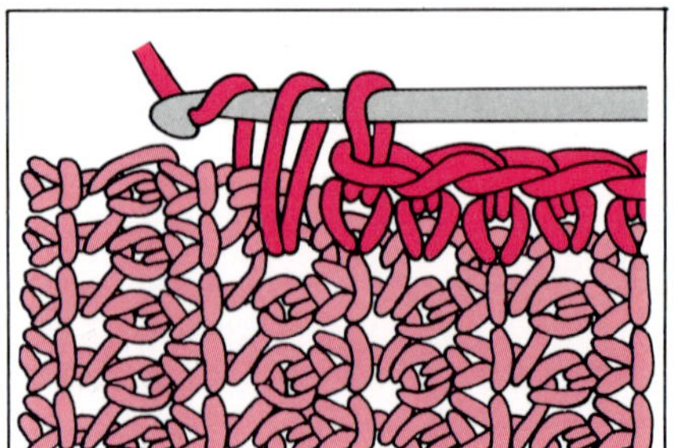

To pick up along an edge, for a front band for example, *insert hook from front to back through edge. Yarn over hook and draw through a loop. Work a double crochet. Repeat from * along edge or for as many stitches as are required. It is easier to pick up the stitches evenly if you divide the length of the edge in half, then in half again and again, so the edge is divided into eighths. Mark each division with a pin. Divide the number of stitches to be picked up by eight and pick up approximately that number of stitches in each section.

Buttonholes and Button Loops

Horizontal Buttonholes

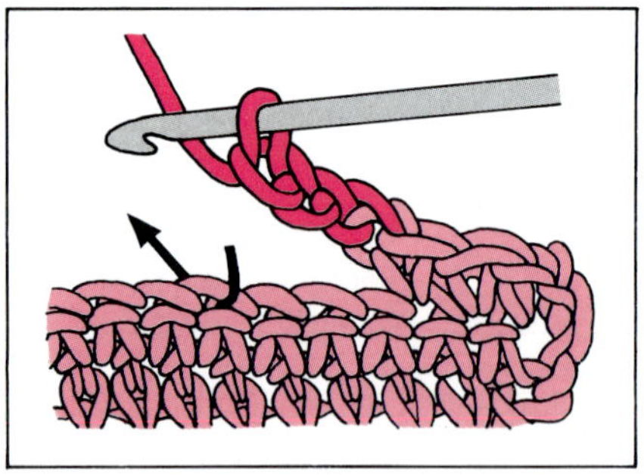

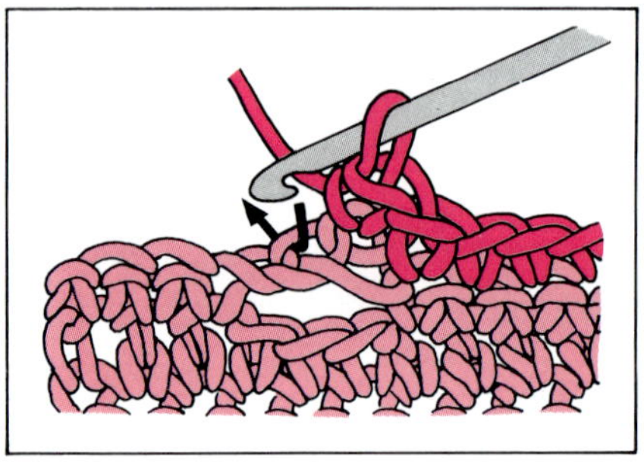

Work to position of buttonhole, make 2 or more chains (depending on size of button), miss the same number of stitches in row below, work to end of row. On next row work in pattern over chains made in previous row.

Vertical Buttonholes

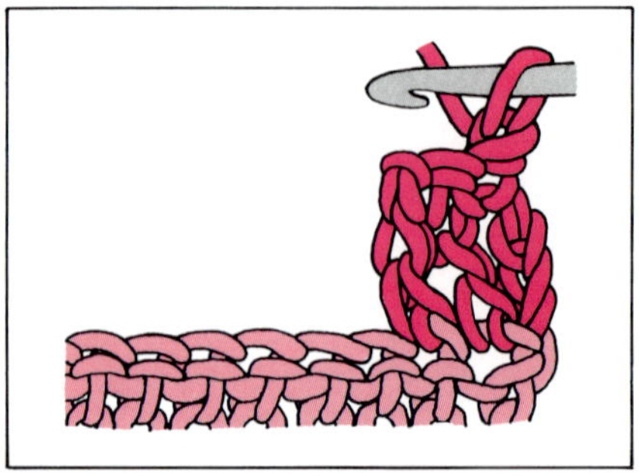

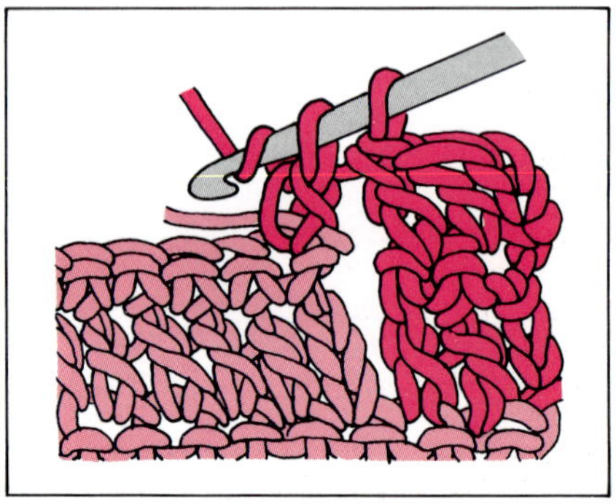

In trebles work to buttonhole position, turn and work required number of rows ending at side edge. Using separate ball of yarn and starting at buttonhole edge, work second side to match ending at division. Break off 2nd ball. Continue with first ball across all stitches, thus closing buttonhole.

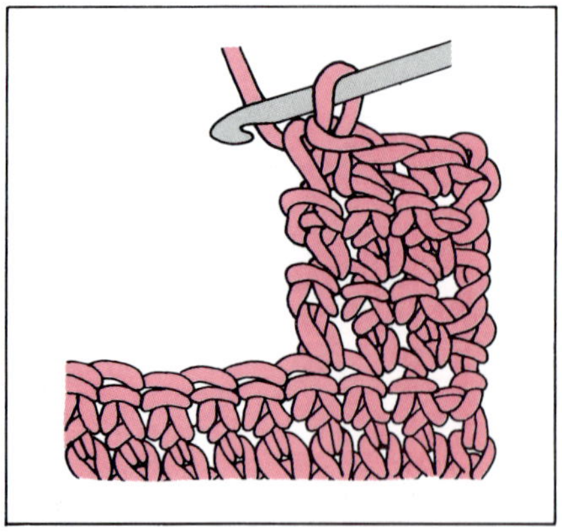

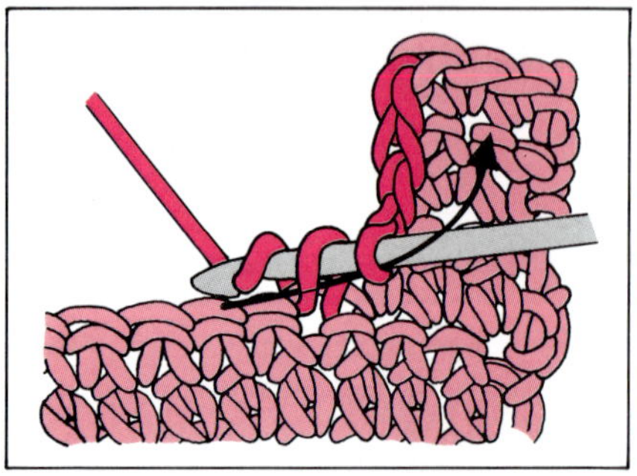

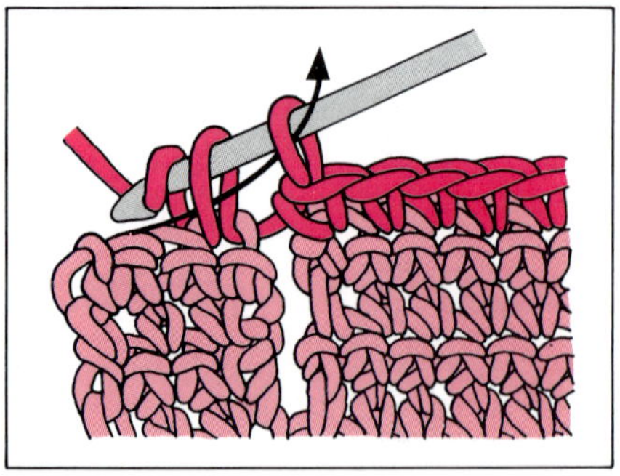

In double crochet work to buttonhole position, turn and work required number of rows ending at buttonhole edge. Slip stitch down side edge to last row before dividing. Work on remaining stitches until level with first side ending at side edge, then work across all stitches.

Button Loops

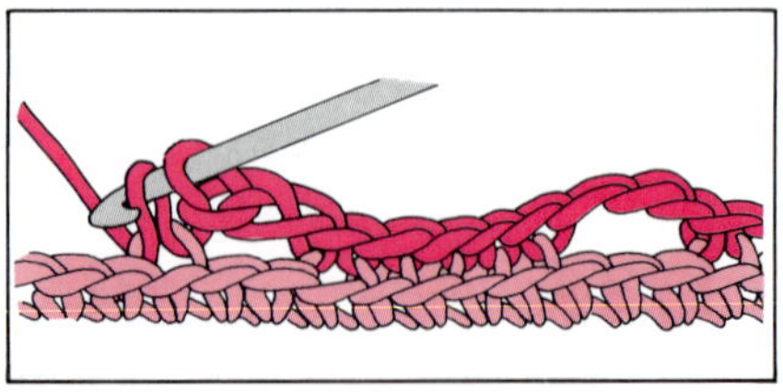

Generally worked on last row of edging. Mark positions with pins. Work to position of buttonloop, *work a slip stitch then the required number of chains. Miss the same number of stitches in row below, work to next buttonloop. Repeat from * to end of row.

Crochet Buttons

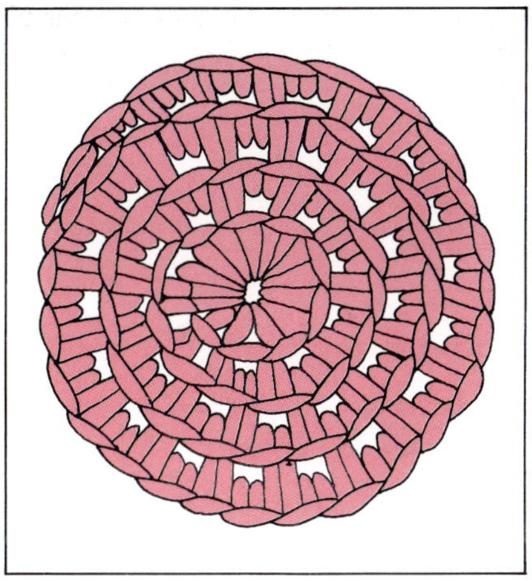

Covered buttons are made by working a circle of double crochet to size of button starting with a loop rather than a ring of chains — see pages 27 and 28. Insert button form then decrease to cover back of button. If button is filled with cotton wool rather than a button form, decrease until a small opening is left, then insert the stuffing. Close opening and finish off. The button can be worked in a contrast colour, or embroidered afterwards.

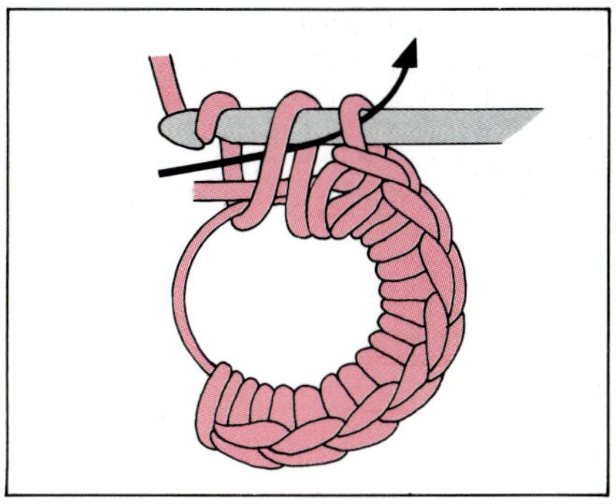

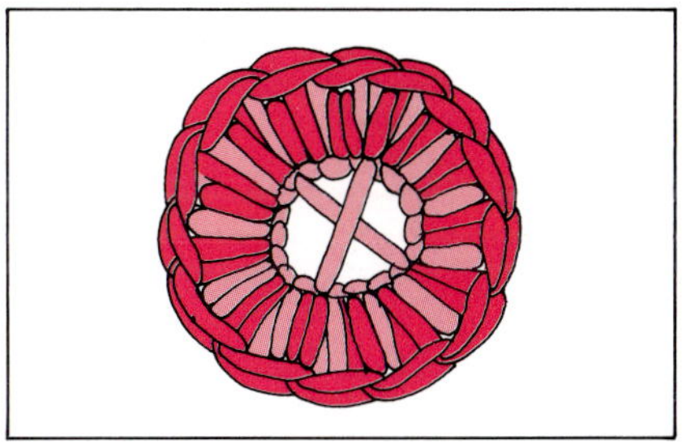

Ring buttons are worked over a plastic ring. Work double crochet around the ring, join with a slip stitch. Turn stitches to centre of ring and sew together. A second round of double crochet can be worked over the first, for extra decoration.

Sewing in Zips

Putting a zip into a crochet garment is done in exactly the same way as for a knitted garment. See page 16.

Sewing in Set-in Sleeves

Work as for a knitted garment (see page 16).

Elastic Waistbands

See page 16 in the Knitting Section.

Sewing in Front Bands

Method is same as for a knitted garment — see page 16.

Extra Hints

Most of the ideas and techniques mentioned in the knitting section (see page 16) can be applied to, or used with, crochet. Don't be afraid to experiment, however, as many different and interesting effects can be used to make **your** garment just that little bit more 'special'.

Sample Crochet Stitches

Here is a selection of sample stitches to help you get used to different patterns, and also to give you ideas for creating your own designs.

Multiples

All but the simplest crochet stitch patterns are built around repeated sequences of stitches. In order to make sense of the instructions you must have exactly the right number of stitches in your base row. This number is a multiple of the number of stitches required for one complete sequence — sometimes plus an extra edge stitch, or two — and is given at the beginning of each set of instructions.

The number of chains you need for the foundation chain, in order to be able to create the appropriate number of stitches in the foundation row is also given. For example, 'Multiple of 2 sts + 1, (add 1 for foundation chain)' = make 4, 6, 8, etc chains for a foundation row of 3, 5, 7, etc, stitches; or 'Multiple of 8 sts + 3, (add 2 for foundation chain)' = make 13, 21, 29, etc, chains for a foundation row of 11, 19, 27, etc, stitches.

Clover Fan Pattern

Special Abbreviation

CVC (Clover Cluster) = [yo, insert hook, yo, draw loop through loosely] twice as indicated for first leg, (5 loops on hook), and twice more as indicated for 2nd leg, (9 loops on hook), *yo, draw through all except last loop, yo, draw through remaining 2 loops.

Note: For CVC with 1 leg only, omit 2nd leg and complete as given from * to end.

1st row (wrong side): 1dc into 2nd ch from hook, *miss 2ch, 5tr into next ch, miss 2ch, 1dc into next ch; rep from * to end.

2nd row: 3ch (count as 1tr), 2tr into first st, *miss 2tr, 1dc into next tr, 1ch, miss 2tr and 1dc, work CVC with 1 leg only into next tr, [2ch, 1CVC inserting hook into same place as previous CVC for first leg and into next CVC for 2nd leg, missing 2ch between] 5 times, 2ch, work CVC with 1 leg only into same place as 2nd leg of previous CVC, miss 1ch, 1dc and 2tr, 1dc into next tr, miss 2tr, 5tr into next dc; rep from * ending last rep with only 3tr into last dc, miss turning ch.

3rd row: 1ch, 1dc into first st, *miss 2tr, 1dc and 1ch, work CVC with 1 leg only into next CVC, [2ch, 1CVC inserting hook into same place as previous CVC for first leg and into next CVC for 2nd leg, missing 2ch between] 5 times, 2ch, work CVC with 1 leg only into same place as 2nd leg of previous CVC, miss 1ch, 1dc and 2tr, 1dc into next st; rep from * to end.

4th row: 1ch, 1dc into first st, 1dc into each st and each ch to end, miss turning ch.

5th row: 1ch, 1dc into first st, *miss 3dc, 5tr into next dc, [miss 2dc, 1dc into next dc, miss 2dc, 5tr into next dc] twice, miss 3dc, 1dc into next dc; rep from * to end, miss turning ch.

Rep 2nd, 3rd, 4th and 5th rows.

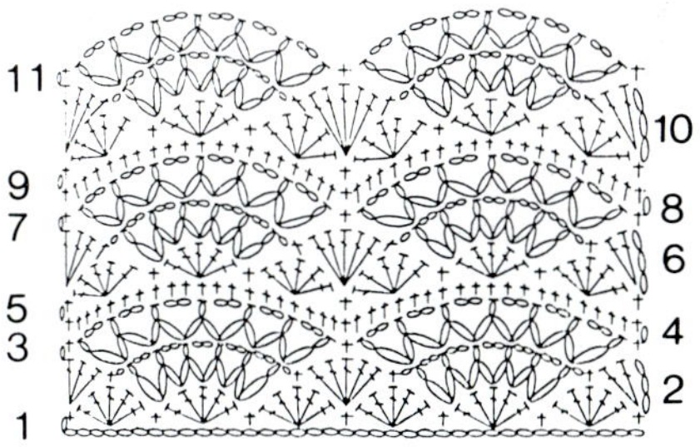

2. Wavy Shell Pattern

Multiple of 14 sts + 1.
(add 2 for foundation chain)

1st row (right side): Miss 2ch (count as 1tr), 3tr into next ch, *miss 3ch, 1dc into each of next 7ch, miss 3ch, 7tr into next ch; rep from * ending last rep with 4tr into last ch instead of 7 tr.

2nd row: 1ch, 1dc into first st, 1dc into each st to end, working last dc into top of turning ch.

3rd row: 1ch, 1dc into each of first 4 sts, *miss 3 sts, 7tr into next st, miss 3 sts, 1dc into each of next 7 sts; rep from * to last 11 sts, miss 3 sts, 7tr into next st, miss 3 sts, 1dc into each of last 4 dc, miss turning ch.

4th row: 1ch, 1dc into first st, 1dc into next and each st to end, miss turning ch.

5th row: 3ch (count as 1tr), 3tr into first st, *miss 3 sts, 1dc into each of next 7 sts, miss 3 sts, 7tr into next st; rep from * ending last rep with 4tr into last dc instead of 7 tr, miss turning ch.

Rep 2nd, 3rd, 4th and 5th rows.

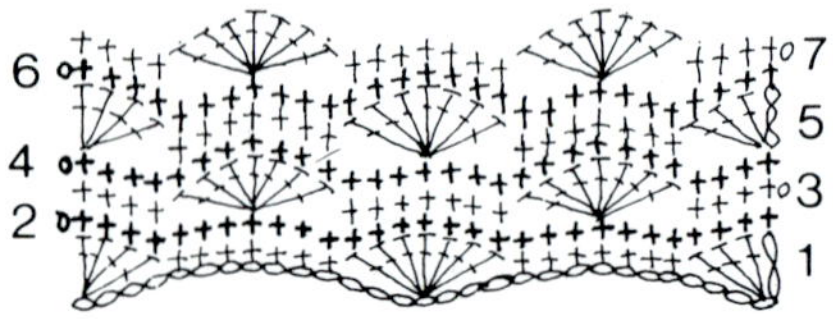

3. Catherine Wheel

Multiple of 10 sts + 6.
(add 1 for foundation chain)

Special Abbreviation

CL (Cluster) = work [yo, insert hook, yo, draw loop through, yo, draw through 2 loops] over the number of sts indicated, yo, draw through all loops on hook.

1st row (wrong side): Using A 1dc into 2nd ch from hook, 1dc into next ch, *miss 3ch, 7tr into next ch, miss 3ch, 1dc into each of next 3ch; rep from * to last 4ch, miss 3ch, 4tr into last ch.

2nd row: Using B 1ch, 1dc into first st, 1dc into next st, *3ch, 1CL over next 7 sts, 3ch, 1dc into each of next 3 sts; rep from * to last 4 sts, 3ch, 1CL over last 4 sts, miss turning ch.

3rd row: Using B 3ch (count as 1tr), 3tr into first st, *miss 3ch, 1dc into each of next 3dc, miss 3ch, 7tr into loop which closed next CL; rep from * to last 5 sts, miss 3ch, 1dc into each of last 2dc, miss turning ch.

4th row: Using A 3ch (count as 1tr), miss first st, 1CL over next 3 sts, *3ch, 1dc into each of next 3 sts, 3ch, 1CL over next 7 sts; rep from * to last 2 sts, 3ch, 1dc into next st, 1dc into top of turning ch.

5th row: Using A 1ch, 1dc into each of first 2dc, *miss 3ch, 7tr into loop which closed next CL, miss 3ch, 1dc into each of next 3dc; rep from * to last 4 sts, miss 3ch, 4tr into top of turning ch.

Rep 2nd, 3rd, 4th and 5th rows.

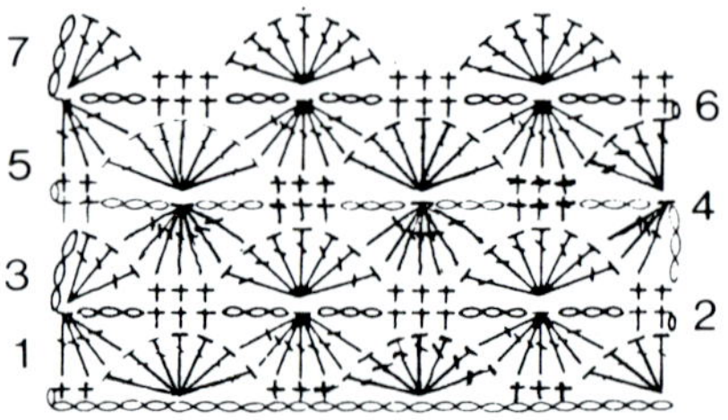

4. Bullion Pattern

Multiple of 6 sts + 2.
(add 1 for foundation chain)

Note: For description of bullion st see page 34. Make Bullion sts with [yo] 7 times.

1st row (wrong side): 1dc into 2nd ch from hook, 1ch, miss 1ch, 1dc into next ch, *2ch, miss 2ch, 1dc into next ch; rep from * to last 2ch, 1ch, miss 1ch, 1dc into last ch.

2nd row: 3ch (count as 1tr), miss first st, 1tr into next ch sp, *1tr into next dc, 1 Bullion st into each of next 2ch, 1tr into next dc**, 1tr into each of next 2ch; rep from * ending last rep at ** when 1 ch sp remains, 1tr into next ch, 1tr into last dc, miss turning ch.

3rd row: 1ch, 1dc into first st, 1ch, miss 1 st, 1dc into next st, *2ch, miss 2 sts, 1dc into next st; rep from * to last 2 sts, 1ch, miss 1 st, 1dc into top of turning ch.

4th row: 3ch (count as 1tr), miss first st, 1 Bullion st into next ch sp, *1tr into next dc, 1tr into each of next 2ch, 1tr into next dc**, 1 Bullion st into each of next 2ch; rep from * ending last rep at ** when 1ch sp remains, 1 Bullion st into next sp, 1tr into last dc, miss turning ch.

5th row: As 3rd row.

Rep 2nd, 3rd, 4th and 5th rows.

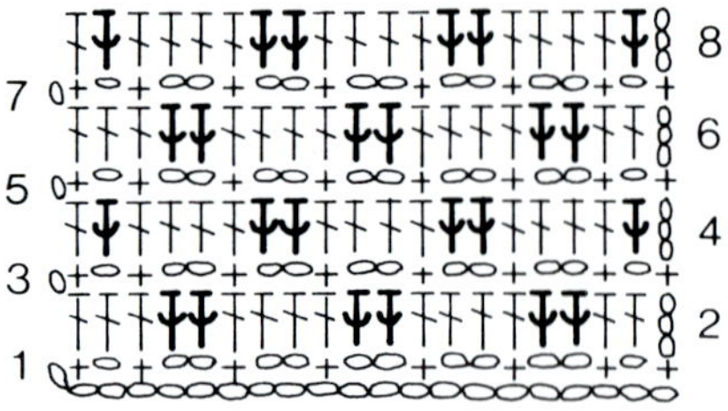

Diagram Note

Bullion Stitch with [yo] 7 times.

5. Spike Cluster Pattern

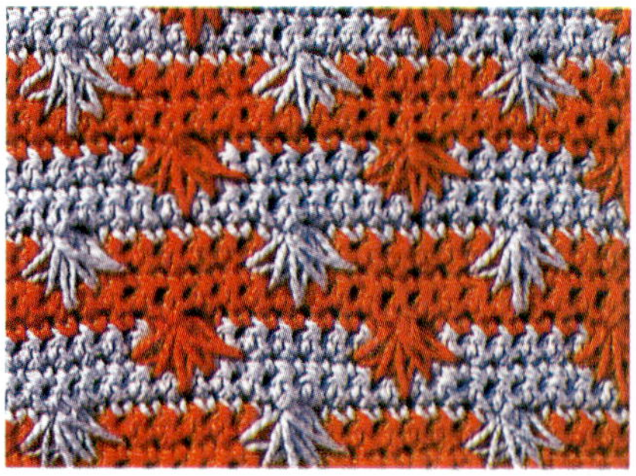

Multiple of 8 sts + 5.
(add 1 for foundation chain)

Special Abbreviation

SPC (Spike Cluster) = over next st pick up 5 spike loops by inserting hook as follows: 2 sts to right of next st and 1 row down; 1 st to right and 2 rows down; directly below and 3 rows down; 1 st to left and 2 rows down; 2 sts to left and 1 row down, (6 loops on hook); now insert hook into top of next st itself, yo, draw loop through, yo, draw through all 7 loops on hook (see also page 37).

Foundation row (right side): Using A 1dc into 2nd ch from hook, 1dc into each ch to end.

Commence Pattern

1st row: Using A 1ch, 1dc into first and each st to end, miss turning ch.

2nd and 3rd rows: As 1st row.

4th row: Using B 1ch, 1dc into each of first 4 sts, *1SPC over next st, 1dc into each of next 7 sts (Hint: be careful not to pick up any of the spikes of the previous SPC); rep from * to last st, 1dc into last st, miss turning ch.

5th, 6th and 7th rows: Using B work as 1st row.

8th row: Using A 1ch, 1dc into each of first 8 sts, *1SPC over next st, 1dc into each of next 7 sts; rep from * to last 5 sts, 1SPC over next st, 1dc into each of last 4 sts, miss turning ch.

Rep these 8 rows.

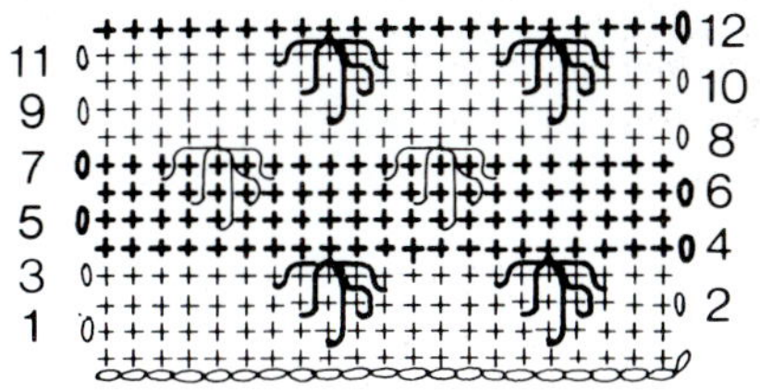

6. Shell Trellis

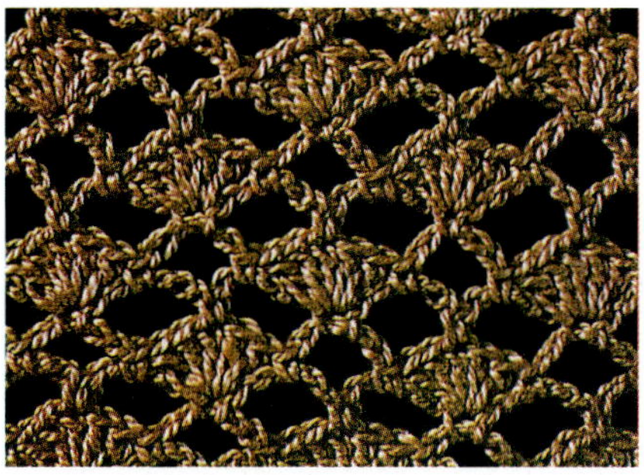

Multiple of 12 sts + 1.
(add 2 for foundation chain)

1st row (right side): 2tr into 3rd ch from hook, *miss 2ch, 1dc into next ch, 5ch, miss 5ch, 1dc into next ch, miss 2ch, 5tr into next ch; rep from * ending last rep with only 3tr into last ch.

2nd row: 1ch, 1dc into first st, *5ch, 1dc into next 5ch arch, 5ch, 1dc into 3rd tr of next 5tr; rep from * ending last rep with 1dc into top of turning ch.

3rd row: *5ch, 1dc into next 5ch arch, 5tr into next dc, 1dc into next arch; rep from * ending 2ch, 1tr into last dc, miss turning ch.

4th row: 1ch, 1dc into first st, *5ch, 1dc into 3rd tr of next 5tr, 5ch, 1dc into next 5ch arch; rep from * to end.

5th row: 3ch (count as 1tr), 2tr into first st, *1dc into next arch, 5ch, 1dc into next arch, 5tr into next dc; rep from * ending last rep with only 3tr into last dc, miss turning ch.

Rep 2nd, 3rd, 4th and 5th rows.

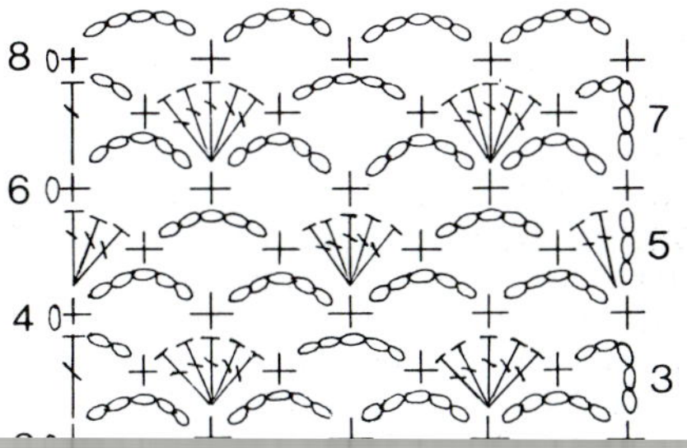

7. Star Motif

Make 6ch, join with sl st.

1st round: 1ch, [1dc into ring, 3ch] 12 times, sl st to first dc.

2nd round: Sl st into each of next 2ch, 1ch, 1dc into same 3ch arch, [3ch, 1dc into next 3ch arch] 11 times, 1ch, 1htr into top of first dc.

3rd round: *6ch, 1dc into next 3ch arch**, 3ch, 1dc into next 3ch arch; rep from * 4 more times and from * to ** again, 1ch, 1tr into htr which closed previous round.

4th round: *[5tr, 2ch, 5tr] into next 6ch arch, 1dc into next 3ch arch; rep from * 5 more times ending last rep in tr which closed previous round, sl st into next st. Fasten off.

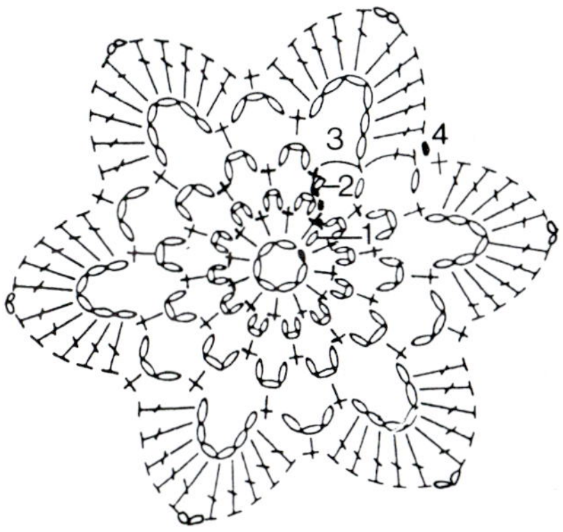

8. Filet Rose Motif

Foundation row

Multiple of 3 sts per square + 1

Pattern = 39 squares

See Filet Crochet page 38.

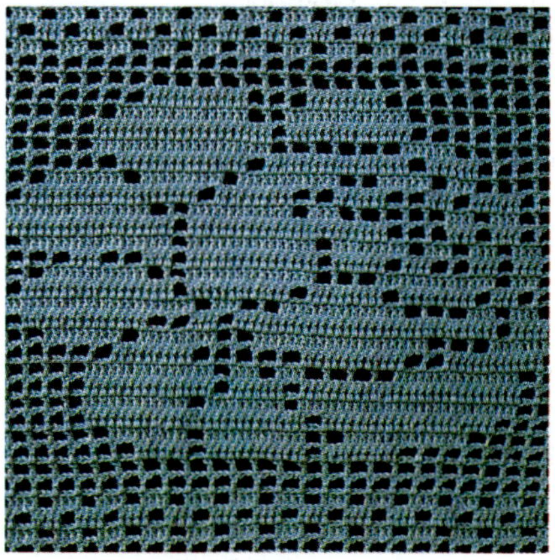

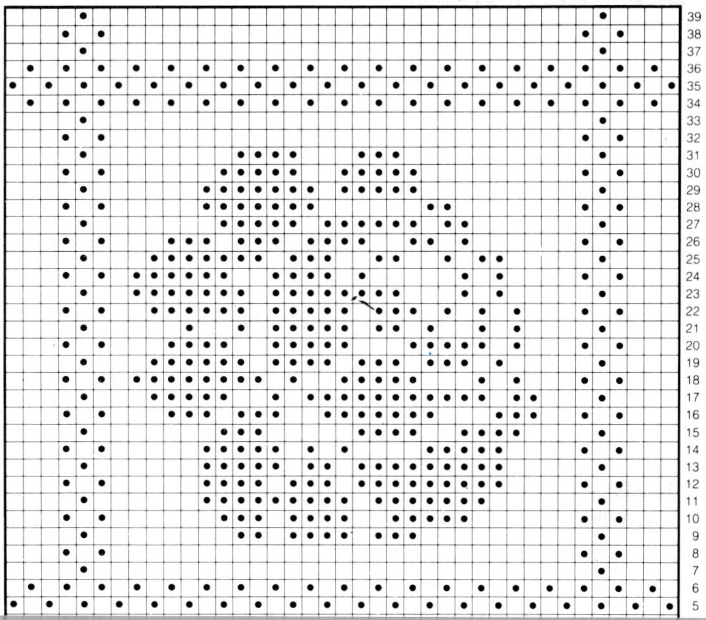

9. Basket Weave

Multiple of 8 sts + 2.
(add 2 for foundation chain)

Note: For description of tr/F and tr/B see page 31.

Foundation row (wrong side): Miss 3ch (count as 1tr), 1tr into next and each ch to end.

Commence Pattern

1st row: 2ch (count as 1tr), miss first st, *1tr/F round each of next 4 sts, 1tr/B round each of next 4 sts; rep from * to turning ch, 1tr into top of turning ch.

Rep the last row 3 times.

5th row: 2ch (count as 1tr), miss first st, *1tr/B round each of next 4 sts, 1tr/F round each of next 4 sts; rep from * to turning ch, 1tr into top of turning ch.

Rep the last row 3 times.

Rep these 8 rows.

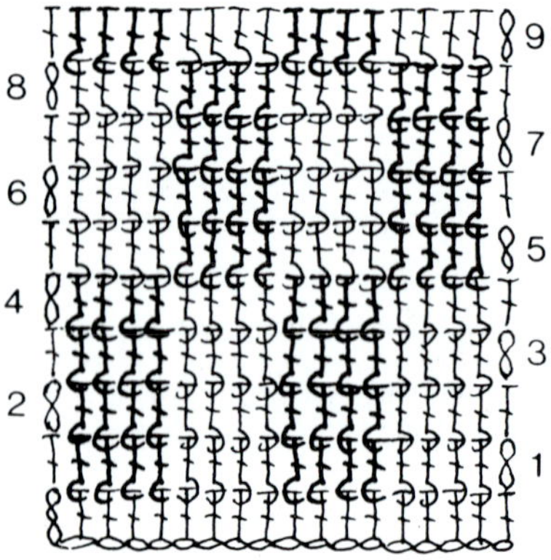

10. Chevron Pattern

Multiple of 10 sts.
(add 2 for foundation chain)

1st row: Miss 2ch (count as 1tr), 1tr into each of next 4ch, *miss 2ch, 1tr into each of next 4ch, 2ch, 1tr into each of next 4ch; rep from * to last 6ch, miss 2ch, 1tr into each of next 3ch, 2tr into last ch.

2nd row: 3ch (count as 1tr), 1tr into first st, 1tr into each of next 3 sts, *miss 2 sts, 1tr into each of next 3 sts, [1tr, 2ch, 1tr] into 2ch sp, 1tr into each of next 3 sts; rep from * to last 6 sts, miss 2 sts, 1tr into each of next 3 sts, 2tr into top of turning ch.

Rep 2nd row.

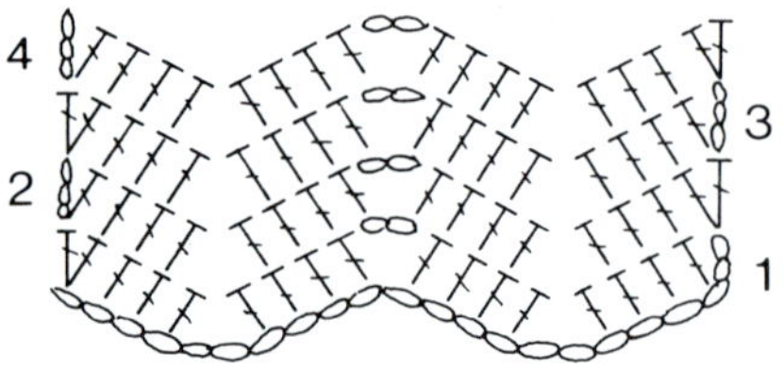

11. Puff Stitch Plaits

Multiple of 8 sts + 1.
(add 1 for foundation chain)

Note: For description of htr3tog see page 33 (Puff Stitch).

1st row (right side): Miss 2ch (count as 1htr), 1htr into each of next 2ch, *1ch, miss 1ch, htr3tog all into next ch, 1ch, miss 1ch**, 1htr into each of next 5ch; rep from * ending last rep at ** when 3ch remain, 1htr into each of last 3ch.

2nd row: 2ch (count as 1htr), miss first st, 1htr into each of next 2 sts, *htr3tog into next ch sp, 1ch, miss 1 st, htr3tog into next ch sp**, 1htr into each of next 5 sts; rep from * ending last rep at ** when 3 sts remain including turning ch, 1htr into each of last 3 sts.

3rd row: 2ch (count as 1htr), miss first st, 1htr into each of next 2 sts, *1ch, miss 1 st, htr3tog into next ch sp, 1ch, miss 1 st**, 1htr into each of next 5 sts; rep from * ending last rep at ** when 3 sts remain including turning ch, 1htr into each of last 3 sts.

Rep 2nd and 3rd rows.

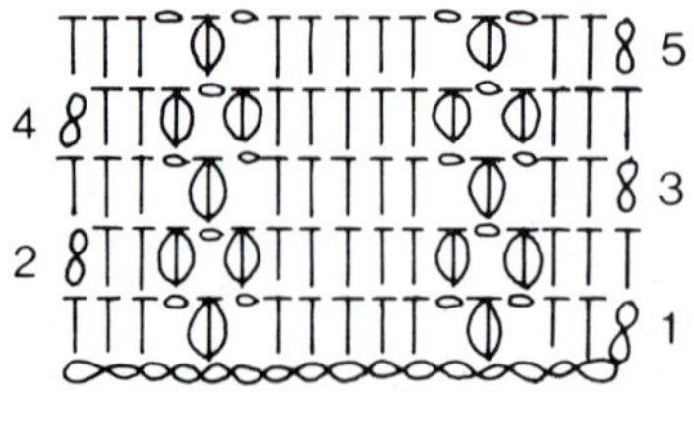

12. Solomon's Knot

Multiple of 2 Solomon's Knots + 1.
(add 2 Solomon's Knots for foundation 'chain')

Special Abbreviations

(see also page 35)

ESK (Edge Solomon's Knot): These form the foundation 'chain' and edges of the fabric and are only two-thirds the length of MSK's.

MSK (Main Solomon's Knot): These form the main fabric and are half as long again as ESK's.

Foundation 'chain': 2ch, 1dc into 2nd ch from hook, now make a multiple of 2ESK's (say, 2cm), ending with 1MSK (say, 3cm).

1st row: 1dc into dc between 3rd and 4th loops from hook, *2MSK, miss 2 loops, 1dc into next dc; rep from * to end.

2nd row: 2ESK and 1MSK, 1dc into dc between 4th and 5th loops from hook, *2MSK, miss 2 loops, 1dc into next dc; rep from * ending in top of ESK.

Rep 2nd row.

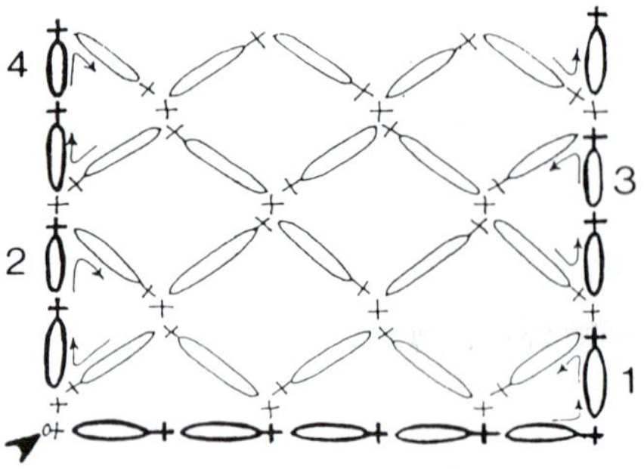

13. Openwork Cross Stitch

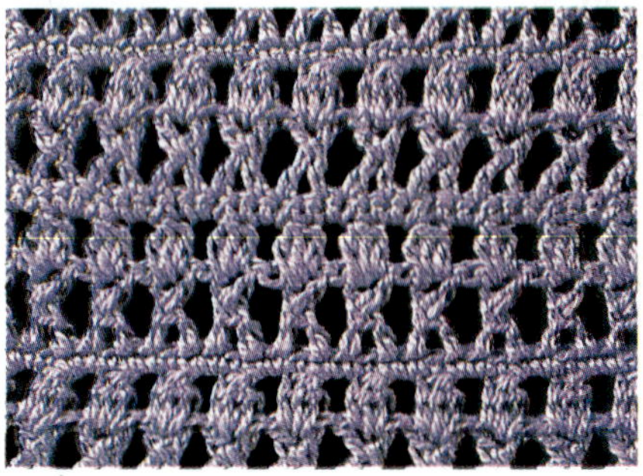

Multiple of 3 sts + 2.
(add 1 for foundation chain)

Special Abbreviation

DtrX (double treble 'X' shape — worked over 3 sts) = [yo] twice, insert hook into next st, yo, draw loop through, yo, draw through 2 loops, miss next st, yo, insert hook into next st, yo, draw loop through, [yo, draw through 2 loops] 4 times, 1ch, yo, insert hook half way down st just made where lower 'legs' join, yo, draw loop through, [yo, draw through 2 loops] twice (see also page 32 'X' Shapes).

Note: For description of tr3tog see page 30.

1st row (wrong side): 1dc into 2nd ch from hook, 1dc into next and each ch to end.

2nd row: 4ch (count as 1dtr), miss first st, *DtrX over next 3 sts; rep from * to last st, 1dtr into last st, miss turning ch.

3rd row: 4ch (count as 1tr and 1ch), *work tr3tog into next 1ch sp**, 2ch; rep from * ending last rep at **, 1ch, 1tr into top of turning ch.

4th row: 1ch, 1dc into first st, 1dc into next ch, *1dc into next cluster, 1dc into each of next 2ch; rep from * to end.

Rep 2nd, 3rd and 4th rows.

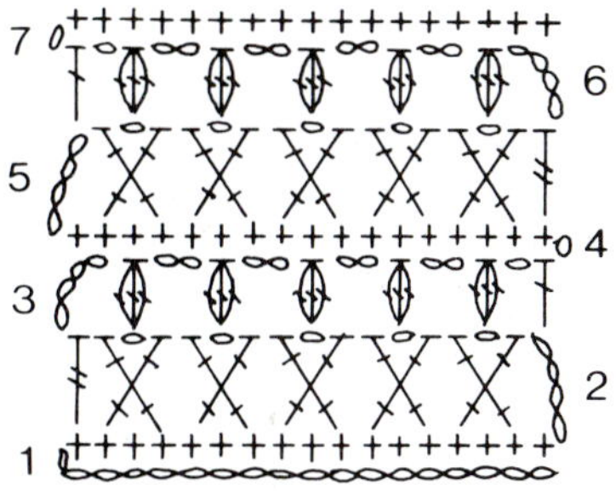

14. Traditional Hexagon

Note: For description of tr2tog and tr3tog see page 30.

Using A make 6ch, join with sl st.

1st round: Using A 3ch, tr2tog into ring (counts as tr3tog), [3ch, tr3tog into ring] 5 times, 1ch, 1htr into top of first cluster.

2nd round: Using B 3ch, tr2tog into arch formed by htr (counts as tr3tog), *3ch, tr3tog into next sp; rep from * 4 more times, 3ch, tr3tog into last sp, 1ch, 1htr into top of first cluster.

3rd round: Using C 3ch, tr2tog into arch formed by htr (counts as tr3tog), *3ch, work [tr3tog, 3ch, tr3tog] into next sp**, 3ch, tr3tog into next sp; rep from * 4 more times and from * to ** again, 1ch, 1htr into top of first cluster.

4th round: Using D 3ch (counts as 1tr), 1tr into arch formed by htr, *3tr into next sp, [3tr, 2ch, 3tr] into next sp**, 3tr into next sp; rep from * 4 more times and from * to ** again, 1tr into next sp, sl st to top of 3ch.

5th round: Using E 1ch, 1dc into same place, 1dc into each tr and each ch all round, ending sl st to first dc.

Fasten off.

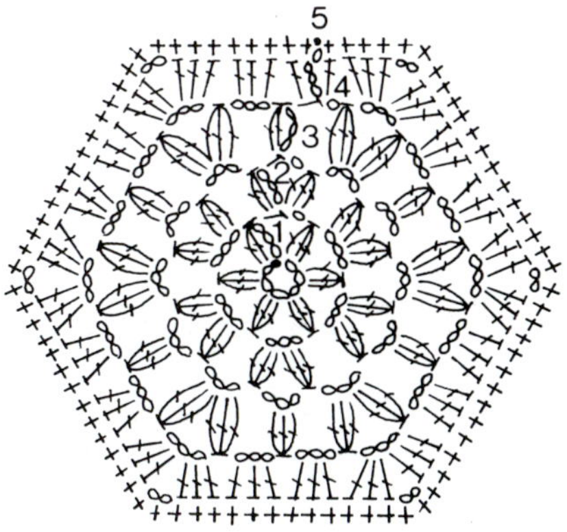

15. Granny Square

Using A make 4ch, join with sl st.

1st round: Using A 5ch (count as 1tr and 2ch), [3tr into ring, 2ch] 3 times, 2tr into ring, sl st to 3rd of 5ch.

2nd round: Using B sl st into next ch, 5ch (count as 1tr and 2ch), 3tr into same sp, *1ch, miss 3tr, [3tr, 2ch, 3tr] into next sp; rep from * twice, 1ch, miss 3 sts, 2tr into same sp as 5ch at beg of round, sl st to 3rd of 5ch.

3rd round: Using C sl st into next ch, 5ch (count as 1tr and 2ch), 3tr into same sp, *1ch, miss 3tr, 3tr into next sp, 1ch, miss 3tr**, [3tr, 2ch, 3tr] into next sp; rep from * 3 times and from * to ** again, 2tr into same sp as 5ch, sl st to 3rd of 5ch.

4th round: Using D sl st into next ch, 5ch (count as 1tr and 2ch), 3tr into same sp, *[1ch, miss 3tr, 3tr into next sp] twice, 1ch, miss 3tr**, [3tr, 2ch, 3tr] into next sp; rep from * twice and from * to ** again, 2tr into same sp as 5ch, sl st to 3rd of 5ch.

Fasten off.

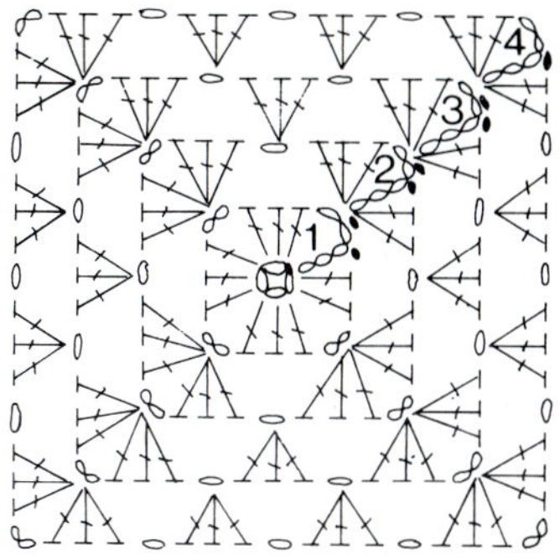

16. Wavy Puff Stitch

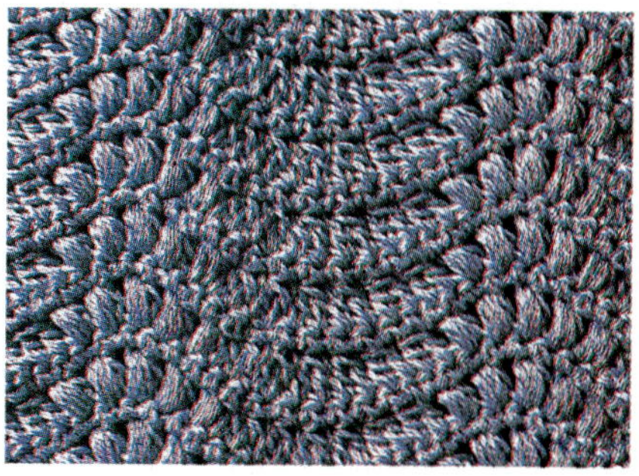

Multiple of 17 sts.

(add 2 for foundation chain)

Note: For description of tr2tog and htr4tog see page 30 (Clusters) and page 33 (Puff Stitch).

1st row (right side): 1tr into 4th ch from hook (counts as tr2tog), [tr2tog over next 2ch] twice, *[1ch, work htr4tog into next ch] 5 times, 1ch**, [tr2tog over next 2ch] 6 times; rep from * ending last rep at ** when 6ch remain, [tr2tog over next 2ch] 3 times.

2nd row: 1ch, 1dc into first st and then into each st and each ch sp to end excluding turning ch.

3rd row: 3ch, miss first st, 1tr into next st (counts as tr2tog), [tr2tog over next 2 sts] twice, *[1ch, work htr4tog into next st] 5 times, 1ch**, [tr2tog over next 2 sts] 6 times; rep from * ending last rep at ** when 6 sts remain, [tr2tog over next 2 sts] 3 times, miss turning ch.

Rep 2nd and 3rd rows.

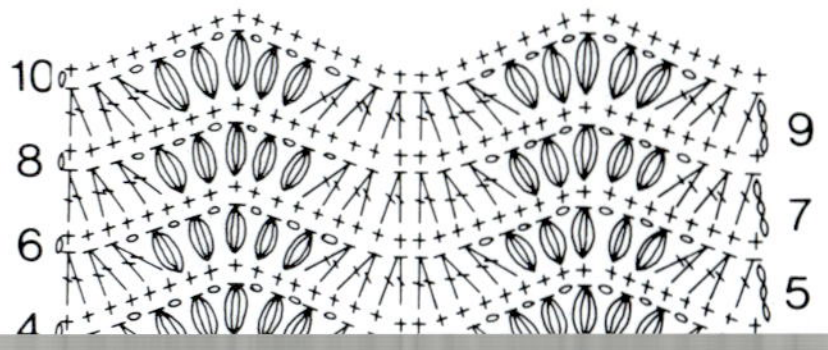

Choosing Your First Knitting or Crochet Project

If you are a raw beginner look for a simple pattern to start with, and go for the thicker yarns as these make up more quickly and you will be able to see the results of all your hard work sooner. Be wary of trying to be too ambitious to start with, as nothing will put you off faster than getting into a mess with your first project!

Look for a sweater that is mainly a plain stitch with a simple panel for a first attempt at a whole garment. Cardigans or jackets are generally more involved than sweaters. If you find your chosen pattern too easy after a while, **don't give up!** You will be getting practice at knitting or crocheting to an even tension.

Choosing yarn

Yarn is the term used for strands of spun fibre which are twisted together into a continuous thread of the required thickness. Yarn can be of animal origin (wool, angora, mohair, silk, alpaca), vegetable origin (cotton, linen) or man-made (nylon, acrylic, rayon). Knitting or crochet yarn may be made up from a combination of different fibres.

Pure New Wool

Wool is warm in winter, gives good insulation, is soft, comfortable and absorbent. It usually costs more than man-made fibres, and the yarn is generally heavier, and therefore will not go as far per 50g ball. It is, however, still the best choice for hand made garments.

Man-Made Fibres and Mixtures

Acrylic is the most commonly used man-made fibre. It is lighter than wool, and therefore more economic per 50g ball, but is less absorbent. When blended with wool, however, it combines the best properties of both fibres, being warm yet stronger and lighter than pure wool. Nylon is mainly used in a blend with acrylic for a hard wearing, light and easy-to-clean yarn for baby garments.

Cotton and Linen

Cotton and linen are highly absorbent fibres which allow the body heat to escape — this makes them ideal for summer wear. Both these fibres have grown in popularity enormously in recent years, and are now available in many weights and textures, from very fine ones traditionally used for fancy lace crochet, to thicker ones suitable for garments. Other fibres can also be mixed with them.

Yarn weights

Each spun single thread of yarn is known as a ply. A number of plys are twisted together to form the yarn. Ply originally meant the actual number of threads twisted together; nowadays it is only a general indication of total thickness. The texture and characteristics of the yarn may be varied by the combination of fibres and by the way in which the yarn is spun. The twist of the yarn can be varied too. A tightly twisted yarn is firm and smooth and makes up into a hard-wearing fabric. Loosely twisted yarn has a softer finish when knitted or crocheted.

Yarn is available in many different thicknesses. Each country has its own standard terms for certain weights.

UK	Australia
4 ply	5 ply
Double Knitting	8 ply
Aran or Triple	12 ply
Chunky or Double Double	14 ply

Speciality yarns produced for a particular purpose or a special fabric effect (with 'slubs' or bobbles in a contrast colour or yarn), often do not conform to a 'standard' tension, and are knitted or crocheted to whichever tension shows them to their best advantage.

Buying yarn

Yarn is most commonly sold ready wound into balls of specific weight measured in grams or ounces. Some yarn, particularly very thick yarn, is also sold in a coiled hank or skein and must be wound up into a ball before you begin working.

Yarn manufacturers (called spinners) wrap each ball with a paper band on which is printed a lot of necessary information. The ball band states the weight of the yarn and its composition. It will give instructions for washing and pressing and will sometimes state the ideal range of needle or hook sizes to be used with the yarn. The ball band also carries the shade number and dye lot number. It is important that you use yarn of the same dye lot for a single project. Different dye lots vary subtly in shading which may not be apparent when you are holding two balls, but which will show as a variation in shade on the finished piece.

Hints and Tips

Always keep the ball band as a reference. The best way is to pin it to the tension swatch and keep them together with any left over yarn and spare buttons or other trimmings. That way you can always check the washing instructions and also have materials for repairs.

Word of Warning

Don't buy expensive wool, mohair or cotton for your first garment in case of disaster!

Pressing

With the vast range of yarns available today with varying characteristics it would be impossible to give standard pressing instructions. For individual yarns these instructions are usually given on the ball band. However, a general guide to the method of **blocking** would be as follows:

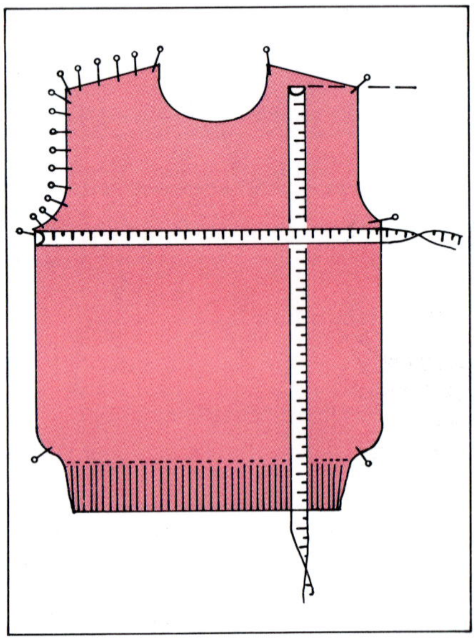

With wrong side facing pin out each piece to the correct size and shape on a padded surface. Take care that fabric is not stretched. Do not pin out ribs or welts, to avoid loss of elasticity. Press lightly following instructions on ball band, and avoiding ribbing or welts.

If there are no pressing instructions available, a general guide would be as follows:

Wool: Lay a damp cloth over piece of work then steam thoroughly without allowing the weight of the iron to rest on the work.

Synthetic yarns: Do not press yarns that are 100% synthetic. For yarns that are a mixture of synthetic and wool fibres, press lightly on wrong side using a cool iron over a dry cloth.

Cotton or Linen: Lay a damp cloth over piece of work then steam thoroughly without allowing the weight of the iron to rest on the work.

All yarns: Allow pieces to dry thoroughly before removing pins.

Washing and Caring for your Handmade Garments

Your handmade garments need to be looked after carefully in order to avoid disasters. In general they are not so resilient as ready made garments, as the tension is usually looser and more likely to stretch. Also they can appear to shrink if not correctly pulled to size after washing.

For best results handwashing is strongly recommended. With yarns that are mostly, or all wool, wash gently in plenty of lukewarm water (30°C/86°F) using a mild soap. Rinse well in 3 changes of cold water or until the water is clear. Squeeze out gently by hand taking care not to allow weight of water to stretch garment. Roll garment in a towel to remove excess water. Lay garment out flat on a dry towel and reshape to correct measurements. Allow to dry naturally away from artificial heat and direct sunlight.

If your garment requires pressing after washing, turn it inside out and press on wrong side carefully following the instructions on ball band, or as given opposite.

Some yarns are now machine washable (check on ball band). If the yarn is suitable, there are some general rules to follow:

(a) Make sure the water is not hotter than the recommended temperature.

(b) Use the wool cycle, or a gentle cycle such as delicates. Most modern machines have the International Care Symbols which are also printed on most ball bands. All you have to do is match the programme to the symbols printed. If you have an older machine it may be more difficult to ensure the correct combination of temperature, agitation and time. If in doubt, handwash!

(c) Once the cycle is finished remove the garment immediately or it will become creased. Reshape to correct measurements on a towel, and leave to dry naturally. Do not use a tumble dryer. These tend to dry the yarn far too quickly and at too hot a temperature, and therefore shrink the garment, usually beyond repair!

International Knitting and Crochet Terms

English	Français	Deutsch	Español	Italiano
Alternate(ly)	Tous les 2 rangs/ toutes les 2 mailles	Im Wechsel	Alternando	Ogni due righe/maglie
Back/front loop (of stitch)	Brin avant ou arrière	Vorderes/hinteres Maschenglied	Hebra delante/atrás	Maglia presa da dietro/davanti
Cast(ing) on	Montage (monter)	Anschlag (anschlagen)	Montaje (montar)	Avvio (avviare)
Cast(ing) off	Rabat (rabattre)	Abketten	Terminaciòn (cerrar)	Chiusura (chiudere)
Chain	Chaînette	Luftmaschenkette	Cadeneta	Catenella
Chain stitch	Maille en l'air ou maille chaînette	Luftmasche	Punto en el aire/punto cadeneta	Maglia volante/maglia catenella
Crochet or crochet hook	Crochet	Häkelnadel	Ganchillo	Uncinetto
Crossed stitch	Maille croisée	Verkreuzte Masche	Punto cruzado	Maglia incrociata
Decrease	Diminution (diminuer)	Abnahme (abnehmen)	Menguados/disminuyendo puntos (disminuir)	Diminuzione (diminuire)
Double treble	Double bride	Doppelstäbchen	Presilla doble	Punto alto doppio
Double crochet	Maille serrée	Feste Masche	Punto prieto	Punto basso
Draw through a loop	Tirer une boucle	Schlinge durchholen	Sacar un bucle	Estrarre un'asola
Fasten off	Arrêter	Den Faden abschneiden	Rematar	Fermare
Flat knitting	Tricot (à) plat	Flachstriken	Punto plano	Lavoro in piano
Front or right side (of work)	Endroit (de l'ouvrage)	Vorderseite	Derecho (del trabajo)	Diritto (del lavoro)
Half Treble	Demi-bride	Halbes Stäbchen	Media presilla	Mezzo punto alto
Hem	Ourlet	Saum	Dobladillo	Orlo
Increase	Augmentation (augmenter)	Zunahme/zunahmen	Aumento (aumentar)	Aumento (aumentare)
Join into a ring	Fermer en rond	Zur Runde schließen	Cerrar en redondo	Chiudere in tondo
Knitting	Tricot	Stricken/Strickarbeit	Punto de malla	Lavoro a maglia
Knitting needle	Aiguille à tricoter	Stricknadel	Aguja de punto	Ferro da calza
Knit stitch	Maille endroit	Rechtsmasche	Punto al derecho	Maglia diritta
Left	Gauche	Links	Izquierdo/a	Sinistra
Left needle	Aiguille gauche	Linke Nadel	Aguja izquierda	Ferro sinistro
Loop	Boucle	Schlinge	Bucle	Asola
Miss (a stitch)	Sauter	Übergehen	Saltar	Saltare
Needle	Aiguille	Nadel	Aguja	Ferro/Ago
Pattern stitch	Point	Muster	Punto	Punto
Previous row	Rang précédent	Vorreihe	Hilera precedente	Riga o ferro prec.
Purl stitch	Maille envers	Linksmasche	Punto al revés	Maglia rovescia
Repeat from	Reprendre à	Ab ... wiedenholen	Volver a coger	Ripetere da
Right	Droite	Rechts	Derecho/a	Destra
Right needle	Aiguille droite	Rechte Nadel	Aguja derecha	Ferro destro
Round (4 needles)	Tour (4 aiguilles)	Runde	Vuelta	Giro

English	Français	Deutsch	Español	Italiano
Slip stitch knitwise	Maille glissée endroit	Masche rechts abheben	Punto levantado a la derecha/deslizado	Maglia passata a dir/ passare una maglia a dir
Slip stitch purlwise	Maille glissée envers	Masche links abheben	Punto levantado al revés	Maglia passata a rov/ passare una maglia a rov
Slip one, knit one, pass slipped stitch over	Surjet simple	Einfacher Überzug (1 M abheben, 1 M abstricken und die abgehobene über die gestrickte Masche ziehen)	Pasar el dezlizado sobre el punto al derecho	Accavallamento sempl.
Slip one, knit 2 tog., pass slipped stitch over	Surjet double	Doppelter Überzug (1 M abheben, 2 M zus. stricken und die abgehobene über die gestrickte Masche ziehen)	Pasar el deslizado sobre los dos puntos al derecho	Accavallamento doppio
Stitch	Maille	Masche	Punto	Maglia
Stitch cast off	Maille rabattue	Eine Mascheabketten	Punto rematado	Maglia accavallata
Stitch holder or cable needle	Aiguille auxillaire	Hilfsnadel	Aguja de repuesto	Ferro ausiliario
Take yarn round needle or hook	Jeter (le fil)	Faden um die Nadel schlagen	Echar (el hilo)	Gettare il filo sul ferro/uncinetto
Through	A travers	Durchziehen	A través	Attraverso
Through back of loop	Derrière (par)	Von hinten einstechen	Detrás	Dietro (dal)
Times	Fois	Mal	Veces	Volta/volte
To cross	Croiser	Kreuzen	Cruzar	Incrociare
To drop one stitch	Lâcher une maille	Eine Masche fallen lassen	Soltar un punto	Far cadere una maglia
To knit	Tricoter	Stricken	Hacer punto o tejer	Lavorare a maglia
To knit up or pick up (stitches)	Relever	Auffassen	Levantar	Riprendere
To pick up dropped stitches	Rattraper des mailles perdues	Aufheben gefallener Maschen	Levantar puntos perdidos	Ricuperare delle maglie cadute
To return	Revenir	Zurückstricken	Volver	Ritornare
To slip	Glisser	Abheben	Levantar sin tejer	Passare una maglia senza lavorarla
To turn (the work)	Tourner l'ouvrage (travail)	Arbeit wenden	Dar vuelta (labor)	Voltare il lavoro
Together (stitches)	Ensemble (mailles)	Zusammen (Maschen)	Juntos (puntos)	Insieme (maglie)
Top of stitch (crochet)	Tête de maille	Oberes Maschenglied	Punto de cabeza	Testa della maglia
Treble	Bride (simple)	Stäbchen	Presilla sencilla	Punto alto
Twisted or crossed stitches	Maille torse	Verdrehte oder verschränkte Masche	Punto torcido	Maglia ritorta
Under	Sous	Unter	Debajo	Sotto
Work	Travail	Arbeit	Trabajo	Lavoro (lavorare)
Wrong side (of work)	Envers (de l'ouvrage)	Rückseite	Revés (del trabajo)	Rovescio (del lavoro)
Yarn	Fil	Garn oder Faden	Hilo	Filo
Yarn forward, or yarn around the needle, or over	Jeté (faire un jeté)	1 Umschlag	Crecido (hacer un)	Gettato (fare un)

Crochet hook and knitting needle charts:

Some charts vary slightly in stating which sizes are equivalent. The important thing to remember is that the size hook or needle to use is the one which gives you the stitch tension quoted in the pattern.

CROCHET HOOK SUGGESTED EQUIVALENT CHART

Canadian & U.K. Sizes	000	00	0	2	3	4	5	6	7	8	—	9	10	11	—	12	13	14	
Metric Sizes	10.0	9.00	8.00	7.00	6.50	6.00	5.50	5.00	4.50	4.00	3.75	3.50	3.25	3.00	2.75	2.50	2.25	2.00	
U.S. Sizes	—	—	—	—	K 10½	J 10	I 9	H 8	7	G 6	F 5	E 4	D 3	—	C 2	—	B 1	—	

KNITTING NEEDLE SUGGESTED EQUIVALENT CHART

Canadian & U.K. Sizes	000	00	0	1	2	3	4	5	6	7	8	9	—	10	11	12	13	14	15
Metric Sizes (for U.K.)	10	9	8	7½	7	6½	6	5½	5	4½	4	3¾	—	3¼	3	2¾	2¼	2	1¾
U.S. Sizes	15	13	11	11	10½	10½	10	9	8	7	6	5	4	3	3	2	1	0	—

Coats Patons Pty. Limited
89-91 Peters Avenue
Mulgrave North 3170 Victoria
AUSTRALIA

Patons & Baldwins Limited
McMullen Road,
Darlington, DL1 1YQ
ENGLAND

5432 Printed in Belgium.